Advance

GEHL *v* CANADA

"Gehl embodies essential Indigenous wisdom, bravery, and responsibility in her work to dismantle the systems of colonial oppression. Her work serves as a beacon in a network of pathways for our people to make their way home."
—Chief Wendy Jocko, Algonquins of Pikwàkanagàn First Nation

"The legal decision in *Gehl v Canada* will have profound effects for the future, ensuring that hundreds of thousands of Indigenous mothers will be able to pass their status on to their children. This victory, the product of decades of struggle by Lynn Gehl, is chronicled here. Read it and learn!"
—Bonita Lawrence, author of *Fractured Homeland:*
Federal Recognition and Algonquin Identity in Ontario

"What a humbling honour and privilege to be able to read Dr. Gehl's profound and wise contribution and take her direction regarding the vital action required of all who are committed to promoting equality and justice."
—Senator Kim Pate

"The status of women under the *Indian Act* had been disputed for decades. Lynn Gehl led an important part of that struggle bravely and sometimes without much support. This book takes us deeply through the history of this critical struggle for women's rights."
—Judy Rebick, author of *Heroes in My Head*
and founding publisher of *rabble.ca*

"Congratulations are due to Dr. Lynn Gehl for her successful challenge of the Indian Registrar's refusal to allow her to be registered under the *Indian Act*. The refusal was based on the fact that because Lynn could not prove who her paternal grandfather was or that he was entitled to be registered, she could not be registered. The Court of Appeal for Ontario found that requiring her to prove the unprovable (the name of her ancestor) was unreasonable and that there was circumstantial evidence showing that he was 'likely' an Indian and a member of the community. On that basis she had established all she could or needed to, and it was unreasonable of the Registrar to demand more. The majority of the judges declined to strike out the requirement as a breach of the equality rights provision of the *Charter*, because they didn't have to in order to rule in her favour. Good win, Lynn!"

—The Honourable Murray Sinclair, author of *Honouring the Truth, Reconciling for the Future: Summary of the Final Report of the Truth and Reconciliation Commission of Canada*

Praise for
CLAIMING ANISHINAABE

"[C]lear, insightful, and desperately needed..."

—Lorraine F. Mayer, author of *Cries from a Métis Heart*

"Gehl is at the cutting edge with her concepts and ideas....She is on a journey and she documents it well."

—Lorelei Anne Lambert, author of *Research for Indigenous Survival*

"[T]he discussion of the heart and mind knowledge, as well as the discussion on the Anishinaabeg Clan System of Governance, [are] major contributions to the research."

—Marlyn Bennett, co-editor of *Pushing the Margins*

Gehl *v* Canada

CHALLENGING SEX
DISCRIMINATION
IN THE INDIAN ACT

Lynn Gehl

University of Regina Press

Printed and bound in Canada at Imprimerie Gauvin. The text of this book is printed on 100% post-consumer recycled paper with earth-friendly vegetable-based inks.

Cover design: Duncan Campbell, University of Regina Press
Interior layout design: John van der Woude, JVDW Designs
Copy editor: Alison Jacques
Proofreader: Rhonda Kronyk
Indexer: Siusan Moffat

Library and Archives Canada Cataloguing in Publication

Title: Gehl v Canada : challenging sex discrimination in the Indian Act / Lynn Gehl.
Other titles: Gehl vs. Canada
Names: Gehl, Lynn, 1962- author.
Description: Includes bibliographical references and index.
Identifiers: Canadiana (print) 20210230339 | Canadiana (ebook) 2021023864x | ISBN 9780889778252 (softcover) | ISBN 9780889778269 (hardcover) | ISBN 9780889778276 (PDF) | ISBN 9780889778283 (EPUB)
Subjects: LCSH: Gehl, Lynn, 1962- | LCSH: Indigenous women—Canada—Social conditions. | LCSH: Indigenous women—Legal status, laws, etc.—Canada. | LCSH: Indigenous peoples—Legal status, laws, etc.—Canada. | LCSH: Indigenous peoples—Canada—Ethnic identity. | LCSH: Canada. Indian Act. | LCSH: Sex discrimination against women—Law and legislation—Canada. | LCGFT: Autobiographies.
Classification: LCC E98.W8 G44 2021 | DDC 305.48/897071—dc23

10 9 8 7 6 5 4 3 2 1

University of Regina Press, University of Regina
Regina, Saskatchewan, Canada, s4s 0a2
tel: (306) 585-4758 fax: (306) 585-4699
U OF R PRESS   web: www.uofrpress.ca

We acknowledge the support of the Canada Council for the Arts for our publishing program. We acknowledge the financial support of the Government of Canada. / Nous reconnaissons l'appui financier du gouvernement du Canada. This publication was made possible with support from Creative Saskatchewan's Book Publishing Production Grant Program.

Contents

Figures and Tables **ix**
Dedication **xi**
Foreword *by Mary Eberts* **xiii**
Preface: Indigenous Ways of Knowing **xxi**
Acknowledgements **xxv**
Acronyms **xxvii**

Introduction **xxxi**

Part One: On Identity Matters
1   Fighting for Recognition **3**
2   The Personal Implications of the Discrimination
     in the *Indian Act* **7**
3   Long Live the "Algonquin Frauds" **10**
4   "Love to Me Is the Kids" **13**
5   Disenfranchised Spirit: A Theory and a Model **16**

Part Two: Some Community Writing
6   Women Protest Bill c-31 Threat to Erase Indians **35**
7   Great Gathering against Bill c-3 **37**
8   *Indian Act* Still Discriminating **40**

9   The *Indian Act*'s Legislative Silence   **43**

10   Canada's Court System: A Hostile Place for Indigenous Peoples   **46**

Part Three: On Cultural Genocide

11   Canada's Unstated Paternity Policy Amounts to Genocide
     against Indigenous Children   **51**

12   Canada Is Carrying Out Cultural Genocide with a Smile   **54**

Part Four: Some Academic Works

13   "The Queen and I": Discrimination against Women in the
     Indian Act Continues   **59**

14   Unknown and Unstated Paternity and the *Indian Act*:
     Enough Is Enough!   **70**

15   Protecting Indian Rights for Indian Babies:
     Canada's "Unstated Paternity" Policy   **79**

16   Ontario's History of Tampering and Re-tampering
     with Birth Registration Documents   **94**

Part Five: A Talk, a Testimonial, and a Submission

17   Law Society of Upper Canada Talk   **109**

18   House of Commons Committee Testimony   **113**

19   Inter-American Commission on Human
     Rights Submission   **118**

Part Six: Bill s-3

20   Understanding "6(1)a All The Way!"   **123**

21   Carolyn Bennett's "Two Million" New Indians   **125**

22   Valuing Discourse: Senators Discuss Indian and Northern Affairs
     Canada's "Unstated Paternity" Policy   **129**

Part Seven: Dishonouring Wenonah's Jurisdiction

23   My Last Chapter: I Am Only a Woman   **135**

Part Eight: Some Final Thoughts
24   Defeating the Wiindigo   **205**
25   I Danced and I Danced; My Heart Was Full   **210**

Afterword: Morals before Knowledge   **215**

Appendix: Timeline of *Gehl v Canada*   **219**
Notes   **235**
Anishinaabemowin Words and Meanings   **249**
Bibliography   **251**
Index   **261**

Figures and Tables

Figure 1   Joseph Gagnon, ca. 1916   **4**

Figure 2   Annie Jane Meness Gagnon with Children,
              ca. 1916   **4**

Figure 3   Harold Ross's Ancestry   **24**

Figure 4   Disenfranchised Spirit   **29**

Figure 5   "6(1)a All the Way!" Art/Poster, 2010
              Marche AMUN   **38**

Figure 6   Unknown and Unstated Paternity   **41**

Figure 7   Letter to Annie Gagnon, 1945   **62**

Figure 8   Tampered Birth Record   **97**

Figure 9   Understanding "6(1)a All the Way!"   **124**

Figure 10   Lynn Gehl's Ancestry   **147**

Table 1   Section 6 of the *Indian Act*   **66**

Table 2   Unwed Mothers in Cairns, Jamieson,
              and Lysyk, 1966   **163**

Table 3   2012 Indigenous and Northern Affairs Canada's Online
              Unstated Paternity Policy   **166**

Dedication

I know all too well that Indigenous identity politics is a context where incredible nastiness can emerge. We need to be better people when it comes to watching others struggle with and through it, me included.

Because of the power of colonization and Indigenous identity destruction, many people are not aware that there is a difference between having a little bit of Indigenous ancestry and being and living as an Indigenous person. It has been my experience that when a person is walking back into who their great-grandparents were, who their grandparents and parents are, and thus who they are, the terrain is rocky and fluid. It is my thinking that we need to provide a safe space for people to come back to who they are, and want to be, as Indigenous Peoples. If they are serious, eventually they will move more deeply into the Indigenous worldview and knowledge philosophy. I say this knowing full well that some people claim Indigenous ancestry for the purpose of education funding, employment, arts funding and awards, and political advancement, which in many ways is cultural appropriation. This really bothers me, but we need to remember that colonial laws and policies forced many Indigenous Peoples underground as a way to survive the misery and genocide their ancestors were faced with, where many no longer know who they are related to, human or otherwise, and what their responsibilities to the natural world are as humans.[1] It is becoming more and more obvious to me that there are people out there in need of someone to help them navigate through the landscape of Indigenous identity politics. This book is dedicated to the Indigenous Peoples who remain in the closet. What I know for sure is that you do not have to be a registered Status Indian to pick up your responsibilities and allow them to guide you forward in being the good human being Creator wants us all to be. I hope this work serves people moving more deeply into serving Indigenous nationhood.

Lastly, there are loads of articles, books, and documentaries about how patriarchy has worked to control women's sexuality, women's bodies, and women's vaginas. Feminists have done this important and hard work. *Gehl v Canada* represents my struggle to get Canada, and Indigenous and Northern Affairs Canada (INAC) in particular, out of the business of, first, thinking it can control the Creator's work that women have been bestowed and, second, thinking it has the right to control the Eastern Doorway, meaning their process of giving birth. The Eastern Doorway will always remain the jurisdiction of women. That is how the Creator intended it to be. *Gehl v Canada* was about more than me. It was so much bigger than me. It was about women, all women, even white settler women, and our right as women to preserve what is ours. Yet here we are in 2021 where men who are more pitiful than women, and the patriarchal women they socialize, continue to think they have the right to control the Eastern Doorway rather than do the moral thing. This book is dedicated to women, all women, and all the children birthed through the Eastern Doorway, because all children, my father and me included, are deserving of love and a sense of belonging regardless of who the man is or is not.

Foreword

Welcome to a very important book.

Dr. Lynn Gehl describes the effort she made to document the sex discrimination affecting her and her family, her decision to challenge that discrimination, and how she applied herself to various proceedings from 1994 until she achieved a victory in the Ontario Court of Appeal in 2017. She offers crucial insights into the struggle of women for equality under the *Indian Act*, the latest stage of which has occupied more than sixty years. With knowledge and experience from years of advocacy before Parliament as well as the courts, and the depth of perception typical of all her scholarly work, Lynn assesses what more is needed before the *Indian Act* system can be truly egalitarian.

This book is unique and inspiring.

The book is unique because it is the only full-length, first-person account of a leading case about discrimination against women in the *Indian Act* of Canada. *Gehl v Canada* is the fifth in a series of iconic court challenges to Canada's long-standing attempt to assimilate Indigenous Peoples by expelling Status Indian women from their communities.

In the 1960s, the battle against discrimination and assimilation was fought largely outside of the courtroom, with activists such as Mary Two-Axe Earley of Kahnawake and Jenny Margetts of Alberta, along with Indigenous women's organizations, raising awareness and seeking amendments to the

Indian Act. In particular, they sought to eradicate the provision that imposed a harsh penalty against a Status Indian woman who married a man without status. She would lose her Indian status and, with it, the right to live in her home community, raise and educate her children there, and be buried there after her death. She could not pass status on to her children. In sharp contrast, a Status Indian man who married a woman without status would endow her with status, and their children would also have status.

Given the deplorable circumstances in which many Status Indians are forced to live, on reserves without adequate housing or clean water, health care or education, and the decades of ill treatment of Status Indians in this country, it seems ironic that so much women's energy has been devoted to asserting a claim to status under the *Indian Act*. But status was (and still is) the golden key to eligibility for a range of services and facilities both on and off reserve. Not having status—that is, registration as an Indian—left women much worse off than their Status Indian sisters, who were eligible for those treaty rights. A woman deprived of status was totally alone in the face of mistreatment or abandonment by her husband and could face poverty, abuse, and rejection in off-reserve society, with no family or community to support her. The women deprived of status, and their children, lacked all opportunity to take part in the decision-making and governance of their First Nations and thus could play no role in the development of governance structures of the future.

Moreover, at the stroke of a pen, Canada was depriving these women and their children of their identity and culture, in order to promote the eventual disappearance of Indians altogether.

This book is inspiring because it tells the story of a woman determined to overcome a lack of resources and the concerted opposition of the Canadian government, in order to claim her place in her family, and in history. It is inspiring because it is set in the context of the long heroic struggle led by Indian women to defeat the use of sex discrimination as an instrument of colonization.

The five women who brought the landmark cases against sex discrimination in the *Indian Act*—Yvonne Bédard, Jeannette Corbiere Lavell, Sandra Lovelace Nicholas, Sharon McIvor, and Lynn Gehl—along with Senator Lillian Eva Dyck, who provided steady leadership during the Senate's efforts to improve Bill s-3, have been dubbed "The Indigenous Famous

Six." The more familiar "Famous Five" are the privileged white women who brought the 1920s court case that resulted in women being held to be persons under the Canadian Constitution. Some women—that is, Indigenous women—did not even have a right to vote in Canadian elections until 1960. The Indigenous Famous Six also seek full personhood, long denied them because Canada had determined that exiling women from home and family was an effective means of weakening, and eventually eliminating, the whole population of Status Indians.

Jeannette Corbiere Lavell, from the Wikwemikong First Nation on Manitoulin Island, and Yvonne Bédard, from Six Nations, had each been deprived of Indian status when they married non-Status men. Their legal challenges reached the Supreme Court of Canada at the same time and were heard together. The Supreme Court's 1974 decision held that the *Indian Act*'s differential treatment of men and women who married non-Status spouses was not contrary to the equality before the law provisions of the Canadian Bill of Rights.

From there, the allegation of discrimination was taken to the United Nations Human Rights Committee (UNHRC) by Sandra Lovelace (now Sandra Lovelace Nicholas), a Maliseet woman from the Tobique reserve in New Brunswick, now a Canadian senator. Also deprived of status because of her marriage to a non-Status man, she had struggled to be accepted on her home reserve after the couple's separation. In December 1977, she submitted to the UNHRC her written argument that the International Covenant on Civil and Political Rights prevented Canada from barring her access to her home community. In July 1981, the committee ruled in her favour, citing Article 27 of the Convention, which prevents states from denying to members of ethnic, religious, or linguistic minorities the right to enjoy their own culture, to profess and practice their own religion, and to use their own language, in community with other members of their group.

The next cases challenging sex discrimination in the *Indian Act* were brought by Sharon McIvor and her son Jacob Grismer, and by Lynn, after passage in 1985 of legislation that the government offered as a remedy for discrimination but that actually continued and complicated the problem.

The new law, known colloquially as Bill C-31, provided that a person could acquire full status only if she or he had two status parents. This requirement perpetuated the power of the father that had been at the root of the prior system, as eligibility for full status depended almost entirely on his decision as to whether he would acknowledge paternity. Moreover, the privilege of families where the husband had conferred status on his wife at marriage was continued by the 1985 amendment: these families were ready to meet this two-parent requirement for any child of theirs born after April 17, 1985, when the new act came into effect. The act provided in section 6(1) a for restoration of status to women deprived of it for marrying a non-status male. However, as the sole status parent in her family, the woman could not pass full status on to her children born after April 17, 1985.

Under the 1985 legislation, a person with one Status Indian parent is assigned a lesser form of status. Status would continue for that person's lifetime, but she or he could not pass it on to a child unless that child also had another status parent. People with this lesser status came to be known as "6(2)s," after the number of the section imposing the lesser status. Their inability to pass status on to a child became known as the "second-generation cut-off." The daughters of women restored to status under Bill C-31 were particularly vulnerable to this treatment: these daughters had the lesser version of status imposed by section 6(2), and unless they could establish that the father of their child was a Status Indian man, their child would have no status at all. The result of "6(2)," and the growing number of children with unknown or unstated paternity, is an expanding class of young mothers and their children exiled from reserves and family just as their mothers and grandmothers had been exiled under the old law.

Section 15 of the *Canadian Charter of Rights and Freedoms* became the weapon of choice against these new forms of gender discrimination. Section 15 came into effect in 1985. It provides that everyone is equal before and under the law and entitled to the equal protection and benefit of the law without discrimination on a number of grounds, including sex and race. The language of section 15 had been crafted in response to fierce lobbying by Indigenous and non-Indigenous women's groups who had been gravely disappointed by the failure of the Canadian Bill of Rights to protect Indian women in the *Bédard* and *Lavell* cases.

Sharon McIvor, from the Lower Nicola First Nation, argued in the British Columbia courts that the *Indian Act*, even in its new version, discriminates against those whose Indigeneity descended, as did hers and her son Jacob Grismer's, down the maternal line. The Supreme Court of British

Columbia agreed with her, in a sweeping decision that cut to the heart of over a century of preference for the male and the male line in determining status. A jittery Court of Appeal pulled back from this ruling, finding instead a minor discrepancy between the treatment of Jacob Grismer, descended through the female line, and the treatment of someone whose mother and grandmother had both acquired status by marrying a status male. The government hurriedly passed what is known as Bill C-3, targeting only the small instance of discrimination identified by the Court of Appeal.

In 2009, fully twenty years after Sharon McIvor first challenged Canada's adverse ruling on the status of her and her son, the Supreme Court of Canada refused to hear her appeal from the decision of the BC Court of Appeal. However, Sharon and her son took their case to the UNHRC under the International Covenant on Civil and Political Rights. On January 11, 2019, the committee agreed with their submissions, finding that Canada had violated Articles 3 and 26 of the Covenant, in conjunction with Article 27. Article 3 obliges states to ensure the equal right of men and women to the enjoyment of all civil and political rights set out in the Covenant. Article 26 states that all persons are equal before the law and are entitled without any discrimination to the equal protection of the law. Article 27 is the section of the Covenant on which the UNHRC had relied to rule in favour of Sandra Lovelace's submission over thirty-five years before. In its 2019 *McIvor* ruling, the committee required Canada to provide full reparations to those whose Covenant rights had been violated, including extending to them full status under section 6(1)(a) of the *Indian Act*.

Lynn's litigation includes a strong focus on the issue of unknown paternity, which has become one of the major trouble spots of the 1985 legislation. Lynn's family tree, carefully researched, contains the fact of her paternal grandfather but not his name. That was unknown, or at least undisclosed. Although the facts of her case predate April 17, 1985, when Bill C-31 came into effect, her arguments have become a mainstay of those challenging the injustice that Bill C-31 visits upon those who cannot or will not name the father of their child. Justice Robert Sharpe of the Court of Appeal acknowledges that while there can hardly be any doubt about maternity, there may be considerable doubt about paternity. He also acknowledges that there may be reasons why a woman may not want, or be able, to name the father of her child; these include both rape and incest. Government policy should, accordingly, take account of the equality-enhancing values and remedial objectives underlying the 1985 amendments.

Noting that the identity of Dr. Gehl's paternal grandfather was unknown, Justice Sharpe states there was evidence in the record to support an inference that he had Indian status. He holds that it was sufficient for Dr. Gehl to establish facts that supported her contention that her grandfather was a Status Indian, and that she did not have to name him, as Canada had been requiring. When Bill s-3 was passed in December 2017, it included a clause modelled on this ruling, providing that the provisions of the *Indian Act* dealt with by Bill s-3 are to be liberally construed to remedy any disadvantage to a woman or her descendants born before April 17, 1985, and to advance the equal treatment of women and men and their descendants under the *Indian Act*.

The passage of Bill s-3 followed the 2015 ruling of the Quebec Superior Court in the case of Stéphane Descheneaux, Susan Yantha, and Tammy Yantha. These three had been forced to litigate because earlier revisions of the *Indian Act* had not addressed the kind of discrimination affecting them, although it was well known at the time. Ruling in favour of their claims to status, Justice Chantal Masse was highly critical of Parliament's habit of crafting remedial legislation very narrowly so as to address only the specifics of a particular judicial decision. In this way, Parliament would avoid a thorough review and repair of the legislation, instead awaiting further judicial decisions before addressing other discriminatory aspects of the *Indian Act*.

When in 2017 Canada brought forward a narrow piece of legislation to address the rulings made by Justice Masse, a spirited campaign to make the statute more comprehensive took place in the Senate. The campaign united behind Lynn's slogan, "6(1)(a) All the Way!," signifying the desire to ensure that all of those who had suffered discrimination on the basis of sex or descent through the maternal line should have full status, of the sort provided by section 6(1)(a). In 2019, the full bill became law; its provisions were considerably broader than those originally proposed by Canada. In fact, Canada now claims that Bill s-3 removes all the historical sex discrimination from the *Indian Act*. It did not take long for advocates and activists to discover that this claim is exaggerated. Much historical gender discrimination remains, as well as all of the gender discrimination introduced by Bill C-31 in 1985. The UNHRC remedy in the *McIvor* case remains unfulfilled. Registration of those eligible under Bill S-3 is proceeding at a glacial pace.

A new campaign is mobilizing to secure the promise of "6(1)(a) All the Way." Unsurprisingly, Lynn—author, scholar, activist, litigant—is once again at the forefront of advocacy to finally put an end to sex discrimination in the *Indian Act*.

In the pages of this book, you will find not just an inspiring story but an inspiring individual. I have known Dr. Lynn Gehl for many years and am proud to be able to call her a friend. I have worked with her on litigation and advocacy. I simply cannot tell you how often I pause for a moment and give thanks that this brave, determined, and principled individual has chosen to do the work she does.

Mary Eberts, O.C.
February 23, 2021

Mary Eberts has been litigation counsel for the Native Women's Association of Canada for over twenty years and was a co-founder of the Women's Legal Education and Action Fund.

Indigenous Ways of Knowing

As Indigenous Peoples decolonize and attempt to survive Canada's ongoing genocide, there is a call to bring back to the table the Indigenous knowledge that processes of colonization pushed off, but is the space really being carved out? I, for one, am making space for it here with this book and with how I have come to write it or, in other words, my methods and methodology.

I am Indigenist. As I previously discussed in my book *Claiming Anishinaabe: Decolonizing the Human Spirit*, Indigenous knowledge is a complete knowledge system that is grounded in its own assumptions, beliefs, theories, methodologies, methods, and practices. It stands to reason that Indigenous knowledge also has its own ways of creating, generating, preserving, and disseminating knowledge. These methods include prayer, song, dance, ceremony, heart knowledge, mind knowledge, personal knowledge, experiential knowledge, introspection, valuing personal and multiple truths, learning by doing, apprenticeship, practice, the Oral Tradition, memory, storytelling, listening, repetition, repetition, responsibility, respect, bravery, mentorship, helping, giving back, role modelling, caring, and valuing morality before knowledge. These methods are better known as Indigenous ways of knowing and being, and they remain intact today as a complete knowledge bundle—as opposed to being delineated in such a way that, for example, morals (or what western scholars call axiology) can be extracted from the knowledge creation and production process.

Given that Indigenous knowledge is a complete knowledge bundle with its own ways of knowing and being, it stands that Indigenous knowledge also has its own criteria set for evaluating what is considered valid knowledge production. With this in mind, it is important to value that just because a thinker, or scholar, or any person is an Indigenous person with brown eyes, this does not mean they are rooted in Indigenous knowledge, rooted in understanding an Indigenous criteria set of knowledge production, and thus able to evaluate what is legitimate Indigenous knowledge. Let's face it; through colonial power many Indigenous Peoples have been colonized and assimilated into western ways of knowing.

While some Indigenous Peoples may be practitioners in terms of ceremony this does not mean they are philosophers of Indigenous knowledge and/or critical thinkers capable of the conscious critical Indigenous thought needed to properly evaluate Indigenous knowledge productions. It is important for us to value that there are practitioners and there are philosophers and theorists. While some people can do both, not all people can. This is not an insult—not at all. It is just the way it is. We need to think through our assumptions. Different people have different gifts and thus different knowledge. This principle of valuing personal gifts is inherent in the Anishinaabe Clan System of governance.[1]

The point I am getting at is this: when an Indigenous person has produced Indigenous knowledge through Indigenous ways of knowing and being, it would be inappropriate to evaluate their work through a western knowledge criteria set that includes such methods and requirements as rationality to the exclusion of heart knowledge, objectivity to the exclusion of heart knowledge, one absolute Truth, and positivism where tangible evidence is prioritized. When reviewers, Indigenous reviewers included, who are not conscious of their discipline's paradigm use criteria sets from western knowledge disciplines—arguing for such things as evidence, repetition of results, artifacts, more literature review, more intellectual rigour—they in fact colonize and oppress through epistemological means. Through epistemological oppression they deny what Indigenous knowledge brings to the knowledge feasting table and force Indigenous scholars to follow western criteria sets and rules of knowledge production. When this takes place, the result is that Indigenous knowledge is treated as an add-on, like salt and pepper or red candies added to a white cake, versus a complete knowledge system from the ground up. It also means Indigenous Peoples have to work harder for the western paradigm. This leads to the question, Why should Indigenous Peoples bring Indigenous knowledge to the table if it is going to be judged through a colonial lens? The best example I can provide to encourage the reader to personally introspect and understand what I am getting at here is the following: If believing in the sacred and associated practices of prayer, song, and dance is more valid, rational, and sustainable than western positivism—knowledge traditions such as historical, legal, economic, and scientific positivism—why would anyone deny Indigenous ways of knowing and being? Why would anyone put it through a western lens? We really need to value Indigenous knowledge for what it is and for the gifts it spreads out on the knowledge feasting table. Indigenous knowledge is not an add-on to western knowledge. Rather, it is a complete knowledge system from the ground up that has to be left alone.

Another thing I have been thinking about lately is that academics should no longer consider knowledge production for the sake of knowledge production alone. What I mean by this is that knowledge production has to be more than a personal effort that satiates the ego. Rather, it must first be moral and serve the natural world before it is considered worthwhile and valid knowledge. This is what I mean when I say "morals before knowledge" and this is what is meant by the Anishinaabe teaching that we all need to walk our knowledge productions back to Creation to make sure they are moral in terms of the natural world and in terms of where women, in the work they do, and children sit closer to Creator.

All this said, I have never had as much clarity in terms of the value of Indigenous methods as valid and legitimate in their own right until this task of writing and telling my story about the ongoing sex discrimination in the *Indian Act* was sitting in front of me. Moving the knowledge from my body, heart, and mind was brutal. While I am grateful for this clarity in knowing that Indigenous ways of knowing are not to be thought of simply as an add-on to the methods of western knowledge philosophy, I am not grateful for the misery that colonization embodied within me. I am in loathe of Canada for what it has done and continues to do to me. Daily I bear the weight of colonial genocide, and the load is heavy. My point for readers and thinkers is that insisting I ought to have taken a mixed-method or rigorous approach to this topic and thus offered a better legal analysis would be ignorant of the effort inherent in the Indigenous methods on which I rest my knowledge and would be yet another miserable colonial imposition. Moreover, it would risk this very knowledge production of mine from being completed, published, and added to the historical archive of what Indigenous women have to continue to live with despite the human rights movement.

Acknowledgements

It is counterintuitive for me to thank people who helped me experience misery; regardless, convention dictates I should.

First and foremost, chi-miigwetch to Nikolaus Karl Gehl for all the help with my process through the torture of Canada's court system.

Miigwetch to Karen Clark of University of Regina Press for working with me on the earlier version of this work. Also, miigwetch to the reviewers of an earlier version of my manuscript. Miigwetch to Alison Jacques for copyediting this work. Collectively, all your suggestions have improved this work.

Chi-miigwetch also to Kimberly Murray, Amanda Driscoll, Christa Big Canoe, Emilie Nicole Lahaie, and Mary Eberts. Miigwetch also to so many other lawyers who worked in the *Gehl* court case, such as Jonathan Rudin, Brian Eyolfson, Katherine Hansel, Lori Mishibinijima, Suni Matia, Amy Britton-Cox, Karen Spector, Amanda Sheane, Marisha Roman, and Mandy Wesley. I apologize if I forgot to add your name to this list. I know all too well what it is like to be disenfranchised. This process has been way too hard for me to be on top of all the important people who had a hand in *Gehl v Canada*.

Miigwetch also to Kirby Whiteduck, Michelle Mann, and Karen Lynn for your contributions to this effort. Miigwetch also to Lerina Koornhof.

Miigwetch to Senator Lillian Eva Dyck, Senator Marilou McPhedran, and Senator Kim Pate for your work and allyship and for serving the "6(1) a All the Way!" campaign. Miigwetch also to Shelagh Day and Gwen

Brodsky for your allyship and your support of Sharon Donna McIvor in her lengthy effort that extended to the United Nations. Sharon was fortunate to have your long-lasting and continued representation and support. I am sure this constancy made her work a little bit less arduous. Miigwetch also to Pamela D. Palmater for the work you did, too.

Miigwetch to Lorraine Land and John Bird for treating me and Nik so well during this miserable process. Miigwetch to the two peer reviewers of this manuscript. Your suggestions are appreciated and have proven to improve this work.

I also wish to say chi-miigwetch to Francine Bryan for your help with the chapter on tampered birth documents, and also miigwetch for loving me so. Please know that you are often in my thoughts and prayers. And miigwetch to Monica Vida and Pamela Schreiner for listening to my miserable process.

Grateful acknowledgement is made to the following newspapers, magazines, journals, and publishers for respecting my intellectual property rights and for understanding my jurisdictional rights to reprint my work in this book in edited and updated forms: *Anishinabek News*, *Canada's History Magazine*, *Canadian Woman Studies*, *First Peoples Child & Family Review*, *Huffington Post*, *Journal of the Motherhood Initiative for Research and Community Involvement*, *Pimatisiwin*, and *rabble.ca*. This collection spans from 2000 through 2018.

I would also like to thank the Canada Council for the Arts and the Ontario Arts Council for financial support in compiling these works in newly edited form and for supporting my writing of different elements of this book.

I want to acknowledge Gichi-Manidoo, the Great Mystery of all Life. I want to acknowledge the wisdom of the Anishinaabe teaching inherent in the colour black. I want to acknowledge and respect the knowledge located outside the human realm; knowledge that continues to remain unknown to humans; knowledge that humans cannot, or will not, let us know; knowledge that only women have; and knowledge that sometimes mothers do not have. I want to honour the Great Mystery element of the Eastern Doorway and the work mothers do when they give birth to a child.

Acronyms

AANDC   Aboriginal Affairs and Northern Development Canada
AFNWC   Assembly of First Nations Women's Council
ALST   Aboriginal Legal Services of Toronto
APPA   Senate Standing Committee on Aboriginal Peoples
CCPC   Court Challenges Program of Canada
CIRNAC   Crown-Indigenous Relations and Northern Affairs Canada
DoJ   Department of Justice
FAFIA   Canadian Feminist Alliance for International Action
IACHR   Inter-American Commission on Human Rights
INAC   Indian and Northern Affairs Canada / Indigenous and Northern Affairs Canada
INAN   House of Commons Standing Committee on Indigenous and Northern Affairs
ISC   Indigenous Services Canada
LEAF   Women's Legal Education and Action Fund
LOME   Law Office of Mary Eberts
MMIWG   National Inquiry into Missing and Murdered Indigenous Women and Girls
NSRAUUP   National Strategy to Raise Awareness on Unknown and Unstated Paternity
NWAC   Native Women's Association of Canada

ONWA	Ontario Native Women's Association
PoP	proof of paternity
QNW	Quebec Native Women Inc.
RCMP	Royal Canadian Mounted Police
SCC	Supreme Court of Canada
SJM	summary judgement motion
SoC	statement of claim
SoD	statement of defence
TRC	Truth and Reconciliation Commission of Canada
UNHRC	United Nations Human Rights Committee

Love to me is the kids.
—Mrs. Glassford, 1967

I had a vision, that one day, I would be free again, free to be myself, to be an Indian. I lost the freedom 45 years ago; to be buried beside the ancestors in the sacred burial grounds, to be able to own property, to be able to live in freedom on the land the white fathers carved out for our ancestors to call home.
—Mary Two-Axe Earley, 1983

I hear lots of empty political rhetoric about how important the Charter is and the need to protect Aboriginal women from abuse. I have neither heard nor read any concrete examples of how we will be protected by the Charter.
—Patricia Monture-Angus, *Thunder in My Soul*

The State party attempts to excuse its failure to bring the Government's "6(1)(a) all the way" clause into effect...on the grounds that it wishes to consult First Nations. It is not appropriate for the State party to consult about whether it will continue legislated discrimination. The State party has been consulting about this discrimination for decades, and consultation has been a tactic for delaying the elimination of sex discrimination.
—United Nations Human Rights Committee,
re: *McIvor and Grismer v Canada*

Introduction

In 1982 the government of Canada patriated the Canadian Constitution, formally entrenching Aboriginal and treaty rights in the supreme law of Canada. Section 35(1) of the Constitution reads: "The existing aboriginal and treaty rights of the aboriginal people in Canada are hereby recognized and affirmed." At this time the *Canadian Charter of Rights and Freedoms* became part of the Constitution. Section 15(1), known as the equality rights section of the *Charter*, reads: "Every individual is equal before and under the law and has the right to the equal protection and equal benefit of the law without discrimination and, in particular, without discrimination based on race, national or ethnic origin, colour, religion, sex, age or mental or physical disability." This is what this book is about: my equality rights as an Algonquin Anishinaabe-kwe, and my treaty rights as an Algonquin Anishinaabe-kwe. As you read this book, keep in mind that through colonial genocide Canada's Parliament, the Canadian Senate, and the Supreme Court of Canada all squat illegally on surrendered Algonquin Anishinaabe territory. During the construction of Canada, the Algonquin Anishinaabeg were denied the right to a treaty yet our land is the heart of what Canada is. I am an Algonquin Anishinaabe-kwe, and I am in loathe of what Canada has done to the Algonquin Anishinaabeg and continues to do.

When I think through the contribution that this book offers, what comes to my mind and heart is that it represents one woman's (mine) effort at challenging Canada's Parliament to do the right thing and care for Indigenous mothers and children. It represents one woman's effort at challenging an all-encompassing power force that ruined her father's life and consequently her life. It represents one woman's effort at pulling out of poverty, neglect, abuse, and layers of structural barriers such as racism, classism, sexism, ableism, and the intersectional and interactional effects of the layering of structural oppression only to realize the power was and remains an all-encompassing wiindigo—an insatiable gluttonous monster that is not just ignorant but lacks morals. It is my thought that this book's contribution is that it represents one woman's journey of coming to value that humans, or the Canadian state, have forgotten that morals must come before knowledge. It represents me coming to realize that I am only a woman, and while I am pitiful, men—in particular, colonial patriarchs—are more pitiful than women in the important work they do opening the Eastern Doorway.

This compilation of works represents the path, in part, that I travelled regarding my process of challenging the sex discrimination in the *Indian Act*, specifically on the matter of Indian and Northern Affairs Canada's unknown and thus unstated paternity policy, a practice that was invented in 1985. The idea that Canada was administering a practice of genocide that was harmful to Indigenous mothers and babies horrified me. I had to do something. Little did I know that this effort would consume my agency and mind for over thirty years, make me so miserable, and almost kill me. That is what wiindigos do: they kill or, in my case, almost do. Wiindigos, they suck the life out of good things.

I begin here with a story about me as a way of grounding this effort and letting people know where my debwewin (truth) emerges from.

I have told the story many times about my eyesight and my difficulties with reading text. My vision is limited because of a congenital cranial nerve issue, resulting in legal blindness in my right eye, and thus I lack three-dimensional depth perception. The lack of three-dimensional vision is a rare type of blindness that affects about 3 percent of the population. This issue had implications in my learning how to read and write text and has implications in the way I engage text today. I have also told the story about attending community college and completing a diploma in chemical technology, after which I worked in the field of environmental science for twelve years—with a reading level that remained at the primary school range.

The *Indian Act* was amended in 1985 and at the time I was working in the field of environmental science, monitoring the quality of Ontario's waterways. Eventually, and after Nik and I were legally married, I resigned from my position and returned to school—this time, university—at the age of thirty-three. I began my journey into higher learning, taking psychology courses that involved reading textbooks with nice photographs and little vignettes threaded through the pages. Textbooks, that is, with black text on nice white pages, with larger spaces between lines, that served my reading needs and greatly improved my reading ability.

Looking for more answers about the human condition than I could find in psychology, eventually I moved into the critical-thinking discipline of cultural anthropology, where my reading and writing skills were deeply challenged in that at the undergraduate level I had to read journal articles requiring more conceptual and theoretical thinking skills. In 2002 I finished my undergraduate degree *summa cum laude* with a major in cultural anthropology. The first paper I wrote was about my experience with sex discrimination in the *Indian Act*. This paper, titled "The Queen and I," was published in a scholarly journal and is included as a chapter in this book.

After I completed my undergraduate degree I immediately moved into a master's program in Canadian studies and Native studies. At this time my interest was Indigenous identity. Situated within the Algonquin land claim process in Ontario as I was, identity was a hotly debated and contested issue, and as such I was observing many Indigenous people struggle with their identity in ways that were heavily felt by both them and me. Actually, I would go as far as saying I suffered vicariously from what others were struggling with. At the same time my own identity as a non-Status Algonquin person was continuously and constantly contested, although less so because I had family ties to an Indigenous community that was recognized by Canada: Pikwàkanagàn First Nation. While identity was my interest at the master's level, shaped by the field of medical anthropology as I was, I was more interested in the spiritual implications than the political implications of the essentialized discourses of Indigeneity imposed through colonization: blood quantum, phenotype physiology, and Indian status registration. As suggested, it bothered me that so many people were emotionally and spiritually harmed by these narrow understandings of identity. This became the topic of my master's thesis, which I eventually drew from and published with Harold Ross in a journal article. This article is now a chapter in this book, with me as the sole author, where I discuss my very own theory and model of disenfranchised spirit through a community insider and case study analysis. I argue that narrow, exclusive definitions of identity are harmful to the human condition.

In 2005, after completing my master's degree, I moved on to a doctoral program in Indigenous studies, where my focus was on the Algonquin of Ontario land claim process. I hesitate to call these two areas of my work, meaning my master's and doctoral work, as research interests because my need for understanding was more about survival in a miserable world of structural oppression and nation-state-imposed genocide. Actually, I don't like the word "research" because it fails to describe my method/s and methodology/ies of coming to know any particular phenomena. The word is somewhat offensive to me.

Situated within the Algonquin of Ontario land claim process at the community level, and as a non-Status person, I existed within a context where I was unable to access and read articles—news articles, community-based articles, and academic articles—that met my need to know what was going on. There seemed to be a dearth of writing that was meaningful to my lived reality. I had many questions and it was especially frustrating that no one, Elders included, at the community level was able to tell me what I wanted to know, such as whether the land claim process was a good process. I eventually began to ask people, including newspaper editors, hard questions about why there were no materials that could help me understand, and this is what led me to writing for *Anishinabek News*. At that time I did not understand that *Anishinabek News* is the political paper of Anishinaabe First Nations in Ontario. That is how politically ignorant I was. Regardless, it was there where I first began publishing in the public domain. My first article appeared in 2002 during the time of my undergraduate education. It was not easy for me to step into public writing; again, I was a new reader, thinker, and writer and I was, to be honest, politically inexperienced. Up until then my life had been more about scavenging for love, survival, and recovery. Needless to say I was learning quickly as I went along. Many of the lessons were hard, such as dealing with an editor who would pick and choose according to the space available on a bloody page, and an editor who violated my confidentiality with a complete lack of remorse. Nevertheless, I am grateful that even though I was not a registered Status Indian and thus not a First Nation member of the larger political body known as the Anishinabek Nation my work and thinking was given some space to be expressed. There remain times today when still I publish with *Anishinabek News*, though now more fully aware that some of my work may be rejected if it is about a political issue that is contrary to the paper's mandate. Some of my early works are included in this book as short chapters. If you pay attention you will be able to see my writing develop over time.

When I began my process of compiling this collection of my writings challenging the *Indian Act* I was overwhelmed. There were so many. I was busy. The first thing I did was scour my computer's hard drive, collecting the works into one yellow folder. They totalled fifty-nine and consisted of news articles, academic articles, chapters in books, newsletter articles, blog posts, talks, submissions, and art, with a range of publishing dates from 2002 through 2018. After scrutiny and ruthlessness, I narrowed them down to forty-one. Then I organized them into themes rather than by date and again further narrowed them down. As I moved along and read through the compilation, I again narrowed the collection. And then at the formal editing stage, after the manuscript was pitched, I yet again narrowed them to what is in this book. Collectively, these chapters represent in part my very brave public learning; what I gave back to community members as I journeyed through Canada's court system, including the Ontario Superior Court and the Court of Appeal for Ontario; and my being an expert witness for the Senate and House of Commons committees.

While this explains my method of selecting my works that appear in this book, it does not address my methods of gathering the knowledge contained in the chapters. It is always important to reflect on a knowledge holder's methods. The methods I relied upon are in line with Indigenous methods, or ways of knowing: the Oral Tradition with my kokomis (grandmother), archival research, first-person experience, embodied knowledge, emotional knowledge, observation, reading, writing, role modelling, learning by doing, repetition, repetition, introspection, and storytelling. As suggested in the prologue, these methods are valid Indigenous methods of coming to knowledge. The way that some of these methods relate to my process of knowing are obvious. For example, I lived the experience of being a non-Status person, and I had to read to learn, whereas writing for various venues was a process of learning by doing. In terms of role modelling, I was learning from women such as Jeannette Corbiere Lavell and Sharon Donna McIvor and, at the same time, doing my best to role model learning and writing. Learning how to write in public venues came from a sense of responsibility and the need to be brave. And of course, I was feeling in my heart and thus embodying the knowledge. In this way, I relied on the additional methods of responsibility, bravery, feeling, and embodied knowledge. What is more, it could be said that I came into this world with the embodiment of colonization and nation-state genocide imposed on me by Canada.

Ten Qualifiers: What Readers Need to Know

First and foremost, the term "unstated paternity"—also known as unreported or unnamed paternity—references situations where a child is conceived through sexual violence or incest, where a mother does not record the father's name on the birth registration form or gain his signature because she does not want him to have access to the child.[1] "Unknown paternity" also references situations where a father is not known to the mother, child, and grandchild because the child was conceived through sexual violence such as rape, gang rape, sexual slavery, or prostitution.

Other situations of paternity include unacknowledged paternity, or alternatively unestablished paternity, where a mother records the father's name on the child's birth registration form yet he refuses to sign it, because he wishes to protect his standing in the community and/or maintain a marriage to another woman and/or avoid child-support payments. Another is unrecognized paternity, where a mother records the father's name on the birth registration form but, because the father's signature is not obtained, a government official blanks out his name. Alternatively stated, the father's name is removed.

In considering this we must also value that in some situations the father is not present during the birth of the child, such as when the mother is flown out of her community to give birth. Furthermore, sometimes the father dies prior to the birth of the child.

Regardless of all these potential situations around paternity, conception, and birthing, the government of Canada has relied on the discourse of "unstated paternity," a discourse that blames mothers. After considering this crucial discourse analysis of issues related to paternity it is important for me to qualify here that, although my use of terms has been fluid in the duration of my work, today when I talk about my court case I rely on the discourse of "unknown and thus unstated paternity" because this is my reality. I do not know who my paternal grandfather is, or was, because he is unstated on my father's birth registration record. It is vital to keep in mind an understanding of this discourse analysis and my current position when reading this book about my section 15(1) *Canadian Charter of Rights and Freedoms* equality rights challenge.

Second, I completely understand that Indigenous jurisdiction and land and resource rights extend beyond the First Nation reserve system and the *Indian Act*; I am also aware that the land claim process is not a valid avenue that respects Indigenous rights and jurisdiction. Again, the latter was the topic of my doctoral work and so I do understand this. My point is that I am aware that Canada continues to eliminate Indigenous rights through the land claim process, or what Canada calls the "modern treaty process." Some people think I am ignorant about this reality. I am not.

People who judge me as ignorant about the larger context of colonization and the need for Canada to get rid of the *Indian Act* should know that, yes, I agree that we need to get out of the *Indian Act*, but this has to be done in a way that respects Indigenous jurisdiction. Contrary to what many people may think, and despite the current Liberal government rhetoric, we are not in an era of reconciliation where nation-to-nation relationships are being honoured. The only effort Canada is making is through the land claim process that forces Indigenous Nations to extinguish our land and resource rights (or define our rights completely). Canada's colonial policy of genocide continues to this day through both the second-generation cut-off rule in the *Indian Act* and through the land claim and self-government process! It is my thought that until the day comes that the *Indian Act* is gone, the need exists to protect the most vulnerable members in our communities. For me this came to mean continuing to challenge Indian and Northern Affairs Canada's unstated paternity policy that did, and in some situations continues to, target mothers and their babies. In large part this is where my thinking and agency has been located—certainly not in my need to be a registered Status Indian, and certainly not within an ignorant void of understanding of Canada's broader policy of elimination and genocide that the

2015 Truth and Reconciliation Commission and the 2019 National Inquiry into Missing and Murdered Indigenous Women and Girls have concluded. Related to this, some people also assume I suffer from a colonized understanding of Indigenous rights where, as such, this was the only reason that I wanted to be a Status Indian. In my thinking about this I have come to know that some people have a hard time deciphering the seeming contradiction of my effort at challenging the cultural genocide inherent in the history of sex discrimination in the *Indian Act* yet also speaking out about the cultural genocide the land claim process imposes. Ultimately, they have to think through this seeming contradiction if they want to understand where I stand. Simple dichotomous thinking will not work here.

Third, I began my effort to become registered as a Status Indian when I was twenty-three years old. Although young, I am not so sure I was interested in becoming registered myself. As I moved along and more fully realized Canada's lies about the claim of removing the sex discrimination in the *Indian Act* in 1985, and Canada's creation of new forms of sex discrimination in 1985, I was morally outraged and disgusted. I also felt embarrassed that Canada was harming young mothers and their babies. In the Anishinaabe knowledge tradition it is valued that morals move through the heart. All Canadians, I felt, should feel embarrassed about what Canada was doing. In this way my motivation was less about me and more about feeling for mothers and babies. My mother had eight babies.

Fourth, while reading this book it is also important to know that what I generally refer to as Indian and Northern Affairs Canada has undergone a few name changes, including Aboriginal Affairs and Northern Development Canada and, more recently, Indigenous and Northern Affairs Canada. The latter name confused matters, having the same acronym (INAC) as the earlier Indian and Northern Affairs Canada. In 2011 the Conservative government changed Indian and Northern Affairs Canada to Aboriginal Affairs and Northern Development Canada. Then in 2015 the Liberal government changed it to Indigenous and Northern Affairs Canada. Further, in 2019 the Liberals dissolved the department and formed two new departments: Crown-Indigenous Relations and Northern Affairs Canada (CIRNAC), and Indigenous Services Canada (ISC). In the chapters that follow, readers will notice I shift between these names. Don't let this shifting distract or irritate you. Also keep in mind that in my legal challenge, *Gehl v Canada*, it was always Indian and Northern Affairs Canada that I was taking to court regardless of all the name changes at the nation-state political level.

Fifth, the 1985 amendment to the *Indian Act* brought forward what is called the second-generation cut-off rule. Many people have difficulty understanding this rule. But it can be simplified, which I do here at the get-go because if I do not, readers will get lost: when a Canadian couple moves abroad, to Britain, let's say, their children will be entitled to Canadian citizenship, but their grandchildren will not. This is similar to the second-generation cut-off rule in the *Indian Act*. Of course the difference is that this land is Indigenous land, not Canada's land. I offer more on this later but the short story is, this rule was applied immediately to the descendants born before 1985 of Indian women who were reinstated with Indian status in 1985 as compared with the descendants of Indian men for whom the rule began to apply after 1985. I caution readers now that the sexist application of the second-generation cut-off rule is an essence that this book fleshes out. What is more, an earlier version of the second-generation cut-off rule was called the double-mother clause. As with Indigenous ways of knowing, the content of this book is repetitious, so if you don't get it now, with some further reading and additional cognitive effort you will soon understand.

Sixth, understanding the process of enfranchisement is also an important matter. Enfranchisement is a process that the pre-1985 Indian Acts and Canada relied on to eliminate Indians and assimilate them into white society. Eventually, enfranchisement was achieved through sex discrimination, and it is this very process that generations of Indigenous women have been challenging. It should be stated here that although it is argued that the enfranchisement process was eliminated in 1985, it is my position that in fact what Canada did was remove the word "enfranchisement" from the legislation and re-codify it as the second-generation cut-off rule. It is best to understand that Canada relied upon the method or tool of legislative obfuscation through "instrumental learning" to further eliminate Indians and their rights to land and resources.[2]

Seventh, this compilation of works has been edited for consistency, typos, new knowledge, new insights, and errors. In the event that a gross error in an original publication—either mine and/or that of editors—needed to be corrected, I have taken the time to qualify it with an endnote. I am sorry if these errors have caused anyone frustration.

Eighth, I use the terms "Aboriginal," "Indigenous," and "Native" interchangeably throughout this book. Sometimes these terms are used as adjectives and sometimes they refer to the Original Peoples. I rely on the term "Indian" when talking about people registered as Indians as defined by the *Indian Act*.

Ninth, in *Gehl v Canada* I was the plaintiff. Readers interested in a deeper legal analysis of the issue of sex discrimination in the *Indian Act* should read beyond this work, seeking out legal thinkers such as Sharon Donna McIvor, Mary Eberts, Gwen Brodsky, and Pamela Palmater. My bibliography is your source.

Tenth, of course this book offers something new beyond the compilation of my previous works in a new and neatly organized and edited way. Part 5 of this book consists of never before published talks that I did. Part 7, titled "My Last Chapter: I Am Only a Woman," is my personal story of the entire journey intact as one complete story, where I add my analysis and thoughts on the judgements and how the *Charter* failed to protect me.

How this Book Is Organized

To this end, in line with my methods of knowing, the chapters in this book do not necessarily unfold in a linear nature. Succinctly, time is not my organizing framework. Part 1 of this book begins with a collection of articles that address identity in a broad way and also narrows to a discussion of INAC's treatment of children born out of wedlock. Most of the chapters are short so the reader will be motivated as they move through them quickly. I like short chapters. However, one of the chapters is lengthy and will require some deeper conceptual thinking. I have, in order to create some cohesiveness between the chapters, revised them slightly to reflect their new place, gathered in this book.

Part 2 is a collection of short community-based chapters that for the most part remain chronological in terms of their original publication. Because these chapters are short, readers will feel motivated and accomplished as they move through them. While reading them, it is important to keep in mind that the *Indian Act* was amended in 1985 through Bill C-31, in 2011 through Bill C-3, and again in 2017 through Bill S-3. I suggest that readers imprint that information in their minds so they are less frustrated with the events that unfold in the chapters that make up this book. Remember, obfuscation is a tool of colonial genocide.

Part 3 contains two short pieces on genocide. This is the most controversial aspect of my thinking and writing. Many people struggle with my use of the word "genocide" because the sex discrimination in the *Indian Act* is a bloodless genocide that is better understood as cultural genocide—and then other people struggle with my use of "cultural genocide." Regardless, cultural genocide through law and policy is genocide and I will always rely on both terms when I talk and write about what Canada has done and continues to do to Indigenous Nations and Peoples.[3]

Part 4 contains a collection of longer, more academic chapters beginning with my first university essay, already mentioned, titled "The Queen and I." Again, keep in mind here that the reader will encounter repetition from previous parts and chapters of this book. Some people will like this and some people will loathe it.

Part 5 is, for the most part, a small collection of never before published writings that were originally presented orally via a script. With this collection the reader will be able to see the growth of my learning. Thirty years is a long time.

Part 6 is a collection of works on Bill s-3, which led to the most recent version of the *Indian Act*. Stéphane Descheneaux, Susan Yantha, and Tammy Yantha challenged additional sex discrimination related to the way the second-generation cut-off rule was applied to them as descendants of an enfranchised woman. Their court case, known as *Descheneaux*, led to Bill s-3 and this is also where the *Gehl* clauses were added to the amended *Indian Act*. Again, the reader will learn more about this process as they move through these chapters.

Part 7 is where I offer my "Last Chapter: I Am Only a Woman," in that it represents what I hoped would be the last thing I write on this life-sucking matter. I caution readers now with saying this last chapter is lengthy and divided by subtitles to organize the story. I wanted this chapter to remain intact as one complete piece; as such, it offers many elements. It begins with me revisiting my methods and methodology because it was here where my process shifted more deeply into Indigenous ways of knowledge and being. It also offers a linear timeline framework of my process, my analysis of the final judgements, my analysis of the court's manipulation of my agency through the *Gehl v Canada* litigation, and a discussion of Canada's waste of taxpayer money, with a compilation of my greatest insights threaded throughout. People who have followed *Gehl v Canada* may want to focus on reading just this last chapter rather than the entire book.

Part 8 ends with two short happy stories because this is the convention readers need: a happy ending. You can be sure that I am not happy about the perpetuation of Canada's genocide. And lastly, the afterword runs deep into the crevices of my thinking on truth, knowledge, morals, and relationships.

PART ONE

On Identity Matters

Chapter 1

Fighting for Recognition

I N THE ALGONQUIN ANISHINAABE TRADITION, DBAAJIMOWINAN,
or personal storytelling, is valued as a legitimate method of gaining and
conveying knowledge. Dbaajimowinan is wholistic in that it values
knowledge that is more than just what is rational: it is emotional and spiritual too.[1]

For me, most days, and especially Remembrance Day, are a bundle
of contradictions in that my lived experience is laden with the genocide
of colonial Canada—both historically and in a contemporary sense. The
Algonquin Anishinaabeg are a Nation of people who straddle what is now
called the Ottawa River watershed. Through processes of colonization we
are now divided into provinces and by language, law, and religion. We were
denied a treaty during the historic treaty process, and Canada's Parliament
squats on our land.

My great-grandfather Joseph Gagnon (also Gagne) served in the First
World War (1914–18). On September 12, 1910, in Eganville, Ontario, Joseph
married Algonquin Anishinaabe-kwe Annie Jane Meness (also Menesse),
the daughter of Mary Ann Bannerman and the adopted daughter of Frank
Meness. Joseph and Annie Jane were members of the Golden Lake Indian

LEFT: *Figure 1.* Joseph Gagnon, ca. 1916. RIGHT: *Figure 2.* Annie Jane Meness Gagnon with Children, ca. 1916

Reserve, now called Pikwàkanagàn First Nation, raising their five children: Viola, Cecelia, Gordon, Kenneth, and Steve. Viola, their first child, was my kokomis.

Through archival research I gained a copy of Joseph's attestation papers that are dated May 12, 1916. His last name is spelled "Gagnon," and his birthdate was recorded as April 7, 1890, making him twenty-six years old at the time of his enlistment. He was recorded as 5 feet, 7¼ inches tall; he had brown eyes and brown hair, with a medium complexion, and was listed as a Roman Catholic. Joseph enlisted in the 207th Battalion and then transferred to the 2nd Battalion; he served in Canada, England, and France. I learned that his port of embarkation out of Canada was Halifax, and he left on my kokomis Viola's sixth birthday, May 28, 1917. His port of disembarkation was Liverpool, England, on June 10, 1917, and he was demobilized on January 24, 1919, remaining a private, service number 246266, for the duration of the war. According to the record, Joseph received the British War Medal and the Victory Medal. Family oral history, though, informs me that he may also have received the Military Medal. I have never seen these medals, and I am not sure where they ended up. The feelings that the military records and the Oral Tradition evoke—of a dutiful, decorated soldier—are real enough for me.

After the war ended, Joseph returned to his family and home community, the Golden Lake Indian Reserve. From my family oral history I have learned that shortly after, in the 1920s or early '30s, the RCMP escorted him and his family out of their community because his Indigenous identity was borne by his mother's ancestral line rather than his father's. The Indigeneity of his wife, Annie Jane, was irrelevant because women, according to British law, were mere appendages of their fathers and husbands. Apparently this practice was commonly imposed on Indigenous veterans and their families. When they came home from serving as the British Crown's loyal allies, some lost all their treaty rights as Indigenous Peoples.

While the Algonquin Anishinaabeg are the traditional Indigenous landholders of the Ottawa River Valley, through colonial practices, policies, and laws many of us were, and remain, denied the right to pass on to our families our national identity and our rights as Indigenous people, such as the right to own land and resources and, via this, the right to live mino-pimadiziwin (the good life). Rather, as historians have argued, we were stripped of our national identity and many were relegated to living in reserve communities until we could prove we met the British criteria of what it meant to be civilized.[2] The reason for this was that British Canada did not view the Algonquin as real people but rather as pre-human beings without legitimate identity, culture, or governance traditions; consequently, we also lacked a valid holding on the land.[3]

In concrete terms, the legacy of these colonial policies and laws also manifests today in the intergenerational transfer of landholdings, in the form of what is, and what is not, willed to the children and grandchildren of settler families and Indigenous families. The short story is that many settler families continue to benefit from Indigenous land and the denial of land rights. In this way, settler Canadians, you should know that my great-grandfather went to war for *your* rights, not mine.

When I reflect on this reality, I am saddened that Joseph Gagnon fought for a country that took so much away from his family—from his children, grandchildren, and great-grandchildren. As Indigenous people of this land, my ancestors deserved the right and the responsibility to care for their children and to provide for them mino-pimadiziwin. This is my story. Learning, sharing, and remembering should not be this hard and yet you will see as we continue that my story has been a difficult and ceaseless intergenerational challenge in defeat of the wiindigo that Canada's foundation rests on.

Chapter 2

The Personal Implications of the Discrimination in the *Indian Act*

LTHOUGH THE *INDIAN ACT* WAS AMENDED IN 1985 THROUGH
Bill C-31 to bring it in line with gender equality under the
Constitution's 1982 *Charter*, many Aboriginal Peoples appre-
ciate that much sex discrimination continued despite these amendments.
Consider a few more details here of my personal story and struggles to
resolve this continued discrimination in my fight against Canada.

I grew up not knowing who I was or what my place was within the Canadian
mosaic. The contradiction was that I secretly knew I was an Algonquin. As
a young person, I spent many years in critical contemplation of what was
happening around me. You see, through processes of policy and legislation,
my father, his mother (who is my kokomis), my great-grandmother and my
great-great-grandmother, and I were denied who we were and are.

My father and grandmothers before him were Algonquin peoples and
thus I too am an Algonquin person. Due to the gendering of Indigenous
identity via the *Indian Act*, my great-grandmother, Annie, and my
kokomis were escorted off the reservation of Golden Lake, known today as
Pikwàkanagàn First Nation. In 1945 Annie wrote a letter to Ottawa asking

if she was counted as an Indian. Just a few weeks later, Indian agent H. P. Ruddy replied explaining that when Annie married Joseph Gagnon, a white man, she became a white woman. I hold this very letter today and it does indeed say, "and you became a white woman."

Interestingly, Joseph Gagnon was Indigenous through his mother. Because his father was white, he too was considered a white person, and he in turn made my great-grandmother, Annie, a white person when she married him. Alternatively, my great-grandmother became a white person because her mother-in-law had married a white man.

When the *Indian Act* was amended in 1985, I began the process of establishing a relationship with my kokomis to determine who I was and where the Algonquin came from. I sent away for the necessary birth and marriage documents and eventually had my great-grandmother and kokomis reinstated as Indians under sections 6(1)c and 6(2), respectively.[1] You see, today we have different kinds, or different levels, of Indians. According to the *Indian Act*, 6(1) Indians are more Indian than 6(2) Indians. At this time, my father was denied registration because he was hit with what is known as the second-generation cut-off rule, which denies status to Native People after two generations of parenting with non-Status people.[2] The Registrar of Indian Affairs applies these new rules retroactively to the children and grandchildren of enfranchised women, which of course is a problematic practice.

In any case, I knew what I had to do and so, despite my visual limitations, I began an archival research project at 77 Grenville Street in Toronto, then the location of the Archives of Ontario, searching for my great-great-grandmother's family. My kokomis told me a little about her; for example, her name was Angeline Jocko, she was a "black Indian," meaning her skin was lovely and dark, and she had adopted a little white boy.

After years of research I found the necessary document to have my great-great-grandmother, Angeline, established as a 6(1)c Indian and thus her son Joseph Gagnon as a 6(2) Indian. As a result, my kokomis was upgraded to a 6(1)f Indian as both her parents, Annie and Joseph, were now considered Indians.

My father, though, was only registered as a section 6(2) Indian because we do not know who his father is or was. As a result of his unknown paternity, I was now hit by the second-generation cut-off rule.

Interestingly, there are no provisions in the current *Indian Act* regarding how the Registrar is to address issues of unknown paternity. Rather, the Registrar simply applies a negative presumption of paternity to my unknown grandfather; that is, the Registrar makes the assumption that my grandfather is or was a white person.

In February 1995, after ten years of work, I was denied entitlement to registration. I filed a protest with Indian and Northern Affairs Canada (INAC) and in February 1997, the Registrar informed me that my name had correctly been omitted from the Indian Register. In 2005, my lawyers at Aboriginal Legal Services of Toronto (ALST) told me that my case was heading toward discoveries in January 2006 and that it may proceed to trial in the year 2007.[3] At that point it had been over twenty years and I am still waiting to have this matter resolved.

I have given you a lot of information, so let me simplify it all. If my grand-mothers were instead grandfathers, I would be registered as an Indian and my children, if I had any, would also be entitled to registration. Specifically, we, my children and I, would be entitled to 6(1)a Indian status. This is the very sex discrimination in the *Indian Act* against which I have fought and continue to fight.

Needless to say, as a litigant and community member, I was left per-plexed for several reasons. First, because my reality of not knowing who my grandfather was (or is, for that matter) is not a reality codified in the current *Indian Act*, I was denied status registration and I literally slipped through the space between the printed words on a page that someone else wrote. Second, I did not understand why the Registrar had applied this new vagueness regarding issues of paternity in the 1985 *Indian Act* to my father's birth in a retroactive manner. My father, Rodney Peter Gagnon, was born in 1935, and at that time, children of unknown paternity born to Indian mothers were considered Indians. Third, if the *Indian Act* was amended in 1985 to bring it in line with the *Charter*, one would think that the denial of my registration resulting from my father's unknown paternity would have been contrary to the original intent and spirit of the amendments—that is, of being treated fairly and fully with no sex discrimination.

Chapter 3

Long Live the "Algonquin Frauds"

I N THE SPRING OF 2015, THEN APTN JOURNALIST JORGE BARRERA published an article on the comprehensive land claim process of the Algonquins of Ontario.[1] The land claim relies on federal policy to eliminate Indigenous jurisdiction and land and resource rights. Canada manipulatively calls this process the "modern treaty process." I would like to speak about the very contentious statements that have been made about who is and who is not Algonquin, as well as to speak to the issue of the Algonquin communities in Ontario that Barrera provided an analysis of.

First, I do not agree with Eagle Village Chief Madeleine Paul and Wolf Lake First Nation Chief Harry St. Denis in their arguments that non-Status Algonquin are not really Algonquin. Not all Indigenous Bands gained First Nation/*Indian Act* recognition by the federal government and as such it is not true that non-Status Algonquin are not Algonquin. We are. I am.

Second, it is well known and long established that one of the main goals of the *Indian Act* has been, and continues to be, to unmake Status Indians as a way to eliminate Canada's treaty responsibilities. As a result, there are more non-Status Algonquin Indians than Status Algonquin Indians. Clearly Indian status registration is not, and cannot be, the sole criterion of who is Algonquin. Most know this to be true.

Third, due to the colonial agenda of erasing Indigenous Peoples, as a mechanism of survival many Algonquin grew up not explicitly discussing and claiming who they were as Algonquin People. While many Algonquin did this in an effort to better ensure they were able to gain land and/or employment, this does not mean they, and their descendants, were not and are not Algonquin. We are.

Fourth, the contribution that Indigenous knowledge brings to the arena is valuing that knowledge is not just in one's mind and consciousness. Indigenous knowledge—and as such, being Algonquin—is also located in our hearts and in our practices.[2] To suggest that being Algonquin is only what is conscious and explicitly discussed is in fact a colonial understanding of what knowledge is. We were and are Algonquin and you cannot take that away from us.

Fifth, while the nine Algonquin communities in Ontario may not have been solidified and structured as the First Nations bands that Aboriginal Affairs recognizes, this in itself does not mean these Algonquin People did not have some semblance of community life—albeit a different one, owing to different colonial pressures. The fact is these Algonquin People were there at the community level doing what they did as Algonquin People. For some Algonquin this may have been a conscious and explicit experience and way of life, while for other Algonquin it may not have been, and still other Algonquin may have actually existed in a state of conscious denial. Regardless of these varied Algonquin experiences they were all there being Algonquin, and they remain Algonquin whatever their experience was, even if this experience was a void.

Sixth, while I do not agree with Chiefs Paul and St. Denis on these matters, I did and do continue to agree that the Algonquin of Ontario communities have been formalized and structured through the colonial process known as the Algonquins of Ontario. Sadly, and most unfortunately, the Algonquins of Ontario are operating under colonial policies that terminate Algonquin land rights, and in this way these communities and their leaders and/or Chiefs have been co-opted by the Canadian state. In this way, Chiefs Paul and St. Denis may be correct when they call these communities "policy fictions." However, this may not be the entire truth on this matter.

In summary, like Chiefs Paul and St. Denis I am not happy about the non-sense of the Algonquins of Ontario's land claim process, but I must defend who I am as a non-Status Algonquin brought on by the long-time sex discrimination in the *Indian Act*. I also need to speak to the reality that even though many Algonquin Bands were never federally recognized, these people, like me, are indeed Algonquin.

It is my thought that the real issue here is that we need to focus on the termination of who the Algonquin are through the comprehensive land claim process, not on who is and who is not Algonquin. Contradictorily, if what Pikwàkanagàn First Nation Chief Kirby Whiteduck argues is true— that there are many questionable Algonquin, potentially resulting in a no vote—some people may be prone to think, long live the "Algonquin frauds."

Chapter 4

"Love to Me Is the Kids"

M ANY PEOPLE HAVE COME TO KNOW THAT I HAVE BEEN IN the long and arduous process of a section 15 *Charter* challenge regarding the never-ending sex discrimination in the *Indian Act.* I qualify here that the sex discrimination I am challenging is not actually explicitly codified in the act; rather, there exists a silence, or a gap in the legislation, on the matter of what to do in situations where a father's signature is not on a child's birth certificate, whereby the Registrar then interprets this silence in a way that prevents women who are registered under section 6(2) of the *Indian Act* from passing on Indian status registration to their children.

While some people know this, what many people do not know is that in the Indigenous tradition the practice of mothering and the love that mothers provide to children was particularly cherished in Indigenous communities and societies, so much so that it was valued that mothering was more of a social process, not constrained by biological constructs and determinations. This means that mothering children who were not one's own biological offspring was a common practice. In this way, mothering is best understood through both a vertical and horizontal model. The historical record, the Oral Tradition, and our sacred stories inform us of this inclusive reality of mothering.

The Historic Record

Although not without limitations, the historical record is a useful source in discussing the Indigenous family model. In his work titled *Travels through Canada and the United States of North America, in the years 1806, 1807, & 1808*, John Lambert offered, "Among some of the groups of women I noticed three or four European children with light hair, whom they were nursing, and was informed that they frequently adopted the natural offspring of the white people whenever the latter abandoned them. Such instances, I think, may serve to show the fondness of the Indian women for children, and indeed no mothers can appear more tender of their offspring than they do. It is an amiable trait in their character, and must make the Europeans blush for that false pride and inhumanity which induce them to forsake their children."[1] Further, after assessing the Indigenous Peoples of Lower Canada (now the province of Quebec and, in part, traditional Algonquin Anishinaabe territory), the 1844–45 Bagot Commission Report assessed Indigenous child-rearing practices and the matter of so-called illegitimate children. Charles Bagot, then the governor general of British North America, explained that a child born outside the institution of marriage does not cast a stigma on the mother or the child, but rather the child is "usually adopted into the tribe."[2] Similarly, in his 1915 work on the Algonquin Anishinaabe Nation of the Ottawa River, Frank G. Speck reported that it was the Chief's responsibility to take care of orphaned children, and in 1979, historian Gordon Day noted, "The basic unit of Algonquin society was the family: the father and mother, grandparents, children and adopted children."[3] Thus, we see that in the Indigenous tradition all children were valued and included as members of the Nation, not cast aside as unworthy bastard children.

The Oral Tradition

While the historical record reveals these valued tidbits of knowledge, my knowledge of the Indigenous family model also emerges from the oral stories my kokomis told me. Originally from Pikwàkanagàn First Nation, Ontario, my kokomis was an Anishinaabemowin-language speaker and storyteller. Several times she recited to me the story of her kokomis Angeline Jocko, a Mohawk woman from the Lake of Two Mountains born around 1825, who in 1844, when she was nineteen years old, married Joseph Gagnon Sr.[4] Despite having several biological children of her own, my kokomis explained, Angeline adopted two little boys named little Paul Jocko (a sibling's son) and Moses Martell.

Our Sacred Stories

In addition, within the Anishinaabe knowledge tradition there are many ancient and sacred stories about Ashkaakamigo-Kwe (Mother Earth), Kokomis Dibik-Giizis (Grandmother Moon), Giizhigoo-Kwe (Sky Woman), Manitou-Kwe (Spirit Woman), and Wenonah (The First Breast Feeder). Anishinaabe stories teach us that these mothers, in their role as creators and nurturers of life, loved all children regardless of what western culture refers to as illegitimacy and non-paternity disclosure. Through these ancient stories the Anishinaabeg continually learn that all children are valued gifts from Creator and are deserving of the love needed to achieve mino-pimadiziwin, meaning the good life. Mothering and the work that mothers do was and is valued in Indigenous communities. It is said that through the work that mothers do they are located closer to the Creator and natural law and that is where their truth emerges from.

While my work to end sex discrimination in the *Indian Act* has become quite well known, many do not know or see it as connected to the Anishinaabe way of mothering and my attempt to protect Indigenous mothers and babies. And while the court date to hear my *Charter* challenge was originally scheduled for May 2014, through some unknown administrative glitch this date was lost. My new court dates—on which the summary judgement motion (SJM) would be heard in the Superior Court of Justice, located at 393 University Avenue, Toronto—were set for October 20, 21, and 22, 2014.

Chapter 5

Disenfranchised Spirit
A Theory and a Model

Identity is, of course, a key element of subjective reality, and like all subjective reality, stands in a dialectical relationship with society.
—Peter L. Berger and Thomas Luckmann,
The Social Construction of Reality

SOME PEOPLE THINK OF INDIAN STATUS REGISTRATION WITH INAC as merely an illusion created by the government of Canada and thus argue it is not real.[1] In my life, in the work I do, and through critical introspection, I have come to appreciate that it is best to understand Indian status not as an illusion but rather as a fictional story, which through systems of colonial power has taken on very real meaning for some people.

Through colonization, the government of Canada has and continues to dismantle Indigenous culture.[2] At the same time, Canada continues to impose a legal definition of "Indian." Through this process, Canada has and continues to distort and deconstruct traditional Indigenous cultural meaning systems of identity such as traditional naming systems and the Clan System of governance.[3] The manipulation and appropriation of traditional cultural meaning systems of identity, and the imposition of Indian status registration as the source of one's identity, have had—and, for that matter, continue to have—very real implications in terms of healthy identity production of Indigenous Peoples and consequently the ability to achieve mino-pimadiziwin. For some people this remains the case today. In this way, the fictional story of "Indian," mediated through imposed systems and structures of colonial power, has become a lived entity.[4]

Much has been written by me and others on the sex discrimination in the *Indian Act* and the amendments that took place in 1985 and then in 2011. This focus continues today in that, despite the amendments, much sex discrimination continues.[5] Even though this is the case, nothing has been written on the wellness potential that individuals experienced as a result of identity restoration once they became entitled to Indian status as a result of the amendments.[6] Certainly, the question of whether gaining Indian status makes a difference in one's ability to live a good life is worthy of exploration, especially given the amount of time that has passed since the 1985 amendment, and certainly there are stories that are illustrative and worthy of telling. After all, why did others before me—Mary Two-Axe Earley, Jeannette Corbiere Lavell, Yvonne Bédard, Sandra Lovelace Nicholas, and Sharon Donna McIvor—work to assure that they, their children, and their grandchildren gain Indian status registration?

Operating through a personal relationship, and existing on the continuum of collaboration, this chapter offers a case study analysis of Harold (Skip) Ross's story. Both Skip and I are Algonquin Anishinaabeg from the Ottawa River Valley. Through our collective effort, Skip eventually gained Indian status through the 1985 amendment to the *Indian Act*. While the archival research took place several years ago, offering Skip's story here illustrates the long-term wellness implications of having one's identity restored through entitlement to Indian status.

I begin with an analysis of western theorists' positions on identity and then offer an analysis of an Anishinaabe perspective on the human condition that values the emotional and spiritual dimensions.[7] With the help of Indigenous scholarship I then link colonial power to Indigenous identity destruction and its implications on the human spirit. Next, I offer a story about Skip's quest for Indian status, his successful entitlement through the method of archival research, and subsequently his entitlement to First Nation Band membership.

Then, relying on western theories of identity, Anishinaabe understandings of the human condition that value heart knowledge, the effects of colonial power on Indigenous identities, and Skip's story, I synthesize a theory and model that illustrates his powerful transformation to living a better life. I have titled this theory and model "disenfranchised spirit," and through it I illustrate how Indian status took on real meaning for Skip and thus cradled the transformational power he needed to begin to live a better life.

Having offered this introduction, it is important that I explain that I was the primary archival researcher in this project, while Skip was my helper. In addition, I was the primary writer of this work and creator of the theory and model of disenfranchised spirit. While this was the case, it is also important that I stress that Skip read several drafts and offered several suggestions along the way. Further, Skip gave his final approval before the article was published. It is in this way that this work was a collaborative effort.

Western Theories of Identity

Stuart Hall distinguishes between three common theories of identity: the enlightenment subject, the sociological subject, and the postmodern subject.[8] According to Hall, the enlightenment subject is both centred and unified, and is gifted with the ability to reason. The enlightenment subject also has consciousness and the ability to act on it where their inner core is present at birth and unfolds autonomously with maturity. With the sociological subject, there is a shift. Here, a person's inner core is contingent on family and community relationships, as well as on social interaction. With the sociological subject, the gap between the self and other members of society is bridged as the subject is now sutured into various social structures. In terms of the postmodern subject, it is Hall's contention that the structural changes that began transforming the world also transformed people and our identities. Hall contends that the continuous changes brought on by globalization, where no single fundamental articulating organizing principle exists, are also changing people. As such, he argues, the postmodern subject has no fixed, essential, or permanent identity. Rather, within us are contradictory identities pulling in different directions.

Notwithstanding these theories of identity, Hall further argues that one's ethnicity is a critical component of one's subjective sense of who one is, in that one's history, language, and culture are inherent in ethnicity.[9] That said, although Hall does not deny the value of strategic political essentialism—where members of a group bond through their ethnicity to challenge systems of oppression—as a strategy of political resistance, he does challenge the practice of always reducing individuals to an essential subject.[10] In this way, and despite what may appear to be a contradiction, Hall remains an ardent anti-essentialist, meaning he does not agree with the practice of reducing a person's entire being to a rigid and narrow definition through, for example, policy or law.

Hall also theorizes identity as a production that unfolds, where power shapes who we are. Specifically, he argues for the need to understand identity as a fluid production that is rooted in history and politics and thus mediated by power. In particular, he maintains, identities emerge within the play of specific modalities of power.[11] Speaking from his experience as a Black man living in England, Hall expresses the horrors of issues with identity control by powerful others, which is applicable to the Indigenous experience in Canada, when he argues that the inner expropriation of cultural identity by others "cripples and deforms."[12]

Richard Jenkins also theorizes identity.[13] He stresses that although some may treat identity as something that one has, he, or is born with, like Hall he theorizes identity as a process of becoming, or as a production. Jenkins's foundational template of identity production consists of an internal-external dialectic of relationships. Emily A. Schultz and Robert H. Lavenda describe this dialectic as "a network of cause and effect, in which the various causes and effects affect each other" where "the properties of parts and wholes *co-determine* one another" (emphasis in original).[14] In this way, Jenkins asserts, identity is never unilateral. Rather, it is within the dialectic of both primary and subsequent socializations that individuals come to define and re-define who they are. In this way, identities are relational and fundamentally dependent on one another in that "what people think about us is no less important than what we think about ourselves." Jenkins stresses, "It is not enough to assert an identity. That identity must also be validated (or not) by those with whom we have dealings. *Social identity is never unilateral*" (emphasis in original).[15] Further, and again similar to Hall, Jenkins appreciates that politics and power are central to one's identity formation and production. It is his contention that it is within institutions and organizations that specific individual identities are bestowed and flow. It is in this way that, according to Jenkins, "the capacity to exercise self-determination...is systematically related to wealth, in terms of both material and cultural resources."[16]

In sum, although theories of identity have shifted, through Hall and Jenkins we learn identity is best understood as a production that unfolds throughout one's life and yet is shaped by social relationships and by and through systems of power. When one understands identity in this way—as a fluid production that unfolds, shifts, and changes within a context of relationships and where power mediates—it becomes apparent why Hall discourages essentialist practices that reduce identity to a narrow, rigid definition. Having offered these western theories of identity, next I turn to Anishinaabe understandings of the human condition, which value the emotional and spiritual realm of who we are as human beings and their role in our identity productions. I also offer an analysis of what Indigenous scholars have concluded about the relationship between colonial power, Indigenous identity productions, and the spiritual implications.

Anishinaabe Theories of the Human Condition

The Indian Act *was repeatedly used to destroy traditional institutions of Indian government and to abolish those cultural practices that defined Indian identity.*
—Joe Mathias and Gary R. Yabsley, "Conspiracy of Legislation"

Through his ethnographic research in the 1930s, Diamond Jenness argued that the Anishinaabeg are more spiritual than European peoples.[17] According to Jenness, the Anishinaabeg understand themselves as consisting of both a body and a soul, where the soul, located in the heart, is capable of travelling outside the body for brief periods of time. Jenness also wrote that the Anishinaabeg understand the soul, and thus one's heart, as the intelligent component of the human condition where reason occurs, which therefore serves to facilitate an understanding of the world. Despite this wandering ability of the soul and the role of one's heart in the knowing process, illness occurs when the soul fails to return to one's heart, because the soul and heart must work in harmony with the body for an individual to live a good life.

Jenness also stated that while an insane person has lost their soul, and thus the intelligence of their heart, and is without the ability to reason, an intoxicated person has only temporarily lost their soul and heart intelligence.[18]

Decades later, A. Irving Hallowell also related an Anishinaabe explanation of the human soul.[19] Similar to Jenness's observations, Hallowell stated that when an Anishinaabe child is born, it is believed that the child comprises both a body and a soul, where the soul has moments of independent existence. The Anishinaabeg believe the soul has the ability to leave the body during sleep and can and will occupy different positions in both time and space. In this way, the body and soul are not always synonymous. Hallowell, in line with Jenness, also explained that the soul has a fundamental role in establishing a good life. The Anishinaabeg believe death can occur when and if the soul leaves the body for too long a period of time. In the Anishinaabe tradition, soul loss explains untimely or unanticipated deaths.[20]

In moving to contemporary Anishinaabe understandings of what it means to be a human being, it is often said that humans consist of four interconnected components: physical, mental, emotional, and spiritual. It is understood that the spirit emerges through one's heart. This significance of the heart is in line with older ethnographic accounts. Thus, as in the past, the Anishinaabeg continue today to recognize the importance of the emotional and spiritual realm in wellness. It is said that healthy individuals manifest when all four of these components are appreciated, allowed to actualize, and kept in balance. This wholistic philosophy of the human condition is often symbolized in the contemporary world as the Medicine Wheel, where the physical, mental, emotional, and spiritual components of the human condition are equally represented. Anishinaabe traditional teacher and leader Edward Benton-Banai speaks about this wholistic understanding of the human condition when he argues that healing has "to take place not only in a physical sense but in a spiritual sense as well," as the body and spirit have to be treated together in order for healing to be effective.[21]

While Indigenous Peoples have their own understandings of the human condition, of what makes for healthy individuals and, by extension, Indigenous identity, in her research Bonita Lawrence speaks about the implications of what colonial Canada has done to Indigenous identity productions. Having explored Indigenous identity and its relationship to colonial power, Lawrence argues that laws "defining and controlling

Indianness have for years distorted and disrupted older Indigenous ways of identifying the self."[22] Lawrence further argues that the *Indian Act*, as a regulatory regime, has manufactured ways of understanding Indigenous identity that are so pervasive that at the community level they have become internalized and thus naturalized. Lawrence's work brings to the fore how it is that Indigenous identity in Canada has been mediated by and through an abuse of colonial power.

Interestingly, in making her decision in the Sharon Donna McIvor court case, Justice Ross of the British Columbia Supreme Court expressed agreement with the role and meaning that Indian status has taken on. In her ruling, Justice Ross argued that the "concept of Indian" has come to exist as an important component of one's identity, cultural heritage, and sense of belonging.[23] Lawrence's argument and Justice Ross's statement serve to illuminate the distortion of Indigenous identity by colonial power. This aligns with identity theorists Hall's and Jenkins' views on power.

In their research Eduardo Duran and Bonnie Duran locate the origin of dysfunction of community people firmly in the colonial process. More particularly, they argue, colonization has systematically inflicted "a wound to the soul" that is "felt in agonizing proportions to this day."[24] They conclude that the only meaningful construct that applies to this dysfunction is "soul wound."[25] In this way, they identify the emotional and spiritual realms as being affected. Val Napoleon makes a similar observation when she argues that the process of colonization in Canada has been "soul crushing," where many First Nations are dealing with addiction, poor health, and unemployment.[26]

In sum, Jenness and Hallowell offer that the Anishinaabeg consider human beings a combination of both body and soul, where the soul, which is located in the heart, is viewed as holding the intelligent or rational dimension of the human condition. Alternatively stated, the soul and heart serve in our understanding of the world. Further, the Anishinaabe worldview encompasses the potential for soul loss as an explanation of sickness and, at times, unexpected death, while intoxication is a form of temporary soul loss and thus the loss of one's ability to reason and live well. In this way, the health of an individual depends on a presence, a balance, and the appreciation of both one's soul, located in the heart, and one's body. Specifically, all four components of the human condition—physical, mental, emotional, and spiritual—must remain present and in balance if one is to remain healthy.

Regardless of Hall's warning of the dangers of identity essentialism, the government of Canada has distorted the lives of Indigenous Peoples and their identity productions through the imposition of an essential legal definition of "Indian." As Lawrence explains, "Indian" as it is defined in the *Indian Act* has taken on meaning at the community level and proven destructive to the human psyche. Justice Ross agrees, as do Duran and Duran and Napoleon, who rely on the constructs "soul wound" and "soul crushing" to explain the effects in their communities.

Skip Ross's Story

Contrary to what many here in Canada may think about Indigenous people—that we all live in First Nation reserve communities or descend from First Nation reserve communities—Skip Ross knows otherwise. Skip was born in 1932 on the banks of the Petawawa River, traditional Algonquin Anishinaabe territory.[27] Skip says his parents were not interested in living on the reserve at Golden Lake. Apparently, they had several concerns, such as leaving their main source of subsistence along the Petawawa River, being narrowly defined by the colonial system as Status Indians, and the possibility that the residential school system could take away their children.

It was in a different colonial temporal context, on May 3, 1999, that Skip submitted his application to INAC for Indian status. He was motivated to become officially registered as a Status Indian after members of his extended family had been registered through the 1985 amendment to the *Indian Act*. While many people have critiqued the limitations of the 1985 legal remedy, many women once enfranchised (a process by which they lost Indian status) because they had married non-Indian men are now entitled to be reinstated as Indians.[28] In addition to this, the 1985 amendment meant that many others who were never registered could now apply, Skip included. By the time I met him, Skip told me, he had been working on the application process for well over ten years. Skip was a drinker; this was obvious.

On April 26, 2000, INAC responded to Skip's application with a letter asking for the marriage certificate of his maternal grandmother, Sarah Jocko (possibly Plouffe).[29] The request further stated, "In the event she was never married, I [INAC Registrar] will then require a letter from Vital Statistics confirming that a search has been made for a marriage" between 1907 and 1912. In other words, in order for Skip to gain Indian status through his grandmother Sarah, he had to prove that his mother, Idi Plouffe, was born outside of the institution of marriage. Sarah's maiden name was Jocko; her daughter Idi was born on November 9, 1912. Skip best describes this seemingly backward request: "They want me to look for something that I am hoping is not there."[30] I agreed with Skip; it seemed like a ridiculous request. Regardless, INAC further informed Skip that he would have to search the vital statistics records not only under the name Jocko (including the spellings Jacco and Jacque) but also under Jacob and Plouffe, as Gerald Plouffe was Idi's biological father.[31]

Sarah Jocko was born in 1892, and both of her parents, Skip's great-grandparents, Jean Baptiste Jacco and Elizabeth Jacob, were considered Indians.

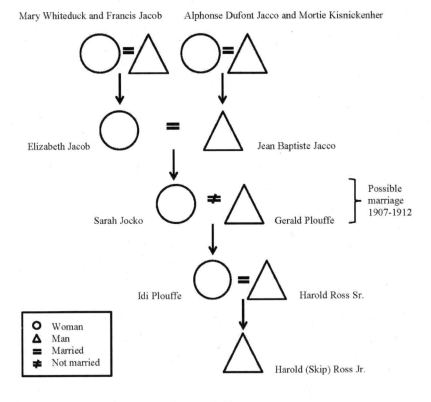

Figure 3. Harold Ross's Ancestry; © Lynn Gehl

As such, although Sarah was not officially registered, as a child of Indians she was also considered an Indian at the time of her birth. When Sarah Jocko gave birth to Idi Plouffe, she was not married to the child's father, Gerald Plouffe. Through the Oral Tradition, Skip understands Gerald to have been an Algonquin from Quebec, and this is all Skip knows about him.

I met Skip in the spring of 2000, possibly in April, at the post office in Golden Lake, Ontario, after a meeting that focused on the Algonquin land claim process. This was one year after Skip had submitted his application to INAC. As Algonquin, we were both learning about our family lineages for the purposes of meeting the criteria of Indian status and the Algonquin enrolment law, the latter being an application process used to identify non-Status Algonquin for the purpose of the land claim mandate.[32] In my process I was at the stage of conducting the necessary archival research. Skip was not. This Indian registration process required me to tie my father, kokomis, grandfather, and great-grandmother to a male ancestor who was once considered an Indian. I was also trying to fulfill the one-quarter blood quantum requirement for the Algonquin enrolment law.[33]

It turns out that Skip and I have a common Jocko ancestor, named Alphonse Dufont Jacco. While Skip is a fourth-generation descendant of Alphonse through Jean Baptiste Jacco, I am a fifth-generation descendant through Angeline Jocko. Possibly needless to say, when I heard Skip's story about what he was trying to accomplish, it resonated. After considering the commitment seriously, shortly after our spring meeting I agreed to do the necessary archival research for Skip. The vital statistics records that INAC had requested required archival research, as the Registrar General of Ontario only holds death, marriage, and birth records for seventy-five, eighty, and ninety-five years, respectively. After these time periods, the records are archived. Since we were interested in a possible marriage record that was between eighty-eight and ninety-three years old, it could only be obtained through the Archives of Ontario.

Although through observation I knew Skip was struggling with an alcohol addiction and therefore, as Jenness and Hallowell explain, an inability to reason to his fullest capacity, I insisted that he come along to witness and participate in the archival research project. This may be viewed by some people as an unreasonable request; however, I was not going to do it any other way. Skip had to be there. I wanted to take the necessary steps to embody within him the knowledge of what I was willing to undertake for him, as well as to embody within him a sense of respect for the archival research process and my effort at helping him. Through years of introspection and my background in medical anthropology, I knew that our archival research project was potentially endowed with deep meaning and thus also cradled, in part, the knowledge and spirit that could change Skip's life. I knew I needed to involve his agency in the process. Within a few weeks, again in the early spring of 2000, Skip and I set a date, May 29, to meet in Toronto, at 77 Grenville Street. Although I lived in the city, Skip had to take a bus from Pembroke, Ontario. He arranged to stay with his nephew, Terry, who lives in Toronto.

I scheduled our day of archival research on a weekday and during office hours as I felt it was best for me to have a trained archivist on hand to help with any questions that may arise. Further, as per INAC's request, I had to have an archivist validate that the vital statistics research was done correctly. That said, in Ontario, marriage registrations are arranged by year and each is assigned an identifying number. The registrations are then indexed by year and in alphabetical order. Because the names of both the bride and groom are indexed, a search can be carried out under either name. As stated above, to cover the different name spellings of the potential bride and the potential groom, we had to search the indexes for Jacob, Jocko, and Plouffe.

As INAC indicated in Skip's letter, the specific marriage record that we were looking for would have been dated between 1907 and 1912. These index records were part of the RG 80-7-0-18 series. Jacob and Jocko marriages were microfilmed on MS934 reels numbered 4, 9, and 10; Plouffe marriages were microfilmed on MS934 reels numbered 6, 9, and 10. With Skip as my helper, we researched for about four hours, making double photocopies along the way of all marriages between people whose surnames began with J or P. Skip supplied the rolls of quarters for the printers. Fortunately, we did not find a marriage indexed for Jacob, Jocko, or Plouffe. In this way, and as odd as this sounds, we were successful in not finding what we were looking for: a marriage record between Sarah Jocko and Gerald Plouffe. After the archival research was completed and the archivist notarized our photocopies, Skip and I had a quick lunch and parted ways. Skip paid for lunch.

Wasting no time, later that night I wrote a letter to INAC on Skip's behalf and emailed it to him so he could send it to the Department. This letter gave me permission to manage his INAC file. I asked him to print off the letter, sign it as soon as possible, and snail mail it to INAC. I then wrote another letter to the Department and enclosed the vital statistics records indicating that no marriage between Sarah Jocko and Gerald Plouffe had taken place during the years 1907 through 1912, thus indicating that Idi was born out of wedlock. Within this second letter I also requested that Skip's file be expedited as he was over the age of sixty-five. I simply did not want Skip to only gain Indian status posthumously. Certainly this has happened before.[34] INAC complied.

A few weeks later, on June 19, 2000, I called INAC to inquire about Skip's application for Status and I was given the good news. I quickly called Skip and passed on the message—that we were successful in our research and thus he was now entitled to be registered as a Status Indian as per subsection 6(2) of the *Indian Act*. After I gave Skip the news, he wasted little time sending me an email. I offer elements of this email here not to engage in an egocentric process but rather because Skip's words are illustrative of the very real significance that Indian status registration has for a seventy-year-old man. In the email, Skip celebrated: "My whole family loves and respects you, even the ones who were already status. They were all hoping and praying for me and you did it all. I will be forever grateful to you. You are now part of my family. I can never thank you enough. Without you I would not have my identity!"

Sure enough, the next day, on June 20, Skip received a letter from INAC confirming the good news. In this letter, Skip was provided with the address of where he could obtain his certification of Indian status: Algonquins of Pikwàkanagàn First Nation. In this letter, Skip was also told that Pikwàkanagàn determines their own membership and he would have to apply with them if he was interested. Shortly after, Skip became a Band member, as Indian status meets Pikwàkanagàn's requirement.

On August 18, 2000, the Algonquins of Pikwàkanagàn hosted a gathering titled "Honouring Chief Tessouat." The gathering was operating under the land claim mandate that had been ongoing since the early 1990s and was an effort to unite status and non-Status Algonquin.[35] Skip and I were told that there would be the opportunity for Algonquin to speak at this gathering, and Skip asked me to help him construct something that he could read. Written collaboratively, in part Skip's speech read, "Until a few weeks ago, I was a member of the non-Status community here on the Ottawa River watershed. I was born and raised here and I always knew that I was an Indian and yet I could not prove it. Thanks to my friend Lynn and the work she did to make me a Status Indian, I can stand here today and say I am no more Indian today than I was yesterday."

What is more, on August 29, 2001, Skip had his last drink, and shortly after he offered tobacco to a traditional person in requesting his spirit name: River Man Running. With his identity now affirmed, and no longer drinking, Skip is able to live a more productive life. Today he works diligently to protect the Petawawa River, the very river he was born, raised, and subsisted on, from being dammed for the purpose of producing two hydroelectric generating stations known as Big Eddy and Half Mile Rapids that were scheduled to be constructed in 2013.[36] The construction of these dams, Skip argues, will place two endangered species at risk: the American eel and the lake sturgeon.[37] Skip asserts these species require a safe passage up and down the Petawawa River, as it is only through their passage that they are able to live the ancient knowledge they are born into. This is the knowledge that these species performed long before European people, and for that matter all human beings, came to Turtle Island. It is precisely for this reason that Skip implores the Ministry of Natural Resources to "drop all plans for development of the Petawawa River." In this way, although as Skip stated he was "no more Indian today than I was yesterday," becoming registered as a Status Indian changed his life.

Having offered this discussion of western theories of identity as well as Anishinaabe understandings of what it means to be human, which recognize emotional and spiritual knowledge, along with Indigenous scholarship on the effects of colonial control and the manipulation of Indigenous identity as causing an effect on the human soul, and further, in adding Skip's experience as a case study, I want to now synthesize these elements in terms of disenfranchised spirit theory to illuminate and bring clarity to Skip's story.

Disenfranchised Spirit:
Offering a Theory and a Model

In articulating disenfranchised spirit, I rely on Hall's and Jenkins's thoughts that identity is a production that unfolds within a larger context of social relationships that is mediated by and through power. I also draw from Hall's warning against the practice of identity essentialism: that it has the power to harm. In disenfranchised spirit theory, the *Indian Act* definition is the essentialism that, in Hall's words, holds the capacity to cripple and deform. In articulating disenfranchised spirit, I also draw on Jenness's and Hallowell's ethnographic accounts of the Anishinaabeg and on Benton-Banai's and Duran and Duran's discussions of an Indigenous understanding of the self: collectively, a conceptualization that values the human spirit and heart knowledge as holding the capacity for reason (also intelligence) and human agency and, by extension, that holds a fundamental role in one's ability to live a good life.

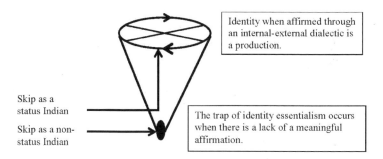

Figure 4. Disenfranchised Spirit; © Lynn Gehl

In the model, the circle represents one's typical identity production. The circle is chosen because it is an Indigenous organizing principle that is rooted in an Indigenous worldview. The four quadrants of the circle represent the physical, mental, emotional, and spiritual components of the human condition. This is in line with the Medicine Wheel, a significant cultural meaning system of Indigenous identity and wellness. The arrows represent one's normal identity production, a process that unfolds throughout one's life. In this model, the disenfranchising potential of an essentialized discourse of identity—in this case, a legal definition of "Indian"—is represented as a narrow rigid point below. This narrow point represents the location where a person who is denied their identity production, as a result of an imposed essentialized definition, is trapped by a pain felt so deep it leads to a soul wound that results in the lack of constructive agency, and thus a healthy identity production is lacking.

Although Indian status did not make Skip any more Indian, it gave him the licence and freedom he needed to be who he is. The external element of the internal-external dialectic was gained through his registration. Alternatively stated, the lack of external affirmation of who he thought he was internally resulted in a state of spiritual disenfranchisement where in turn he lacked the intelligence of his heart knowledge and, therefore, constructive agency to move forward in a healthy identity production. In essence, Indian status took on real meaning for Skip; lacking it he was trapped. In agreement with disenfranchised spirit theory, in his own words he added, "Although the *Indian Act* is made up by the government of Canada, the denial of who I was as an Algonquin Indian was spiritually hurtful and therefore spiritually harmful. Once I became entitled to Indian status, the Algonquin Indian I felt in my heart was affirmed, and this gave me both the motivation and the reason to quit drinking and move on with my life." It is precisely here that disenfranchised spirit theory obtains its name. Disenfranchised spirit theory encompasses the relationship between the need for external validation (in this case, by the Registrar of INAC and Algonquins of Pikwàkanagàn First Nation), one's internal sense of self, one's identity production, an abuse of power, the trap of essentialism, one's spirit and the intelligence of heart knowledge, one's agency, and one's overall well-being.

In summary, as disenfranchised spirit theory illustrates, once Skip was affirmed as an Indian as defined by the *Indian Act*, the intelligence of his heart was animated; he was able to move out of the trap of essentialism, become more productive with his agency, and move on with his life's production as an Algonquin Anishinaabe. Within a year of receiving Indian status, no longer spiritually disenfranchised, Skip gave up drinking and converted the "booze room" in the basement of his home into what he calls "my own personal cultural centre," a source of personal empowerment.

With that explained, there is the need to qualify that I am aware that some people may criticize disenfranchised spirit theory because Skip and I do not explicitly illustrate a relationship between Canada's essentialized definition of "Indian" and Skip's alcoholism. Rather, we make a connection between identity affirmation and his recovery. We hear this critique, and our response to this is that our goal in writing this article, and in offering this theory, is for the purpose of illustrating how identity affirmation holds the power to shape personal agency. Further, some people may wonder why we did not title this concept "enfranchised spirit theory," as this name is more in line with what we did. More specifically, we linked identity affirmation, spiritual wellness, and a healthy identity production. Our response to this potential critique is that in order to honour the Ancestors, and the people living today who continue to be denied their identity because of an abuse of colonial power, we decided to name it disenfranchised spirit theory.[38]

There is also the need to qualify that in no way are we proposing or arguing that the only way to gain the external identity affirmation needed to live a good life is through registration as a Status Indian. Certainly there are other ways to have one's identity affirmed, such as receiving one's traditional name, Clan, song, or colours. This commentary and case study is intended to share Skip's story and, through this sharing process, allow other people to gain insight into the effects of colonization, the *Indian Act*, identity control, identity denial, soul loss, the wellness potential of identity affirmation, and the role of heart knowledge and the soul in one's identity production and one's ability to live mino-pimadiziwin.

It must also be realized that in offering disenfranchised spirit theory we do not claim to have resolved all the issues the theory puts forward. Rather, disenfranchised spirit theory is also intended to offer and encourage thinking about the dangers of an inner expropriation of cultural identity that generations of colonial governments in Canada have unleashed in Indigenous communities.

This understanding and articulation of disenfranchised spirit theory is consistent with Hallowell's and Jenness's observations: in an Anishinaabe worldview there is a relationship between a person's soul (spirit), their heart, their ability to rationalize, and thus their agency to live a good life. Disenfranchised spirit theory is also in line with Benton-Banai's thoughts and Duran and Duran's soul wound as the culprit in Indigenous health issues.

Disenfranchised spirit theory and Skip's story begin to fill the gap in the literature regarding the positive effects of gaining Indian status registration through the 1985 and 2011 amendments to the *Indian Act*. Through Skip's bravery we learn that Indian status registration was for him a meaningful system of identity and thus heartfelt. It is in this way that fictional stories created by the Canadian government, mediated through power, have become endowed with spirit and have become lived entities in our communities. August 2011 marked Skip's tenth year of sobriety—and a continued life of being the Indian he knew himself to be all along.[39]

PART TWO

Some Community Writing

Chapter 6

Women Protest Bill C-31
Threat to Erase Indians

J UNE 28, 2005, MARKED THE TWENTIETH ANNIVERSARY OF THE
implementation of the Bill C-31 amendments to the 1985 *Indian Act*. To
raise awareness of the continued sex discrimination in the *Indian Act*'s
current form, the Quebec Native Women (QNW) and the Native Women's
Association of Canada (NWAC) organized a protest at the human rights
monument in Ottawa followed by a march to Parliament Hill, which, it is
worth noting, remains unsurrendered Algonquin land. Both organizations'
presidents, Ellen Gabriel and Beverly Jacobs, were on hand acting as mod-
erators of the event. Elaine Shipley led the way from the monument to the
Hill while drumming and singing the Strong Women's song. The event was
very well attended, with over 150 women, men, and children taking part.

Interestingly, the human rights monument reads "All Human Beings
Are Born Free and Equal in Dignity and Rights." Despite this very public
display of Canada's sentiments—carved in stone, no less—many women,
men, and children continue to be treated unequally in terms of how the
Registrar of INAC interprets and applies the current *Indian Act*. The children
and grandchildren of Indian women who were once enfranchised are treated

differently than the children and grandchildren of their male counterparts. In addition, many children are being denied status registration because of issues related to their paternity. More specifically, children born of unknown or unstated paternity are potentially denied status depending on whether their mother is a 6(1) or 6(2) Indian. This is because the Registrar makes the assumption that the father is a non-Indian person. This, of course, is a problematic practice.

Both Jeannette Corbiere Lavell and Senator Sandra Lovelace Nicholas were present at this demonstration offering their continuing support in the efforts to eliminate such discrimination. Both women were instrumental in having the *Indian Act* amended in 1985. Jeannette took her concerns regarding section 12(1)b, which stripped Indian women of their status when they married a non-Indian man, to the Supreme Court of Canada (scc). When this effort failed to create the change needed, Sandra took her concerns all the way to the United Nations. The United Nations shamed Canada when it ruled that Canada was in fact discriminating against Indian women.

In 1985 Canada *supposedly* amended the *Indian Act* to bring it in line with the *Charter*. I add "supposedly" to this statement because in amending the *Indian Act* the government took the opportunity to codify a new version of the double-mother clause in the form of the second-generation cut-off rule. At this time, the government also neglected to include provisions regarding unknown and unstated paternity. Instead, there was a silence on this latter matter.

It must be appreciated that the second-generation cut-off rule and the Registrar's practice of interpreting situations of unknown or unstated paternity as non-Indian Peoples serves the government's agenda of eliminating Status Indians. Further, in taking this approach the government enacted a law that eliminates the Indian problem at an accelerated rate over the previous *Indian Act*.

Chapter 7

Great Gathering against Bill C-3

O N May 31, 2010, yet another gathering of Indigenous women took place to challenge the sex discrimination in the *Indian Act*. This time this gathering was intended to bring attention to Bill C-3, which was moving through Parliament in a form that yet again perpetuated sex discrimination. As many as two hundred people attended the feast in celebration of what was called "Marche AMUN." The last leg of Marche AMUN was the walk from Victoria Island to Parliament Hill on June 1. Again, this is unceded Algonquin land.

Marche AMUN, where the Innu word AMUN translates to "great gathering," covered a five-hundred-kilometre trek from Wendake, Quebec, to Parliament Hill in Ottawa. The march was carried out during the May moon, culminating on June 1. The goal of the march was to raise awareness of the problems inherent in Bill C-3 and, as articulated by lead marchers Michèle Audette and Viviane Michel, to inform parliamentarians that they must denounce Bill C-3 because it simply does not eliminate the gender discrimination in the *Indian Act*.

In honour of the marchers, the Odawa Native Friendship Centre and the Indigenous Peoples Solidarity Movement Ottawa (IPSMO) hosted a celebratory feast.[1] Algonquin Elder Annie Smith St. Georges opened the feast in a good way. Traditional foods such as waawaashkesh (deer) and ode'minan (strawberries) were served, after which Sharon Donna McIvor offered her sage advice. Sharon called for a united front among the various women's associations: NWAC, QNW, the Assembly of First Nations Women's Council (AFNWC), the Ontario Native Women's Association (ONWA), and the AMUN marchers. She cogently argued for the government of Canada to eliminate all gender discrimination in the *Indian Act*: "Bill C-3 does not go far enough. The government must withdraw the Bill and introduce one that takes out all of the discrimination against us and our children."[2] Indeed, Sharon is a great thinker and a leader worth following. It was during this time when I created the slogan "6(1)a All the Way!" It was catchy.

NWAC president Jeannette Corbiere Lavell agreed with Sharon, arguing that "forty years of fighting this battle is long enough." There is no need for yet another process of legislative change that fails to resolve all of the gender issues. Jeannette also argued that AMUN marchers Michèle and Viviane were great role models for younger women to emulate. They "have taken on a praiseworthy task," Jeannette continued. Kathleen McHugh of the

Figure 5. "6(1)a All the Way!" Art/Poster, 2010 Marche AMUN; photo by Nik Gehl

AFNWC and Dawn Lavell Harvard of ONWA were also in attendance, and they too stood in agreement with the actions of the AMUN marchers.

As it stands, several things are wrong with Bill C-3. First, there is a 1951 cut-off point that will leave out some people. Second, Bill C-3 applies to the grandchildren of Indian women who lost status by marrying out and fails to include the descendants of unmarried Indian women. Third, a female child of a Status Indian man and a non-Status Indian woman who were unmarried will continue to be excluded from registration solely because the child is female. Fourth, Bill C-3 confers an inferior form of status on the grandchildren of Indian women who married out. In these ways Canada's colonial and sexist policies continue and I and others continue to fight.

Chapter 8

Indian Act Still Discriminating

ANY PEOPLE KNOW IT WAS LARGELY THROUGH SHARON Donna McIvor's efforts that an amendment to the *Indian Act* passed into law in 2011. It is estimated that as many as 45,000 grandchildren of Indian women once enfranchised because they married non-Indian men will gain status registration and consequently be entitled to the treaty benefits that were once denied them.

Despite this progress, through a line of discriminatory reasoning—that being that there was a need to preserve the pre-existing rights of the men and their descendants—several caveats remain. For example, grandchildren born prior to September 4, 1951, who trace their lineage through Indian women will continue to be denied status registration. In addition, descendants of Indian women who co-parented through common-law relationships, and the female children and grandchildren of Status Indian men who co-parented with non-Status women through common-law relationships, will continue to be denied status registration.

As a result, as with the 1985 amendments brought forward through the efforts of Mary Two-Axe Earley, Jeannette Corbiere Lavell, Yvonne Bédard, and Sandra Lovelace Nicholas, this recent legal remedy once again fails to resolve all the discrimination. Like Lovelace Nicholas before her,

McIvor has been forced to pursue the elimination of discrimination in the *Indian Act* beyond the domestic arena. Shortly after Bill c-3 became law, McIvor filed a complaint against Canada with the United Nations Human Rights Committee (UNHRC).

And there is more. When the *Indian Act* was amended in 1985, the government of Canada removed the provisions that had once protected children born out of wedlock. In actuality, the current *Indian Act* is silent on this issue, as it is on the issue of unknown and unstated paternity. Although the *Indian Act* is silent on how the Registrar should address these situations, INAC has developed an administrative policy that is followed when determining if status requirements have been fulfilled.

Through the 1985 amendment, Status Indians are now registered under either section 6(1) or section 6(2). Section 6(1) status allows a parent to pass on Indian status to their children in their own right, while section 6(2) status does not. This means a 6(2) parent must parent with another Status Indian to pass on status registration and the associated treaty benefits. Today, when a child is born and for some reason the father is unable to sign, or does not sign, the birth certificate, the Registrar of INAC applies a *negative assumption of paternity*—meaning the Registrar assumes the child's father is a non-Indian person. As a result of this unfair negative assumption, when the mother is registered under section 6(1) the child is only registered under section 6(2) of the *Indian Act*. This child is entitled to status registration

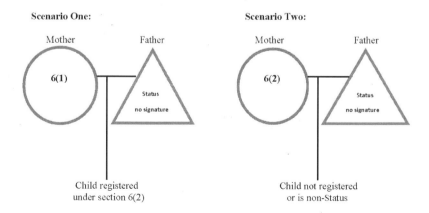

Figure 6. Unknown and Unstated Paternity; © Lynn Gehl

and treaty benefits. However, when the mother is registered under section 6(2) the child is deemed a non-Status person and the consequently loses treaty benefits.

Young mothers and their babies are in need of their status registration and the protection of their treaty benefits—in particular, their healthcare and education benefits. These young mothers and their babies should not bear the brunt of the government of Canada's desire to eliminate Status Indians.

In summary, there are two scenarios that result from this negative assumption of paternity. Scenario one: a child born to a section 6(1) mother and a Status Indian father, either 6(1) or 6(2), who does not sign the birth certificate, is only registered under section 6(2). Scenario two: a child born to a section 6(2) mother and a Status Indian father, either 6(1) or 6(2), who does not sign the birth certificate, is a non-Status person.

Chapter 9

The *Indian Act*'s Legislative Silence

L EGISLATIVE CHANGE MUST NOT BE USED BY A GOVERNMENT AS an opportunity to create new forms of sex discrimination—and mask them through legislative silence. This is exactly what Canada has done.

Canada has treaty responsibilities that it has to live up to. We all know this by now. Yet since 1985, and through an amendment to the *Indian Act*, Canada has been specifically targeting Indigenous children in its goal to eliminate these treaty responsibilities. In 1985 the *Indian Act* was amended to conform to section 15 of the *Charter*, which prevents discrimination based on race, national or ethnic origin, colour, religion, sex, age, or mental or physical disability.[1] Regardless of the implementation of the *Charter*, for several reasons the legislative change was failed remedial legislation in that it did not eliminate the sex discrimination. In many situations, the change shifted the discrimination onto the grandchildren of Indian women.

Through Sharon Donna McIvor's efforts, the *Indian Act* was amended yet again, in 2011, to remove the continued sex discrimination. This process of legislative change, though, was once again failed remedial legislation in that it did not remove all of it. Offering one example here, some children born to Indian women in common-law relationships before 1985 continue to be denied Indian status registration and therefore their treaty rights. This is in part because the SCC refused to hear McIvor's appeal. She is now pursuing this matter at the international level.

Notwithstanding this continued sex discrimination and the long-time efforts to eliminate it, the 1985 changes to the *Indian Act* not only created a legislative silence or gap in law but also took rights away from children born to mothers registered under section 6(2) of the *Indian Act* and whose birth certificates lack a father's signature. What is bewildering about this legislative change is that prior to 1985, "illegitimate" children born to Indian mothers were the same as their mothers: "Indians" as defined by the *Indian Act*. What this means is that what Canada did in 1985 was remove an offensive word in law, that being the word "illegitimate," while at the same time removing the protective measures associated with it. In this way, since 1985 Canada has denied many First Nations children Indian status registration and treaty rights resulting from the lack of a father's signature on their birth certificates.

I must add that post-1985 it does not matter if a child is born inside or outside of the institution of marriage; if a father's signature is missing on a child's birth certificate, the father is assumed to be non-Indian. Disturbingly, this practice also occurs in situations of rape and other forms of sexual violence such as incest, sexual slavery, and prostitution. What is more, the mothers of these First Nations children are not entitled to child-support payments. These children are harmed in both directions.

What makes this situation even worse is that many of these children are born in northern First Nations communities where their basic needs of clean water and sanitation—let's face it, we all hydrate and we all urinate—are not met, and as such they are very much in need of the treaty rights to which they are entitled through Indian status, such as housing, education, and health care. These treaty rights, as many know, are the very rights on which Canada is founded.

I can imagine this knowledge is hard to understand, both in terms of the legal and policy complexity of the issue and, more so, in terms of the absolute absurdity of Canada in doing this. I realize many readers may be asking, "What exactly are you talking about, Lynn? Can you tell me that again?" As stated, to comply with the *Charter*, in 1985 the federal government of Canada removed the word "illegitimate" and associated protective provisions from the *Indian Act* and became silent in law in situations where a father's signature is missing on a child's birth certificate. Then, at the departmental level, Canada developed a policy and practice that denies many Indigenous children whose mothers are registered under 6(2) of the *Indian Act*. When a father's signature is missing, a departmental practice assumes the father is a non-Indian. Through this policy assumption, Canada places First Nations children born to mothers registered under section 6(2), and whose father's signature is missing on their birth certificate, in a worse situation. I estimate that as a result of this negative assumption of paternity, as many as 25,000 children have been denied entitlement to Indian status registration and consequently their treaty rights.

In summary, what this amounts to is that during an important moment of legislative and human rights remedial action, Canada did the very opposite of meeting the standard outlined in the *Charter*, actually making the situation worse. Removing the word "illegitimate" from legislation, becoming silent on an issue in law, and then creating and implementing a policy assumption that is more oppressive is the worst form of legislative and policy manipulation I can think of. Is this what legislative reform in Canada is about, an opportunity to make things worse at the level of policy and practice?

In May 1990 and in December 1991 Canada signed and ratified the United Nations Convention on the Rights of the Child, where article 3 states the best interests of the child must be a top priority. Clearly this process of legislative and policy manipulation is not in the best interest of First Nations children. First Nations children do not deserve to have their needs and their treaty rights manipulated by Canada's legislation and policymakers. What is it about Canada, our parliamentarians, and our law and policymakers? Is Canada a kakistocracy that lies to and manipulates its citizenry? Canada, are you proud?

Chapter 10

Canada's Court System
A Hostile Place for Indigenous Peoples

I APPRECIATE THE PUBLIC INTEREST THAT PEOPLE HAVE IN MY SEC-
tion 15 *Charter* court case, where I am challenging the *Indian Act*'s
continued sex discrimination and denial of Indian status registration in
the case of an unknown paternal grandfather. When a child's birth registration form is lacking a father's signature, and the mother is registered under
section 6(2) of the *Indian Act*, Aboriginal Affairs and Northern Development
Canada's (AANDC, formerly INAC) paternity trap denies the child status registration. As a result, these children, as well as grandchildren, me included,
are also denied treaty rights such as education and health care. Disturbingly,
this practice of denial also occurs in situations where the child is the result of
sexual violence such as rape.

I also appreciate the need to be respectful of the hard work my lawyers
and their legal team at Aboriginal Legal Services of Toronto have done so
far in moving my *Charter* case forward. As such, I need to politely clear up
an inaccuracy reported in a few recent news articles. In these news articles it
was argued that my lawyers filed the statement of claim (SoC) in the wrong
court and, further, that it had to be refiled in the correct court. This is not

true. In 2001 we filed the SoC with the Ontario Superior Court of Justice. This was the correct path to take.

Something did go awry, though. It is my position that the court made an error when it struck my first SoC. In May 2001, and through my SoC, my lawyers correctly challenged the practice by the INAC Registrar of assuming that my unknown paternal grandfather was/is a non-Indian. This approach of challenging the Registrar's practice was taken because there is absolutely nothing in the *Indian Act* that directs the Registrar to carry out this practice; he/she just went ahead and did it. Succinctly, the Registrar made the assumption that my paternal grandfather was/is a non-Indian and applied this assumption to my application for Indian status entitlement as a matter of internal practice, procedure, or policy, whatever the case may be.

The Department of Justice (DoJ), representing the genocidal interests of Canada, filed a motion to strike my SoC and, in November 2001 while in court, argued that we had incorrectly challenged the INAC Registrar's practice and, further, that we needed to challenge the *Indian Act* itself. After admitting she had conducted an internet search on the *Indian Act* the night before court, Justice Swinton of the Ontario Superior Court agreed with the DoJ's position and struck my SoC. In September 2002 we took this decision to the Ontario Court of Appeal, where Justices O'Connor, Catzman, and Doherty (one of whom seemed pretty miserable, tired looking, and bored out of his mind) agreed with and upheld the lower court decision.

In sum, and contrary to news reports, we were in the right court. Further, it is my position that we correctly challenged the Registrar's practice, as the *Indian Act* is silent on the matter of unknown paternity. As such, it is also my position that the DoJ incorrectly argued that we needed to challenge the *Indian Act*. Through its power, the DoJ was successful at throwing in this wrench. Needless to say I have learned that justice remedies are more about power than about what is right and fair.

A person has to ask, Why would two levels of Canadian courts do this, and why would a Canadian court system force me to go through a long process of challenging legislation laden with sex discrimination that generations of Indigenous women have already challenged, especially in light of the fact that we live in a post-*Charter* era? After all, it was in 1857 with the *Civilization Act*, a predecessor to the *Indian Act*, that the sex discrimination was first codified into law. Is not 157 years of sex discrimination long enough?

Furthermore, one has to ask, Would it not be easier for Canada to simply change the Registrar's practice? In offering my response to why this approach is not taken, realize it is quite simple to understand. Mediated by and through the power of a European and thus foreign court system, with its continued motivation to deny Indigenous People their rights, the court, which represents the Crown, also serves to continue to deny Indigenous justice.

Over time, it has become obvious to me that the justice system in Canada is not a place where Indigenous People will achieve justice, or the protection of the treaty rights that Indian status registration provides. Rather, Canada's legal system is a tool of the oppressor. While I may have been naïve of this fact in 1985, when the Bill C-31 amendment to the *Indian Act* was enacted— and when I began my effort to gain Indian status entitlement—I am naïve no longer. I know today that Canada's court system, with its intentionally constructed layers of structural oppression, is without a doubt a hostile place to Indigenous People. I hope others, journalists included, learn from my process. And I hope non-Indigenous readers can understand even more clearly why it is that Indigenous Peoples say and know that in Canada a policy of genocide continues on these lands of ours.

PART THREE

On Cultural Genocide

Chapter 11

Canada's Unstated Paternity Policy Amounts to Genocide against Indigenous Children

CANADA COMMITS THE GENOCIDE OF 25,000 INDIGENOUS children through AANDC's unstated paternity policy and yet relies on language that blames their mothers.

In 1944 Raphael Lemkin coined the term "genocide" and proceeded to define it.[1] Interestingly, what many people do not know is that Lemkin defined genocide in cultural terms rather than in terms of mass murder. More specifically, he defined genocide as having two stages. The first involves the denial of an oppressed group's national pattern, and the second involves the imposition of the oppressor's national pattern.

When the Convention on the Prevention and Punishment of the Crime of Genocide was adopted by the United Nations in December 1948, Lemkin's work was included within the definition.[2] Article 2 of the Convention codifies five genocidal practices and states that any of these acts committed with the intent to destroy, in whole or in part, a national, ethnical, racial, or religious group constitutes genocide. These five practices are as follows: "killing members of the group; causing serious bodily or mental harm to members of the group; deliberately inflicting on the group conditions of life calculated to bring about its physical destruction in whole or in part; imposing measures intended to prevent births within the group; and forcibly transferring children of the group to another group."

That said, when I think about the issue of unknown and unstated paternity and the *Indian Act*, and specifically about AANDC's unstated paternity policy, or internal practice or whatever they want to call it, I realize it is in fact genocide. As many know, Indian status registration is delineated into two subsections of section 6 of the *Indian Act*: subsection 6(1) and subsection 6(2). While mothers registered under subsection 6(1) are able to pass on status to their children in their own right, this is not the case with mothers registered under subsection 6(2), also known as a weaker form of status. In the event that a father's signature is missing or not found on a child's birth registration form, the Registrar of AANDC assumes a negative presumption of paternity, meaning the Registrar assumes non-Indian paternity. This means that the children born of mothers registered under subsection 6(2) are vulnerable, as their children are now considered to be non-Status and thus not entitled to treaty rights such as health care and education, First Nation Band membership, and First Nation citizenship.

Many know by now that, compared with non-Indigenous women, Indigenous women experience a higher rate of sexual violence, including incest, rape, gang rape, sexual slavery, and prostitution. This situation has been brought on through the oppression of colonization, the denial of our rights as Indigenous Peoples, the denial of our land and resources, the residential and day school systems, and the criminalization of our cultures and Indigenous knowledge systems. In any sexist and racist society, young women are particularly vulnerable. Research has shown that 45 percent of the children born to Status Indian mothers fifteen years of age or younger do not have their father's signature on their birth registration form. It is precisely at this moment where Canada's practice falls within the parameters outlined in the international Convention on the Prevention and Punishment of the Crime of Genocide. Specifically, when a father's signature is not placed on a child's birth registration form and the mother is registered under subsection 6(2) of the *Indian Act*, AANDC's unstated paternity policy transfers these children from their First Nation community into mainstream Canadian society (read: commits the genocide).

It is crucial that I point out that in the process of committing genocide Canada relies on language that blames mothers, as in "unstated paternity." While AANDC's unstated paternity policy targets Indigenous mothers for the lack of the father's signature, there are many instances where a mother, for very legitimate reasons, may refuse to obtain a man's signature, such as in the unfortunate situations of incest and rape. In addition, there are many situations where a father will not sign a birth registration form, such as seeking to avoid child-support payments or wishing to preserve a current or previous relationship. Clearly, terms such as "unreported," "unnamed," "unacknowledged," "unestablished," "unrecognized," and "unknown" paternity are better signifiers of women's realities.

AANDC's genocidal policy continues to exist today despite the fact that section 15 of the *Charter* was put in place in 1982 and is supposed to protect Indigenous women from sex discrimination. Furthermore, this genocidal policy exists today despite the long-time heroic efforts of Mary Two-Axe Earley, Jeannette Corbiere Lavell, Yvonne Bédard, Sandra Lovelace Nicholas, and Sharon Donna McIvor. It is clear to me that legislative change, such as the changes to the *Indian Act* that took place in 1985 and 2011, is not an avenue available to Indigenous women. Clearly the government of Canada has merely manipulated moments of legislative change in their favour.

Through the unstated paternity policy, Canada perpetuates the sexual violence imposed on Indigenous women and commits genocide on their children. I estimate that since 1985, when this AANDC policy emerged, as many as 25,000 Indigenous children have been affected by this genocidal practice. In April 2012 Canadians celebrated the thirtieth anniversary of the *Charter*. Do you feel protected? Do you feel fuzzy and warm? I certainly do not and I am sure many Indigenous women and their babies stand with me on this.

Chapter 12

Canada Is Carrying Out Cultural Genocide with a Smile

*It is the First Nations who have the knowledge of what is needed
to ensure our future, not just theirs, but ours too—and all the live
forms that sustain us. Please remove all the sex discrimination in
the Indian status registration provisions of the* Indian Act.
—Mejran Monsef, n.d.

ANADA'S MINISTER FOR WOMEN AND GENDER EQUALITY,
Maryam Monsef, in voting to pass the gutted version of Bill s-3, An
Act to amend the *Indian Act*, is complicit in cultural genocide.[1] As
many know, I have been working on removing the sex discrimination in the
Indian Act for over thirty years. In April 2017, my case went to the Ontario
Court of Appeal, the highest court in Ontario, where I won on the matter
of INAC's proof of paternity (PoP) policy. Unfortunately, a new form of sex
discrimination was imposed on me when the judges determined I was only
entitled to the lesser form of Indian status: 6(2).

Sex discrimination in the *Indian Act* is a form of cultural genocide in that
it is rooted in the need for Canada to eliminate its treaty responsibilities.

We need to keep in mind that Raphael Lemkin defined genocide in cultural terms. Cultural genocide is insidious in that it can take place through law and policy—such as the *Indian Act* and Canada's comprehensive land claim and self-government policies—right in front of people, and they will be unable to see it. The sighted become blind. What is worse is that cultural genocide is so insidious that many people, owing to their socialization, have actually celebrated the genocide during festivities such as Canada 150.[2]

This past spring, after the 2015 *Descheneaux* decision that came out of Quebec, the Senate moved forward with Bill S-3, which addressed the sex discrimination by adding the "6(1)a All the Way!" clauses. These clauses were added after it became apparent to Senate members that INAC and the DoJ were not addressing all of the sex discrimination in the revision process.

Unfortunately, after the Senate moved the bill forward, the House of Commons gutted the bill, removing the "6(1)a All the Way!" clauses and thereby reintroducing the sex discrimination. Prime Minister Justin Trudeau, calling on party solidarity, passed the gutted bill on June 21, 2017. The House of Commons and the Senate then rose for the summer.

Maryam Monsef, MP for Peterborough–Kawartha and Minister of Status of Women, voted to pass the gutted version of Bill S-3. The rationale from Minister of Indigenous Affairs Carolyn Bennet, Prime Minister Trudeau, and consequently Monsef was that they would address the ongoing sex discrimination in phase-two consultations. A phase-two consultation approach was argued in 2010 after the *McIvor* case in British Columbia, yet nothing came of it. On August 23, 2017, during a meeting with myself and Peterborough community members, which I requested, Monsef put forward the argument that the 2010 approach was under the Conservative government. This is a pitiful excuse to say the least when you think that Indigenous women have been working for well over sixty years to eliminate the sex discrimination in the *Indian Act*.

Recently I had a telling experience in terms of Canadians' blindness to cultural genocide. As I moved in my daily activities, talking, holding meetings, and emailing on the very issue of Monsef's voting position against Indigenous women—after all, she is the Minister for Women and Gender Equality—it was suggested by a settler woman that I was attacking a young female politician. "Attacking" was this particular settler's choice of word, when in reality all I was doing was generating discussion and awareness that the minister did not have the best interests of Indigenous women and their descendants as one of her priorities. At first I was taken aback by this accusation, but then I addressed this line of poor reasoning by explaining that the issue is complex and thus a complexity of thought is needed to understand it. It was not an attack—not at all. This was clearly a settler issue, not mine.

As I thought more, I remembered that all too often patriarchs, colonizers, and oppressors actively seek out nice, obliging, accommodating, compliant, young people who have lovely smiles to carry out their oppressive, sexist, racist, and genocidal agendas. What I am getting at is this: How is it that I am blamed for attacking someone when, thinking about the matter more deeply, we come to realize that it is in fact Monsef, in voting to pass the gutted version of Bill s-3, who is attacking and is complicit in cultural genocide? Why is it that this settler woman cannot see the reality that is right in front of her eyes? Is it because, as I suggested, they are blind to the cultural genocide? Is it because Monsef does her political work with a kind and polite smile that people enjoy? Is it because I have less to smile about in the context of oppression and cultural genocide? I ask these questions to generate thought.

Without a doubt we need to decolonize the lovely smiles many people wear, as one may be worn by a person whose agency has been co-opted by a colonial oppressor.

PART FOUR

Some Academic Works

Chapter 13

"The Queen and I"

Discrimination against Women in the Indian Act Continues

How would you answer the question "What is your cultural identity?" There are many people living in Canada today who struggle with issues of identity in terms of their culture, ethnicity, minority status, sexuality, and race. Many people have relocated to Canada against their will, while others, for many reasons, made a conscious choice. These dislocated and relocated people at some point in their lives, if not all their lives, will wrestle with their identity and their sense of belonging. However, for many Aboriginal women and their children this is not a question of belonging and being but rather a question of law. The oppression of Aboriginal women and their descendants is of a particular nature as their cultural identities are entangled with legislation.

In Canada, the federal *Indian Act* determines who is and who is not an Indian. Legislation titled the *Indian Act* was first formalized in 1876. It was early in 1869 when "patrilineage was imposed" on Aboriginal Peoples and "Indianness" was defined as applying to any person whose "father or husband was a registered Indian."[1] Eventually, in 1951, the *Indian Act* underwent one of its infamous amendments, known as section 12(1)b. Here the *Indian Act* dictated that Indian women who married non-Status men were no longer Indian. The goal of the *Indian Act* was one of assimilation and of civilizing the so-called savages—a national agenda. Ironically, what this type of policy did was subjugate women to the status of "chattel of their husbands."[2] It stripped women of their rights socially, politically, and economically and made them dependent people. By European standards, this was the proper location for women on the social evolutionary scale.[3]

The struggle to have the gender inequalities removed from the *Indian Act*, which continues today, has been a difficult process. The paternalism is so well entrenched in Aboriginal communities that women have been struggling internally as well as externally to have their rights acknowledged. The oppressed have often proven to be the oppressor.

One of the first women to speak out publicly about section 12(1)b was Mary Two-Axe Earley in the 1960s.[4] Legally, the first women to argue against the sex discrimination set out in 12(1)b were Jeannette Corbiere Lavell and Yvonne Bédard. In 1973 the Supreme Court of Canada determined that the *Indian Act* was exempt from the Canadian Bill of Rights.[5] Part of the problem in the fight to remove the discrimination was the lack of unity and support the women had from the National Indian Brotherhood (NIB, now called the Assembly of First Nations). The NIB feared changes to the *Indian Act* would jeopardize the federal government's legal responsibility to Status Indians.[6] In 1977 Sandra Lovelace Nicholas took her complaint against 12(1)b to the UN Human Rights Committee, where in 1981 she was not successful.[7] In 1979, the Tobique Women's Group of New Brunswick organized a grassroots march from Oka, Quebec, to Parliament Hill in Ottawa, the country's capital, to raise awareness of Aboriginal human rights specific to Indian women.[8]

In 1985 the *Indian Act* was amended to conform to the equality provisions of the *Charter of Rights and Freedoms*. Regardless, and despite what many people think, much of the sex discrimination still exists in the act. I, my family, and many other First Nations People continue to be excluded from registration as Indians.[9] Aboriginal Peoples who wish to pursue registration as Status Indians with the Department of Indian Affairs and Northern Development must have extensive knowledge of their family history and great determination, as well as awareness of the continued discrimination against women and their descendants perpetuated by section 6 of the current *Indian Act.*

First, I will take you on a genealogical journey of five generations of my family history. Second, I will discuss the difficulties I encountered when forced to fulfill the documentation requirement of the application process for registration with the Department of Indian Affairs and Northern Development. Finally, I will explain how Indian Affairs exercises section 6 of the *Indian Act* in regard to my application for registration and how it continues to discriminate against me and my family on the basis of sex and marital status.

I am often asked, "Why is registration as a Status Indian so important?" This question is difficult to answer because, as my understanding of my identity and my right to identify with the Aboriginal First Nations has evolved, so has my reply. Most people living in Canada are fortunate enough to identify with their place of origin. This is not true for many Aboriginal Peoples, including myself. One can argue that identity to Native Peoples is not a subjective process but rather something that legislation provides. For Native Peoples, registration as an Indian with Indian Affairs is an important component of their cultural identity. Denial of Indian status has excluded many Aboriginal women and their descendants from residing on the reserve and from sharing in the benefits available to the community. Registration as an Indian in Canada is required to participate in rights to land, education, and health care and, most importantly, to share in similar cultural values. Larry Gilbert articulates this challenge well in the preface to his book: "As an Algonquin Indian from Ontario...I am acutely aware of the identity crisis suffered by many aboriginal people separated from their homeland, their tribe or clan, their language and their culture. Seeking and protecting one's identity is a personal and a very human aspiration. It is seldom that the state intervenes and declares persons are not who they really are. That is the legacy and the reality of the *Indian Act.*"[10]

On January 2, 1945, my great-grandmother wrote a letter to Ottawa. She explained that she was having some difficulty with her nationality and was wondering if the government could help in any way. "I would like to know if I am counted as an Indian. Please let me know soon."[11] Four weeks later, she received a reply (see Figure 7).

Prior to the implementation of Bill c-31, the *Indian Act* discriminated against Indian women by revoking an Indian woman's status upon her marriage to a non-Indian man. Essentially what happened was this: "She was stripped of her *Indian identity* [my emphasis] and not able to live on the reserve with her extended family."[12] However, an Indian man was allowed to retain his status and pass it to his non-Native wife. This inequity prevented Indian women from passing Indian status on to their children (in their own right), while permitting Indian men to do so. This is how my great-grandmother lost her status, and as a result, so did my kokomis. Of particular interest is that my great-grandmother's husband was also a Native person

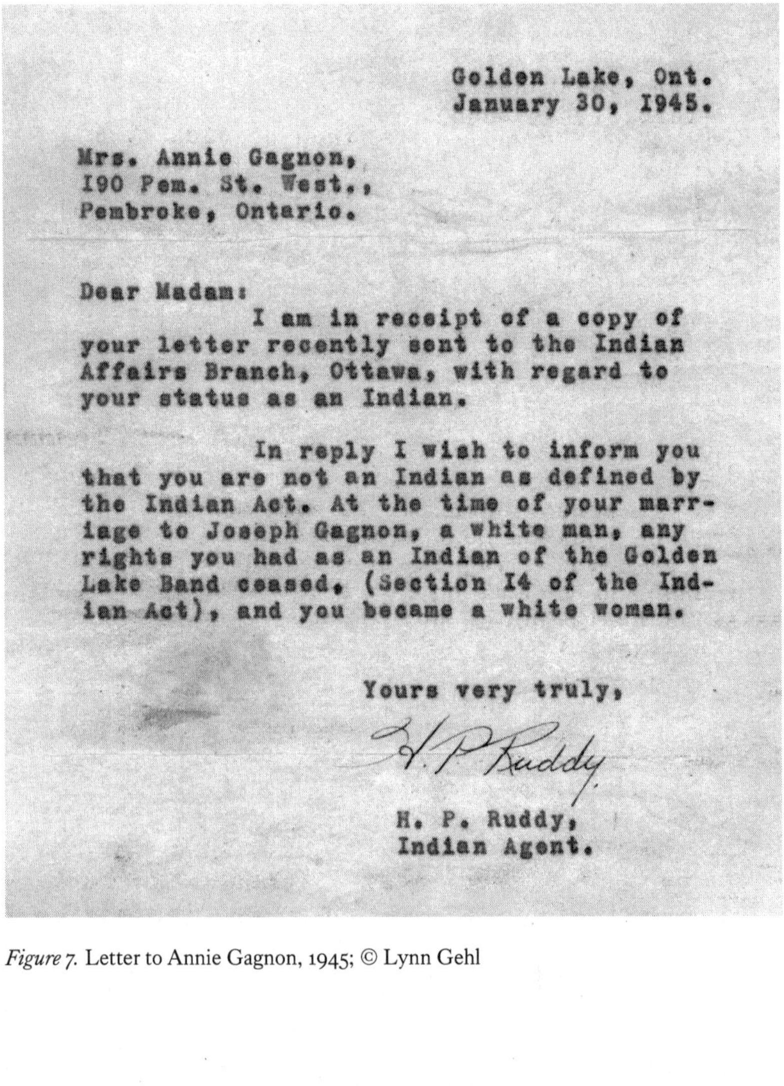

```
                                    Golden Lake, Ont.
                                    January 30, 1945.

Mrs. Annie Gagnon,
190 Pem. St. West.,
Pembroke, Ontario.


Dear Madam:
            I am in receipt of a copy of
your letter recently sent to the Indian
Affairs Branch, Ottawa, with regard to
your status as an Indian.

            In reply I wish to inform you
that you are not an Indian as defined by
the Indian Act. At the time of your marr-
iage to Joseph Gagnon, a white man, any
rights you had as an Indian of the Golden
Lake Band ceased, (Section 14 of the Ind-
ian Act), and you became a white woman.


                        Yours very truly,

                        H. P. Ruddy,
                        Indian Agent.
```

Figure 7. Letter to Annie Gagnon, 1945; © Lynn Gehl

through his mother (my great-great-grandmother), not his father. Hence, because of the male lineage criteria he too was deemed a "white" person. His mother, Angeline, married a white man and became "white" as well.

My kokomis, Viola, was born and raised on the reserve. In 1927, at the age of sixteen, she and her parents were escorted off the reservation of Golden Lake by the RCMP.[13] They lost their home along with most of its contents and, from what my kokomis tells me, they were given nothing to start their new lives as "free" people. Welcome to civilization. After all, this was the intent of the *Indian Act*: to protect the Indians until they had assimilated into white society and then to set them free.[14]

Consequently, when my father was born Viola recorded her racial origin as French despite the fact that both of her parents, Annie and Joseph, were Native. By this time, it had been deeply ingrained in her soul that she was French, or rather, not an Indian person. I was told that my kokomis gave birth to my father where she was born, on the reserve of Golden Lake, where she felt most at home. He was born of unknown paternity. The midwife who attended my kokomis was my father's great-aunt Maggie, and she is who he spent his early years with. His life on the reserve came to an end, just as his mother's had before him, when his Aunt Maggie was also escorted off by the RCMP.

When one considers the legacy of the oppressive legislation, the effects of residential schools, and poverty, it should not be difficult to understand the deleterious effects on Indian women and their children materially, culturally, and psychologically.[15] These effects leave people lacking confidence and self-esteem, making them vulnerable to illiteracy, hostility, alcohol, and suicide. For example, in 1992 Health and Welfare Canada reported that the suicide rate among registered Indians was at least three times the Canadian average.[16] This reality is a scenario all too familiar for Native Peoples. For me, this also proved to be the legacy of the *Indian Act*. My father died suddenly in 1988. I know that it was the direct result of the oppressive nature of the *Indian Act* and the forced assimilation process. A few years later, I proved his eligibility for registration; however, I was too late. I am sure he would have given his other little finger to have his identity affirmed through Indian status registration.

When Bill C-31 came into effect, I was aware that its major changes involved reinstating women previously enfranchised because of whom they had married. My kokomis, Viola, and her mother, Annie, would regain their status. I was also aware that Annie's husband, Joseph, was entitled through his mother, Angeline. This was where the challenge presented itself. In order for me to have my father entitled, I had to prove that both of his grandparents were entitled. That is, I had to prove that both Annie and Joseph were entitled to be registered with Indian Affairs so that status could be passed to my kokomis, Viola, in such a manner that she, in her own right, could pass it to my father; otherwise, he would be affected by what is known as the second-generation cut-off rule, which results in the loss of Indian status after two successive generations of parenting by non-Indians as defined by the *Indian Act*.[17]

I started by spending many hours with my kokomis learning my family history via the Oral Tradition. Without this opportunity I would not have been successful, and for this I am eternally grateful. It was difficult, though, because she was very bitter and often sad about her life on the reserve. She remembered our family history well. She told me about her mother, Annie, and her father, Joseph. I was most interested in finding more information about Joseph's mother, Angeline. My kokomis did not know much about Angeline, although she did repeatedly say that "Angeline was a black Indian from the Lake of Two Mountains who adopted two French boys whose mothers were unwed."

After the family history lesson, I constructed a family tree and began the formidable task of searching for the documents to prove my ancestral link to a past Band member. This proof is required to fulfill the Indian Affairs Registrar's demand that "the applicant connect the ancestor to an existing band as the basis of his [*sic*] entitlement regardless of the date of evidence."[18] I sent away to the Office of the Registrar General for birth certificates of my father, my kokomis, and myself. I also sent away for the marriage certificate of Annie and Joseph as well as the death certificate of Angeline. As discussed previously, the Registrar General holds the records of deaths, marriages, and births for seventy years, eighty years, and ninety-five years, respectively, after which time the records are microfilmed and then held at the Archives of Ontario.

When I first entered the archives library, I was overwhelmed—not surprising when one considers that I am visually impaired. The library essentially consists of numerous filing cabinets stuffed with microfilm. Archivists on staff can assist in your research, from 9:00 a.m. to 5:00 p.m. Needless to say, I was discouraged, especially when I read an outline that was prepared by the archives to explain various Aboriginal sources. It explained the difficulty with Native surnames and how they vary widely in records written by people who did not speak the Native languages. An additional blow was an Archives of Ontario cautionary note that read, "Aboriginal ancestors more than three generations away from you may be hard to document and therefore very difficult to claim status from."[19] I had an enormous task ahead of me with having to research back five or possibly six generations to Angeline's male family members.

A person requires a variety of skills in order to do this type of work, many of which I acquired on the job. I spent many hours using microfilm readers searching, compiling, and analyzing documents. I had to be very organized in my research and, as a result, made many purchases along the way, such as a filing cabinet, a large magnifier, and many reference books on how to do genealogical research. I also had to spend hours becoming proficient on the microfilm readers and printers, as well as learning how the actual microfilm reels are organized. When I would find birth, marriage, death, or census records that I felt might have significance, I would photocopy them; I would then take them home and construct and reconstruct my extended family tree in an attempt to look for clues as to where I could find Angeline's male family members. It became such a difficult task that occasionally I would stop for weeks or even months at a time.

At one point I had stopped for a period of several months when I once again began to act on my desire to be a registered Indian. This turned out to be the day that I found what I needed. It appeared that Angeline was at the home of the birth of her brother's child. The date of the birth was August 20, 1882. For unknown reasons, the child's birth registration was delayed until December 1934, fifty-two years later. It seems his mother was missing and, since Angeline was present at the time of his birth, she was the only person qualified to sign the declaration. This declaration of delayed birth stated her brother's name as the father and herself as the child's aunt. This document was the patrilineal link that tied the two surnames together— Angeline's married name and her brother's—which could connect her to a Band member. I knew that what I held in my hand was the necessary document, and I quickly sent all the documents and required affidavits along with several applications to Indian Affairs.

By this time I was familiar with section 6 of the *Indian Act*. I was certain my great-grandmother, my great-grandfather, my kokomis, and my father would all be reinstated or registered. I was uncertain about myself because I did not know how my father's unknown paternity (UP) would be interpreted. How Indian Affairs applies section 6, the main entitlement section of the current *Indian Act*, is summarized in Table 1.

6(1) + 6(1) = 6(1)
6(1) + 6(2) = 6(1)
6(2) + 6(2) = 6(1)
6(1) + NS or NI = 6(2)
6(2) + NS or NI = NS

NS = non-Status person
NI = non-Indian person

6(1) + UP = 6(2)
6(2) + UP = NS

UP = unknown paternity
NS = non-Status person

Table 1. Section 6 of the *Indian Act*

Indian Affairs applied section 6 to my family in the following manner: Angeline was reinstated as 6(1) status; her son, who was also Annie's husband, was registered as 6(2) status. Annie was reinstated as 6(1). My kokomis, the child of a 6(1) parent and a 6(2) parent, was registered as a 6(1). My father's combination of parents was applied as 6(1) + NS and registered as a 6(2). The Registrar, when applying section 6, assumed a negative presumption for my father's unknown paternity as being a non-Status or non-Indian person.[20] This means that he cannot confer status to me in his own right, because a 6(2) + NS (my mother is a non-Status person) = NS.

All previous registered Indians in the Indian Register as of April 16, 1985, were granted 6(1) entitlement.[21] This was also the situation when reinstating women who had lost status through marriage; "however, their children are entitled to registration only under section 6(2)" of the *Indian Act*.[22] "In contrast, the children of Indian men who married non-Indian women, whose registration before 1985 was continued under section 6(1), are able to pass on status if they marry non-Indians".[23] Alternatively stated, the new rules of section 6 were being applied retroactively to Indian women and their children, creating an inequity, because 6(1) registration permits a person to pass on status to their children in their own right, yet 6(2) does not.

I became acutely aware of the continued sex discrimination within the amended *Indian Act* and how it was affecting me. I was denied registration. With this denial it became evident to me that if my female ancestors had been male, I would be entitled to Indian status today. Had they been male, they would never have lost status registration and they could then pass it to me. Since all previous entitlement continues, I would be a 6(1) in my own right and I could therefore pass status on to my children. In this way the present-day *Indian Act* continues with the theme of discrimination on the basis of sex.[24] Furthermore, the *Indian Act* continues to violate section 15 of the *Charter*. Section 15(1) provides that all individuals are equal before and under the law.

The 1985 amendments (Bill C-31) to the *Indian Act* corrected part of the sex discrimination against women who had lost their status upon marriage to non-Indian men; however, these amendments failed to address the discriminatory aspect that does not allow Indian women who married non-Indian men to pass their status to their grandchildren. The result is that the current *Indian Act* continues to discriminate against the children and grandchildren of Indian women who lost their status. Said another way, the children of Bill C-31 Indian women are treated differently than children born to Indian men. The former are granted status under section 6 subsection (2) when the father is a non-Indian person, whereas the latter are granted status under section 6 subsection (1).

My application was denied entitlement on February 13, 1995. I submitted a letter of protest on March 16, 1995, and on February 4, 1997, I received a letter from the Registrar concluding that my name had correctly been omitted from the Indian Register. I filed an appeal claiming discrimination on the basis of sex and marital status. Indian Affairs denied my appeal in April 1998. I am now content with my identity, partly because of my new understanding of these huge issues and partly because I realized, during the process, that legislation cannot tell me who I am. It is as a matter of principle that I continue to appeal to the appropriate court as outlined in section 14.3 of the *Indian Act*.

In conclusion, I would like to suggest a very simple, fair, logical, and equitable remedy to eliminate the continuum of discrimination within the *Indian Act*. All children, and their descendants, born prior to 1985 to an Indian man or an Indian woman regardless of who they married should be entitled to registration under 6(1). The new rules of entitlement should then, and only then, be applied to all births equally after 1985. This would resolve the continued inequities in the current *Indian Act* between men and women and would then bring it into accord with the *Charter*. This would also resolve the issue of unknown paternity before 1985, as unknown paternity is also being interpreted in an unequal manner.

The biggest challenge in having my family members reinstated or registered was the Registrar's demand that I connect my ancestors to an existing Band member as the basis of my family's entitlement. I found two official documents in which Angeline was recognized and recorded as an Indian: her death certificate and her marriage certificate. This was not enough. I had to further my search until I could prove a link. This is grossly unfair and an unreasonable request when one considers that "there are countless historical records of Indians who never belonged to a band."[25] Angeline was an Indian, regardless.

After reading this chapter, one should be more aware of the research and analytical skills required to prove Aboriginal ancestry: in particular, being able to prove a link to an existing Band member. It is an enormous task. Individuals require time, money, stamina, and great determination to fulfill the Registrar's requirements. Many of Canadas[26] Aboriginal Peoples are poor or unemployed as a result of the forced assimilation process. When the *Indian Act* was amended, assistance in the form of guidance from genealogical researchers should have been made available to the non-Status communities to help them in their quest for their identity as well as registration.

Finally, Sharon Donna McIvor argues that the *Indian Act*, with its paternalism and colonial ideologies, has created a "fictitious body" of Indians.[27] What McIvor implies by this is that the *Indian Act* is a legal construction based on Eurocentric notions of what defines an Indian, excluding many Aboriginal Peoples from that definition in the process.

I will never see myself as a Canadian first, but rather as a First Nations person. My ideas of who I am and who my ancestors were will always extend beyond national policies and boundaries of control and assimilation.

Neither identity nor human behaviour can be constructed through rigid definitions such as the *Indian Act*. My identity as an Aboriginal person was partially achieved through political struggle and the need to realize the potential of my genetic memory. I feel this way despite the fact that I am not a legal Indian.

Chapter 14

Unknown and Unstated
Paternity and the *Indian Act*
Enough Is Enough!

A man may beget a child in passion or by rape, and then
disappear; he need never see or consider child or mother again.
—Adrienne Rich, *Of Woman Born*

I WAS HAPPY WHEN I LEARNED THE EDITORIAL BOARD OF THE
Motherhood Initiative for Research and Community Involvement
(MIRCI) intended to dedicate an entire volume to motherhood activism, advocacy, and agency. Although I am not a biological mother, I truly
believe there is nothing more important than mothers and the work that
they do. It stands to reason then that by extension I also think there is little
that is more important than advocating for the rights of Indigenous mothers
and their children.

Here on Turtle Island, prior to European contact, Indigenous mothers
and their children were situated at the centre of community politics and wellness. While this was the case historically, owing to the sex discrimination in

the *Indian Act*, which continues to exist today, many children who have an unknown or unstated paternity in their lineage—either a father or grandfather—are excluded from gaining Indian status registration and consequently their treaty rights. This is my lived reality. I do not know who my paternal grandfather is. When I think about the denial of who I am, and by extension my treaty rights, I realize further that while I was born into a wealthy Nation, it was Canada that took this away from me. Alternatively stated, it was Canada that legislated my ancestors into an impoverished existence and Canada that continues to deny me my rights as an Indigenous person because of an unknown paternal grandfather.

It is important that I stress that while some people may perceive my effort as more closely representing a resistance effort, and as such see this chapter as a narrative of resistance, I perceive my effort foremost as a desire to belong to my ancestral community and, after this, as an advocacy effort that seeks to protect young Indian mothers, as defined by the *Indian Act*, and their children. That said, my primary goal in telling my story, and in the advocacy work that I have taken on, is to create greater awareness about AANDC's unstated paternity policy. I firmly believe that the more people know about this continued sex discrimination, the better we are able to protect Indigenous mothers along with their children's right to Indian status registration and, as I have been stressing, their treaty rights.

This chapter is structured in three parts. In part 1, I offer a brief discussion of the history of the government of Canada's process of defining Indians through what has become the *Indian Act*, its relationship to treaty rights, and the sex discrimination it has long imposed. I also offer a discussion of the efforts that Indigenous women have taken to eliminate this sex discrimination. This discussion is important as it sets the stage for the matter at hand: unknown and unstated paternity. In part 2, I discuss AANDC's unstated paternity policy as it affects Status Indian mothers, as defined by the *Indian Act*, and their children, offering a model to assure reader clarity, as the matter is somewhat complex. To illustrate the effect of AANDC's unstated paternity policy on these mothers, in part 3 I offer my story as an example of the continued sex discrimination. I also offer a discussion of my ongoing advocacy efforts in challenging this sex discrimination as well as a discussion of some facts and statistics.

History of Sex Discrimination in the
Indian Act and Women's Efforts at Its Elimination

It was through the process of Indian status registration that Indigenous Peoples became, and for that matter continue to be, entitled to their treaty rights: annuity payments, hunting and fishing rights, and education and health care.[1] These treaty rights were negotiated in exchange for Indigenous Peoples allowing settlers to reside in and benefit from our landscapes and the many gifts Mother Earth provides. Interestingly, the initial criteria of Indianness followed an Indigenous model, meaning it was broad and included all people who resided with the Indians. Despite this inclusive beginning, eventually the government of Canada began limiting the number of people entitled to registration through a process called enfranchisement.[2] Through this enfranchisement process, the government of Canada also eliminated its treaty responsibilities.[3] This process of narrowly defining and controlling Indians is commonly referred to as getting rid of the Indian problem.[4]

When it was determined that the process of enfranchising Indians was proceeding at too slow a pace, Indian women and their children became the targets of a racist and sexist regime. As I have explained elsewhere, through a series of legislative acts dating back to the 1857 *Gradual Civilization Act*, Indian women and their children were enfranchised when their husbands or fathers were enfranchised.[5] It was through the 1869 *Gradual Enfranchisement Act* where Indian women, along with their children, who married non-Indian men were enfranchised.[6] Again, with this loss of Indian recognition, treaty rights were lost. In addition, the right to live in one's community, the right to inherit property, and for that matter the right to be buried in the community cemetery were also lost. The process of eliminating registered Status Indians through sex discrimination was last codified in section 12(1) b of the 1951 *Indian Act*.[7]

It would be an understatement to say that Indigenous women have worked tirelessly to eliminate section 12(1)b and its intergenerational effects. In 1966 Mary Two-Axe Earley began to speak out publicly on the issue, and in 1971, Jeannette Corbiere Lavell took the matter of section 12(1)b to court, arguing that it violated the Canadian Bill of Rights.[8] Yvonne Bédard joined Corbiere Lavell's effort, such that in 1973 both cases were heard together by the Supreme Court of Canada (SCC). Unfortunately, relying on a racist and sexist line of reasoning, the scc compared Indian women to Canadian women, ruling that the former had equality with the latter and thus there was no sex discrimination.[9] Regardless of this setback, in 1981 Sandra Lovelace Nicholas appealed to the un Human Rights Committee (unhrc). Because her marriage and resulting loss of status registration had occurred prior to the International Covenant on Civil and Political Rights, the unhrc declined to rule on the matter. It did, however, rule that the *Indian Act* violated section 27 of the International Covenant, which protected culture, religion, and language. Through this ruling, it became evident that Indigenous women had rights that international forums recognized and were willing to protect.[10]

When Canada's Constitution was patriated in 1982, it included the *Charter of Rights and Freedoms*. Section 15 of the *Charter* guarantees the right to live free from sex discrimination.[11] In 1985 the *Indian Act* was amended through Bill c-31, purportedly to bring it in line with the *Charter*. Through this amendment many Indigenous women, once involuntarily enfranchised for having married non-Indian men, were reinstated as Status Indians, whereas their children were registered for the first time. With registration, they also became entitled to their treaty rights.

Nonetheless, through the creation of what is commonly referred to as the second-generation cut-off rule, the grandchildren of the Indian women once enfranchised for marrying out continued to be denied status registration and consequently their treaty rights. The term "second-generation cut-off" references the fact that after two generations of parenting with non-Status partners, status registration is no longer passed on. Sharon Donna McIvor's situation is illustrative of the government of Canada's continued unwillingness to resolve the sex discrimination in the *Indian Act*. Because McIvor's status entitlement moved through her mother line rather than her father line, she was prevented from passing on status registration to her son in a way that he could pass it on to his children. Unfortunately, as was the case in 1985 with Bill c-31, the legal remedy encoded in 2011 in Bill c-3 and brought forward through McIvor's effort also failed to resolve all the remaining sex discrimination. In sum, despite the efforts of Two-Axe Earley, Corbiere Lavell, Bédard, Lovelace Nicholas, and more recently McIvor, the history of blatant sex discrimination in the *Indian Act* continues.

Unknown and Unstated Paternity

An additional form of sex discrimination exists pertaining to the children of Indian women where a father or a grandfather is of unstated, unreported, unnamed, unknown, unacknowledged, unestablished, or unrecognized paternity. Disturbingly, and regardless of the *Charter*, it was the 1985 amendment to the *Indian Act* that introduced this form of sex discrimination. While previously there were provisions in the *Indian Act* whereby both a child born out of wedlock and a child of unknown and unstated paternity would be registered along with their Status Indian mother, the current *Indian Act* is now silent on this very issue. In short, the government of Canada removed the provisions that once protected these children. To address this intentional and carefully crafted legislative silence, Aboriginal Affairs developed an unstated paternity policy, and it is this very policy that the Registrar relies on when determining Indian status entitlement in situations where a father's signature does not appear on a child's birth certificate.[12]

Through this unstated paternity policy, the Registrar is directed to interpret all situations of unstated, unreported, unnamed, unknown, unacknowledged, unestablished, or unrecognized paternity as representing a non-Indian man. Today, when a child is born to a Status Indian mother and a Status Indian father, and for some reason the father's signature is not on the child's birth certificate, AANDC assumes the father is non-Indian.[13] In other words, all situations of non-identified paternity are assumed to be non-Indian. This practice is also referred to as a negative assumption of Indian paternity.

As a result of this negative assumption of Indian paternity, a child *potentially* loses their right to Indian status registration and thus their treaty rights. Some might ask, "Why do you add the word 'potentially'?" This is a good question and this is where the issue becomes somewhat complex. Since 1985 Status Indians are registered either under section 6(1) status or under section 6(2) status. Section 6(1) status is best viewed as a stronger form of status, meaning a mother can pass on status in her own right regardless of her child's paternity. Section 6(2) status, in contrast, is a weaker form of status in that a mother cannot pass on status to her child in her own right.[14] In this latter situation, where the mother is registered under section 6(2) and the father's signature is not on the child's birth registration form, the child is hit with the second-generation cut-off rule, discussed above, and denied status registration.

In sum, two scenarios result from AANDC applying a negative assumption of Indian paternity. In scenario one, a child born to a section 6(1) mother and a Status Indian father who does not sign the child's birth certificate is registered under section 6(2). In scenario two, a child born to a section 6(2) mother and a Status Indian father who does not sign the child's birth certificate is a non-Status person due to the second-generation cut-off rule.

How It Affects Me and My Advocacy Efforts

Certainly I was focused on the events that led up to the 1985 amendment to the *Indian Act*. I was curious as to whether I would be entitled to Indian status registration through this amendment. I was unsure, though, how my unknown paternal grandfather would be factored into the equation of entitlement. As I have discussed previously, I began the process of learning about my ancestry from my kokomis, followed by conducting the necessary archival research.[15] In this oral and archival research I needed to establish a clear link to a male ancestor who was recognized as an Indian through the use of vital statistic records such as birth, marriage, and death certificates. After many years of archival research, I was successful in having my kokomis registered under section 6(1) of the *Indian Act*, the stronger form of status. This meant my father was entitled as well. Said another way, as a 6(1) Indian my kokomis could, in her own right, pass status on to him.

Although prior to 1985 there were provisions in the *Indian Act* that protected children born out of wedlock and of unknown paternity, through my process of applying for Indian status I discovered that in situations of new applications, AANDC's unstated paternity policy is also applied to births that predate 1985.[16] This includes me and my father. I was born in 1962 and my father, Rodney Peter Gagnon, was born in 1935 with unknown paternity.[17] Through AANDC's unstated paternity policy it is assumed my unknown paternal grandfather was, or is, a non-Indian person. Thus, it was determined that my father, as a child of unknown paternity, was only entitled to registration under section 6(2), the weaker form of status, meaning he could not pass status on to me in his own right.[18] Essentially, due to AANDC's policy assumption, I was hit with the second-generation cut-off rule that was codified in the 1985 *Indian Act*. With this denial of Indian status I am also denied my treaty rights, such as the healthcare and education rights, that registered Status Indians are entitled to. Further, I am also denied Band membership and citizenship in the larger Anishinabek Nation.[19] Succinctly, because I do not know who my grandfather was, or is, I am denied my treaty rights and I live in exile because the government of Canada assumes my unknown paternal grandfather is a non-Indian man.

I have taken many steps to become registered as a Status Indian. In May 2001 my legal representative, Kimberly Murray of ALST, filed a section 15 *Charter* challenge on my behalf; even through Murray has since moved on, ALST has retained carriage of my file. This statement of claim was struck, appealed, and subsequently refiled in October 2002.[20] The discovery, affidavit, and cross-examination process is now complete. Further, the expert reports are in. The next step in my *Charter* challenge is filing the summary judgement motion, which I am more than eager to move on with.

It is important that I stress I am not alone in my quest for Indian status registration and, as such, raising awareness about AANDC's horrific policy is a large part of what I now do. Writing this paper is no exception to this important work. Between 1985 and 1999, 37,300 children of so-called unstated paternity were born to mothers registered under section 6(1).[21] During the same period, 13,000 children of so-called unstated paternity were born to mothers registered under section 6(2).[22] These latter 13,000 children lost their right to status registration and their treaty rights. In extrapolating this latter figure forward to 2012, as I have, I calculate that as many as 25,000 children have been denied status registration.

The rates of so-called unstated paternity for mothers registered under 6(1) are disconcerting, and not surprisingly they are higher for younger mothers. For mothers under the age of fifteen years, the rate of so-called unstated paternity is 45 percent; aged fifteen to nineteen years the rate is 30 percent; twenty to twenty-four years the rate is 19 percent; and for mothers aged thirty to thirty-four years the rate is 12 percent.[23] While no figures are provided for mothers registered under 6(2), it is not unreasonable to assume that similar rates apply.

In reviewing these figures, and in thinking about this issue, we must be careful not to assume that mothers are to blame. Raising awareness about this is central to my advocacy efforts. There are many reasons why fathers' signatures are lacking on birth registration forms. For example, some mothers are victims of sexualized violence such as incest. These situations are best known as unstated, unreported, and unnamed paternity, as mothers may not record the father's name on the birth registration form, nor gain his signature, as a mechanism to prevent him from having access to the child. In some cases the child was conceived through sexual violence such as rape, gang rape, sexual slavery, or prostitution. These situations are best known as unknown paternity, as the father is not known to the mother, child, or grandchild.[24] In other situations a father may refuse to acknowledge or establish the paternity of his child: for example, when a mother records the father's name on the child's birth registration form yet, in his desire to avoid child-support payments and/or to preserve another existing relationship, he refuses to accept responsibility for the child. Another situation is unrecognized paternity, where a mother does record the father's name but, because his signature is not obtained, government officials blank out his name. One example of this latter situation is when a father dies prior to the birth of his child.[25]

In an effort to raise awareness about the continued sex discrimination in AANDC's unstated paternity policy, I have sought out and gained endorsements from three Indigenous women's organizations. In February 2008, September 2009, and November 2009, the AFNWC, NWAC, and ONWA, respectively, endorsed the importance of my court case. Further, in September 2010 I ambitiously, although without funding, launched the National Strategy to Raise Awareness on Unknown and Unstated Paternity and the *Indian Act* (NSRAUUP). It is important that I reach the people most affected by AANDC's policy, and as such, as part of my national strategy, I created a personal website dedicating a significant amount of space to articles and posters on this matter. Many of these materials are geared toward reaching community people, such as "Quick Facts on Aboriginal Affairs and Northern Development Canada's Policy on Unstated Paternity."[26] I have also written numerous community articles that have been published in *Anishinabek News* and the ONWA newsletter, and I created a short video, titled "Sex Discrimination and the *Indian Act* (yes the saga continues...)." Further, to reach community people across Canada I also created a Facebook group, "Unknown and Unstated Paternity and the *Indian Act*." As of August 2012, I have over nine hundred members and it is growing every week.

Conclusion

For years, or rather decades, Indigenous women such as Mary Two-Axe Earley, Jeannette Corbiere Lavell, Yvonne Bédard, Sandra Lovelace Nicholas, and Sharon Donna McIvor have worked tirelessly to eliminate the sex discrimination in the *Indian Act*. Regardless of their efforts, and despite living in a post-*Charter* era, two attempts at remedial legislation—in 1985 and 2011—have led to new forms of sex discrimination. Clearly, legislative change intended to eliminate sex discrimination should not result in the government of Canada taking the opportunity to create additional forms of sex discrimination. Indigenous women and their long-time efforts deserve more respect than this. To manipulate their agency, as the government of Canada has, is a national disgrace. As discussed, one such new form of sex discrimination is AANDC's unstated paternity policy. Through this policy, today when a father's signature is not on his child's birth certificate, AANDC assumes the father is non-Indian. I estimate that as many as 25,000 children born to mothers registered under section 6(2) of the *Indian Act* have been denied status registration and consequently their treaty rights because of this policy. Disturbingly, in the unfortunate event where Indian women are victims of sexualized violence that prevent them from being able, or willing, to name fathers and obtain their signatures, AANDC's policy assumption remains. Mothers must not bear the brunt of this unconscionable policy. Indian women and their babies deserve more than being targets of the government of Canada's desire to eliminate Status Indians and the treaty responsibilities on which this country is founded.

Although it has been twenty-seven years since the *Indian Act* was amended to bring it in line with the equality provision of the *Charter*, I have yet to experience the liberation it claims to contain. Moving beyond my personal need, though, it is for young mothers and their children that I do the advocacy work I do. Enough is enough!

Chapter 15

Protecting Indian Rights for Indian Babies

Canada's "Unstated Paternity" Policy

T HROUGH AANDC'S UNSTATED PATERNITY POLICY, MANY Indigenous Peoples and children are denied Indian status registration owing to the lack of a father's signature on their birth certificates. This chapter is mainly for Indigenous community members, Indigenous women's organizations, and people caring for Indigenous women and their children to learn and draw from.

History of the Sex Discrimination in the *Indian Act*

Through the imposition of colonial policy and laws, it was through the process of Indian status registration whereby Indigenous Peoples became, and continue to be, entitled to their treaty rights. It is because of this relationship between Indian status registration and treaty rights that many people conflate "treaty" and "status," as in a "treaty status" Indian. Initially, the legislative process of defining who was an "Indian" followed an Indigenous model, meaning that being an Indian was more about community relationships and affiliation and thus was broad and inclusive. Despite this inclusive beginning, through the application of an increasingly narrow definition of Indian status, the government of Canada began limiting the number of people entitled to Indian status and thereby began eliminating its treaty responsibilities established in 1764 during the Treaty at Niagara.[1] This process of narrowly defining and controlling who an Indian was, and is, is commonly referred to as eliminating the "Indian problem."[2]

When it was determined that the process of enfranchising Indians and eliminating Indigenous treaty rights was proceeding at a snail's pace, Indian women and their children became the target of a patriarchal and racist regime. Through a series of legislative acts dating back to the 1857 *Gradual Civilization Act*, Indian women and their children were enfranchised when their husbands or fathers were enfranchised. It was through the 1869 *Gradual Enfranchisement Act* where Indian women who married non-Indian men (a.k.a. married out), along with their children, were enfranchised, denied Indian status registration, and thus their treaty rights.[3] At this time, as per the European model of the world, women were considered chattel or appendages of their husbands and therefore if, and when, they married a non-Indian man they too became non-Indian persons.[4] Eventually, the process of eliminating Status Indians through sex discrimination was codified in section 12(1)b of the 1951 *Indian Act*.[5] Significant to this discussion is another form of sex discrimination first codified in the 1951 *Indian Act*: the double-mother clause. Essentially, through the double-mother clause a person was enfranchised at the age of twenty-one years if both their mother and paternal grandmother (two generations of non-Indigenous mothers) were non-Indians prior to their marriage.[6]

With this loss of status, Indian women also lost their treaty rights, their right to live in their communities, their right to inherit property, and their right to be buried in the community cemetery. Further, through this sex discrimination "Aboriginal women have been denied opportunities to hold leadership positions within their communities and organizations and have been excluded from high-level negotiations among Aboriginal and Canadian political leaders."[7]

Ogitchidaa Kwewag

As most know, many Indigenous women have worked tirelessly to eliminate section 12(1)b and its intergenerational effects. I think it is appropriate to refer to these Indigenous women as ogitchidaa kwewag, an Anishinaabemowin term that best translates to brave women who are dedicated to the safety, security, and service of their family, community, and Nation. On the national and international scale it was Mary Two-Axe Earley, a Mohawk woman from Kahnawake, Quebec, who in 1966 began to speak publicly about the matter; eventually she approached the Royal Commission on the Status of Women.[8] It was in 1971 that the now icon of Indigenous women's rights Jeannette Corbiere Lavell, an Anishinaabe woman from Manitoulin Island, Ontario, took the matter of section 12(1)b to court arguing it violated the Canadian Bill of Rights. Yvonne Bédard, from Six Nations, Ontario, was also addressing the sex discrimination, and in 1973 both of their cases were heard together at the Supreme Court of Canada (SCC). Unfortunately, the SCC, relying on a patriarchal line of reasoning, ruled that because Indian women who married non-Indian men "had equality of status with all other Canadian married females," there was no sex discrimination to resolve.[9]

Although the 1973 SCC decision was a setback, in 1981 Sandra Lovelace Nicholas, a Maliseet woman from Tobique First Nation, New Brunswick, appealed to the UN Human Rights Committee (UNHRC) regarding section 12(1)b. Because Lovelace Nicholas's marriage and loss of status registration had occurred prior to the International Covenant on Civil and Political Rights, the UNHRC declined to rule on the matter of sex discrimination. Nonetheless, the UNHRC did rule that the *Indian Act* violated section 27 of the International Covenant, which protects culture, religion, and language. Through this ruling it became evident that Indigenous women did have rights that international forums were willing to stand behind and protect.[10]

Largely as a result of the actions of these ogitchidaa kwewag, combined with the patriation of Canada through the Constitution Act, 1982, intact with the *Charter*—in particular, section 15: the sex equality section—the *Indian Act* was amended in 1985. Through this amendment many Indigenous women, involuntarily enfranchised for having married non-Indian men, were reinstated as Status Indians, and many of their children were registered as Status Indians for the first time. Statistics Canada reported that by 2002, more than 114,000 individuals had gained Indian status registration through the 1985 amendment.[11] Through this process, many reinstated women regained, while their newly registered children gained for the first time, First Nation Band membership and entitlement to treaty rights that were protected through the 1764 Treaty at Niagara.[12] Indian status registration entitlement for the grandchildren of these reinstated Indian women, however, is another matter.

Although many think the 1985 amendment to the *Indian Act* served the purpose of establishing equality between men and women—and, foremost, achieved compliance with the equality provisions of the *Charter*—it in fact failed. Through the creation of the second-generation cut-off rule, the grandchildren of women once enfranchised for marrying out continued to be denied Indian status registration and consequently all that went with it, such as Band membership and treaty rights. The second-generation cut-off rule is a process whereby after two successive generations of parenting with a non-Indian parent, either mother or father, the loss of status registration occurs.[13] While the second-generation cut-off rule applies to all births after 1985, including the descendants of Indian men, it was applied immediately and retroactively to the descendants of the reinstated Indian women sooner than to Status Indian men and their descendants. Through this discriminatory process, Corbiere Lavell has stated, "Three of my five grandchildren do not have legal rights to be members of my community."[14]

Understanding this legislative complexity is not a simple task. First, it is important to understand that because of the 1985 amendment, Indian status registration is now stratified into two main subsections: 6(1) and 6(2). While subsection 6(1) status, and its many paragraphs (sub-subsections)—a, b, c, d, e, and f—allows a parent to pass on Indian status to his or her children in his or her own right, subsection 6(2) status does not.[15] This means a 6(2) parent must parent with another Status Indian in order to pass on Indian status registration to his or her children. For this very reason many people refer to 6(1) as a stronger form of status and 6(2) as a weaker form. Certainly, this distinction is useful in conveying some of the legal complexity created in 1985.

Within the stronger form of Indian status registration, paragraph 6(1)a is the best form of status. When the *Indian Act* was amended, Indian men and all their descendants born prior to April 1985, the date of amendment, were all registered under paragraph 6(1)a, whereas the Indian women who had married out were only registered under paragraph 6(1)c and their children were only registered under the weaker form of status registration, subsection 6(2). As a result of this difference in Indian status, and as suggested above, the grandchildren of Indian women became immediate targets of the second-generation cut-off rule. This of course means that sex discrimination was not eliminated from the *Indian Act*. Rather, through Bill C-31 the sex discrimination was passed on to the children and grandchildren of Indian women once enfranchised for marrying out.[16] It is precisely in this way that the 1985 amendment to the *Indian Act* through Bill C-31 was "failed remedial legislation."[17]

As most know by now, the situation of Sharon Donna McIvor, and her son Charles Jacob Grismer, is illustrative of the government of Canada's continued reluctance to resolve the sex discrimination. Through the 1985 amendment McIvor was designated as a 6(2) Indian, the weaker form of status registration, which thus prevented her from passing on status to her children in her own right because the Indian status to be granted descends from her Indian women forebears, not her Indian men forebears.[18] McIvor took this very matter to court. Possibly needless to say, for twenty-five years she continued the important work of eliminating the sex discrimination that continues to face the children and grandchildren of Indian women once enfranchised.[19]

An ally to Indigenous women, relying on her critical legal perspective, Mary Eberts offers her comments and analysis on the *McIvor* decision. Eberts explains that Madam Justice Carol Ross of the British Columbia Supreme Court agreed with McIvor's legal team that the correct comparator group for McIvor was the Indian men who had married non-Indian women, and the children of those men, who on April 17, 1985, were registered as Status Indians under 6(1)a of the *Indian Act*. Through applying this comparator group Justice Ross ruled that the "preference for descent of status through the male line is discrimination on the basis of sex and marital status."[20] She ruled that 6(1)a must be applied equally to Indian men and their descendants and to the Indian women once enfranchised and their descendants. Alternatively stated, the children and grandchildren of both Status Indian men and the Status Indian women who married out should all be registered under 6(1)a of the *Indian Act*. This ruling was cause for celebration.

Unfortunately, through a questionable line of reasoning, the Court of Appeal narrowed the scope of Justice Ross's legal remedy by using a comparator group for Grismer, McIvor's son, rather than for McIvor herself, thereby completely ignoring McIvor's inability to pass on status registration to her grandchildren. Yet it was McIvor, not her son, who had brought the matter of sex discrimination to court. The new comparator group on which Justice Harvey Groberman relied comprised the grandchildren once enfranchised through the double-mother clause codified in section 12(1)(a) iv that came into effect on September 4, 1951. As discussed, through the double-mother clause a person was enfranchised at the age of twenty-one when both their mother and paternal grandmother were non-Indians prior to marriage. This change means that McIvor's son was only entitled to a subcategory of 6(1)c, as in 6(1)c.1, versus registering both Sharon and her son as 6(1)a Indians. Thus, Sharon's grandchildren were only entitled to 6(2) status.[21] In relying on this comparator group, Justice Groberman narrowed the scope such that, as a result, and in line with Bill c-31, the legal remedy found in Bill c-3 fails to resolve all the sex discrimination in the *Indian Act*. It is precisely for this reason that Eberts has argued that the "Court of Appeal decision is a deep disappointment" and further "is, in fact, almost a case-book example of judicial activism producing bad law."[22]

One can determine through Justice Groberman's reasoning that many caveats remain in the *Indian Act*'s current form. First, the grandchildren (born before September 4, 1951, when the double-mother clause was first enacted) of Indian women once enfranchised will continue to be denied Indian status registration, yet the grandchildren of Indian men in this same situation are registered. Second, grandchildren born to Indian women through common-law relationships rather than the institution of marriage will continue to be denied status registration. Third, the female children (and their descendants) of Indian men who co-parented with non-Status women in common-law union will continue to be excluded, yet the male children (and their descendants) of Indian men who co-parented with non-Status women in common-law union have status. Fourth, the grandchildren of Indian women once enfranchised and now reinstated are only entitled to 6(2) status and therefore will not be able to pass on status to their children (born prior to April 17, 1985), yet the grandchildren of Indian men are registered under 6(1)a. Clearly, it is in these ways that matrilineal descendants remain targets of sex discrimination.[23]

Unfortunately, on November 5, 2009, the Supreme Court of Canada refused to hear the appeal in the case of *McIvor v Canada (Registrar of Indian and Northern Affairs)*. Although Gwen Brodsky and McIvor argued Bill C-3 as inadequate remedial legislation, in January 2011 the bill passed into law. Thus, despite the *Charter*—and in particular section 15, which states women have the right to live free from racial and sex discrimination—like Lovelace Nicholas before her, McIvor has been forced to pursue the elimination of the sex discrimination beyond the domestic arena. Shortly after Bill C-3 became law, McIvor filed a complaint against Canada with the UNHRC.[24] In taking on this process McIvor herself has argued, "Canada needs to be held to account for its intransigence in refusing to completely eliminate sex discrimination from the *Indian Act* and for decades of delay."[25] Similarly, the Women's Legal Education and Action Fund (LEAF) has argued that forcing Indigenous women like McIvor "to endure the emotional and financial hardship of years and years of additional protracted litigation to remove the remaining areas of sex discrimination in the status provisions is unconscionable."[26] Notwithstanding these issues and arguments, it is estimated that as many as 45,000 grandchildren of Indian women once enfranchised for marrying out will gain the right to status registration through this more recent amendment.[27] They will now also be more likely to be entitled to First Nation Band membership and their treaty rights.

In sum, despite the efforts of ogitchidaa kwewag—Two-Axe Earley, Corbiere Lavell, Bédard, Lovelace Nicholas, and more recently McIvor—the 156-year (as of 2013) history of sex discrimination in the *Indian Act* continues. This is the case regardless of the fact that Indigenous women have dedicated many decades to its elimination.[28] Although we live in a post-*Charter* era, the equality outlined in section 15 of the *Canadian Charter of Rights and Freedoms* has no real practical value for me, and possibly many others, beyond that of a pitiful and meaningless fictional story. Through living, observing, and thinking about the process of remedial legislation—both in 1985 and in 2011—I have come to realize that Canada manipulates legislative change as an opportunity to create new forms of sex discrimination rather than eliminate it. The next section of this article discusses yet another form of sex discrimination that has not received much attention: unknown and unstated paternity and the *Indian Act*.

Unknown and Unstated Paternity and the *Indian Act*

Traditional Knowledge

As previously discussed in my work, but worthy of repeating, after assessing Indigenous Peoples of Lower Canada, the 1844–45 Bagot Commission, reporting on child rearing and the reality of children being born out of wedlock, observed that "the birth of illegitimate children is less frequent than formerly, but an event of this nature [read: a child of unknown or unstated paternity] does not cast a stigma upon the mother, nor upon the child, which is usually adopted into the tribe."[29] Similarly, in his work on the Algonquin Anishinaabe Nation of the Ottawa River, Frank G. Speck observed it was the Chief's responsibility to take care of orphaned children.[30] Further, historian Gordon Day has stated that "the basic unit of Algonquin society was the family: the father and mother, grandparents, children and adopted children."[31]

In my process of understanding the Indigenous family model, parenting, and community membership, I also turn to Anishinaabe governance laws, in particular the Clan System of governance. Through Clan teachings such as the need to keep our blood clean, men and women were encouraged to seek new genetic material from outsiders as this diversity ensured the health and wellness of the people. In addition, it was common practice for Indigenous Nations to adopt, kidnap, and assimilate young children when membership loss owing to disease and war was great. In this way, parenting and community membership were not always limited to the biological parents. Pamela D. Palmater arrives at a similar realization of the limitations of blood as the primary criterion in determining identity and nationhood when she argues that "blood is not only unnecessary as an indicator of our identities; it is completely irrelevant."[32] Rather, it is the social-cultural aspect that determines who we are, such as deeply rooted connections to our Nations that include family, larger community relations, and traditional territories, as well as the collective history, values, and beliefs that we share with one another.[33] Martin Cannon concurs with this broader understanding of identity and belonging, arguing that there exists in Indigenous culture an "ancient context" that informs us of the importance of respecting women and the responsibilities they carry.[34]

Legislative History

As the historical record, traditional governance practices, and sacred teachings inform us, eventually the *Indian Act* began to impose European definitions and practices on who was and who was not an Indian child, even though the inclusion of all children regardless of paternity disclosure was once traditional Indigenous practice. In 1927 section 12 of the *Indian Act*, which remained in place until September 4, 1951, stated that "any illegitimate child may, unless he has, with the consent of the band whereof the father or mother of such child is a member, shared in the distribution moneys of such band for a period exceeding two years, be, at any time, excluded from the membership thereof by the Superintendent General."[35] This criterion was broad and inclusive in that all that was required was the sharing of Band funds. From September 4, 1951, through August 13, 1956, the criteria determining who was an Indian shifted slightly, where the test was that "the Registrar had to be *satisfied* [my emphasis] that the father was not an Indian in order to omit adding a name to the register"[36]

The requirements shifted once again between August 14, 1956, and April 16, 1985, where section 12(2) stated that illegitimate children were automatically added to the Indian Register whereby the Band had twelve months to protest. This provision protected Indigenous mothers and their children. That said, if and when a protest was made and the Registrar determined that the father of the child was a non-Indian person, then the child's name was removed from the official Indian Register.[37] In summary, although regulated by legislation, and although the inclusive process was once narrowed, it was eventually re-expanded to include all children regardless of non-paternity disclosure unless a successful protest was made. This process of inclusion remained in place until 1985.

Aboriginal Affairs' Unstated Paternity Policy Explained

Along with the issues that McIvor continues to pursue, today there is an additional form of sex discrimination of which few are aware. This sex discrimination is particularly disconcerting as it places many Indigenous children at risk of being denied their entitlement to Indian status registration and consequently First Nation Band membership and treaty rights. It pertains to the Indigenous children whose fathers' signatures are not on their birth certificates. Today, when a child is born and for some reason the father is unable to or does not sign the birth certificate, AANDC assumes the father is a non-Indian person as defined by the *Indian Act*. This unstated paternity policy, which I prefer to call unknown and unstated paternity, is best thought of as the application of a negative presumption of paternity, and it occurs whether the parents are married or not. Succinctly, a father's signature must appear on a child's long-form birth certificate, as it is the long-form birth certificate, and both parental signatures, on which the government relies in determining if a child is entitled to Indian status.

Interestingly, as with the sex discrimination that McIvor continues to challenge, this sex discrimination was created through the remedial action of the 1985 amendment to the *Indian Act*. What is really important here is that today the *Indian Act* is silent on this very matter of missing fathers' signatures. Regardless of this legislative silence, through AANDC's unstated paternity policy these children are placed at risk for the denial of Indian status registration. More particularly, when administrating applications for status, this policy instructs the assumption of a non-Indian father in all cases where a father's signature is lacking. Through this unfair negative assumption of paternity, when a mother is registered under section 6(1)— the stronger form of Indian status—and a Status Indian father does not sign the birth certificate, the child is only registered under section 6(2). While this child is entitled to Indian status registration, when a mother is registered under section 6(2)—the weaker form of Indian status—and a Status Indian father does not sign the birth certificate, the child is deemed a non-Status person.[38]

What is really dubious about this policy assumption is that AANDC relies on a discourse—unstated paternity—and practice that blames and targets mothers and their babies. Clearly there is a need to understand the situation from the perspective of mothers.[39] My own reasoning informs me that sometimes, in cases of an abuse of power and sexual violence such as incest and rape, mothers may not obtain the father's signature on the child's birth registration form because they do not want the father to know about the child or have access to the child. Such situations may be best referred to as unreported and unnamed paternity. Again relying on my own reasoning, sometimes a mother may record the father's name on the child's birth registration form yet he refuses to sign the form because he needs to protect his standing in the community, and/or preserve a marriage to another woman, and/or to avoid having to make child-support payments, and/or prevent the loss of his driver's licence should he fail to make child-support payments. Such situations may be best referred to as unacknowledged and unestablished paternity.

Further, I have been told via the Oral Tradition that in some situations mothers do record the father's name on the birth registration form, but because the father's signature is not obtained, an official of the government of Canada blanks out the name. In other words, an official removes the father's name from the birth form. Still further, I have also been told via the Oral Tradition that in many situations the father may not be present during the birth of the child, such as when the mother is flown outside of her community to give birth as many communities are not equipped to fulfill this necessary area of health care. Moreover, once again my own reasoning informs me that sometimes the father dies prior to the birth of his child. Such situations may best be referred to as unrecognized paternity. What is more, a child may be conceived through the sexual violence of rape, gang rape, or sexual slavery or through prostitution; as a result, the mother may not know who the father is and, possibly needless to say, could care less who he is as she has other matters to address. These latter situations may best be named unknown paternity.[40]

Statistics and Figures

According to Stewart Clatworthy, between 1985 and 1999 as many as 37,300 children of so-called unstated paternity were born to Status Indian mothers registered under 6(1).[41] During this same period, as many as 13,000 children of so-called unstated paternity were born to Status Indian mothers registered under 6(2). Through AANDC's policy, these latter 13,000 children were immediately denied Indian status registration and, therefore, potentially Band membership and treaty rights. Michelle M. Mann provides the rates of so-called unstated paternity respective to age for section 6(1) mothers which, unsurprisingly, are higher for younger mothers.[42] For example, mothers under the age of fifteen years had a rate of so-called unstated paternity of 45 percent. Mothers aged fifteen to nineteen had a rate of 30 percent. Further, mothers aged twenty to twenty-four had a rate of 19 percent, mothers aged twenty-five to twenty-nine had a rate of 14 percent, and mothers aged thirty to thirty-four had a rate of 12 percent.

Although these statistics represent rates for mothers registered under 6(1), it is not unreasonable to assume the percentages are similar among mothers registered under 6(2).

Administrative Remedies Offered and My Thoughts

According to Clatworthy, 53 percent of so-called unstated paternity cases are unintentional, while the remaining 47 percent are intentional.[43] Unintentional situations emerge from compliance issues such as the father's signature not being secured because of his absence during the birth, the dissolution of the relationship, and the inability to pay administrative charges for changes requested after amendment deadlines have passed. Intentional situations emerge because of unstable relationships, a father's denial of paternity, confidentiality concerns of the mother, child custody concerns, a mother's fear of losing Indian status registration or First Nation Band membership, and an unwillingness to pay administrative fees for birth registration changes.[44] Moving from this limiting framework Clatworthy offers a number of administrative remedies: development of a national policy; First Nation leadership development; the production of new resource materials for parents; education initiatives for parents; and the development of birth and status registration kits for parents.[45] For the most part these remedies emerge from an androcentric position.

Jo-Anne Fiske and Evelyn George critique Clatworthy for failing to explore in greater detail why Indigenous mothers might not disclose who the father is. They argue that paternity disclosure can at times place women in "jeopardy, perhaps endanger them, and at the very least cause social conflicts where a man either denies paternity or refuses to acknowledge it to state authorities."[46] Similarly, as NWAC has noted, "Issues related to personal safety, violence, or abuse may provide a reason for a woman deciding to disassociate herself with a former partner or spouse." Continuing, NWAC says, "mothers may wish to avoid custody or access claims on the part of the father: leaving the paternity unstated forms a partial protection against such actions by a biological father who may be unstable, abusive, or engaged in unhealthy behaviours."[47] Mann adds that intentional situations also emerge when a mother knows who a father is yet is unwilling to identify and name the father when the pregnancy is the result of abuse, incest, or rape.[48] Certainly Fiske and George, NWAC, and Mann are getting closer to the issues and reality that many Indigenous women are forced to endure in a sexist and racist patriarchal society.

Mann also offers a discussion of administrative remedies; in some ways, they do pick up where Clatworthy left off. Mann suggests access to travel funding for fathers when mothers have to leave the community to give birth, birth forms signed in the community prior to the mother leaving to give birth, increased administrative support in communities, and alternatives to notarization when there is a need to amend birth registration forms.[49] In offering these remedies, Mann admits that they will serve little in situations where a mother for some very legitimate reason cannot or will not disclose the name of the father. Mann proceeds to offer several recommendations: to allow the use of affidavits or declarations as PoP by either the mother or father, or at the very least allow for affidavits or declarations to identify who the father is when the child is the result of sexual violence such as incest or rape; to provide necessary resources when affidavits or declarations are required; to offer educational initiatives for both men and women; to conduct research to determine additional administrative remedies; and to conduct research where key stakeholders such as First Nation women and First Nation representatives are included throughout the development of policy or legislative change.[50] In this way, her analysis moves in the right direction, extending Clatworthy's limitations. But more thinking and research are required.

Certainly, administrative remedies are within AANDC's jurisdiction, and while these remedies offered by Clatworthy and Mann are on the right track—again, Mann more so—my own thinking informs me that they do not begin to consider and thus address situations where a father, for whatever reason, while accepting paternity refuses to officially acknowledge paternity and sign a child's birth certificate. For example, it is common knowledge that sometimes fathers go through a period of insecurity and jealously when their partner becomes pregnant. I view this state of being as analogous to the postpartum depression–psychosis continuum that some mothers experience after childbirth. While this state of pathology has yet to be identified, named, and defined in the *Diagnostic and Statistical Manual of Mental Disorders*, and thus effectively addressed in our societal structures, many people know that it is during a woman's pregnancy when a male partner is more likely to become neglectful, abusive, and consequently likely to refuse to acknowledge paternity and sign a child's birth certificate.

Nor for that matter, and again drawing from my thinking, do these administrative remedies that Clatworthy and Mann offer address situations where a mother cannot identify the father as a result of rape or gang rape by unknown perpetrators. While in some cases of sexualized violence a mother may know who the perpetrator is, in other situations she may not. Moreover, there may be more than one perpetrator. In addition, and this time drawing from my own experience of being denied Indian status, these suggested administrative remedies do not address situations where an individual such as myself does not know who her grandfather was or is and has no way of determining his identity. Like the ogitchidaa kwewag before me, I am forced to take the matter of an unknown paternity in my lineage, and consequently the denial of Indian status registration, through Canada's legal system.

That said, I think it is also important to understand that these remedies and recommendations offered by Clatworthy and Mann do not address situations where a non-Indigenous woman has a child with a Status Indian man yet for some reason is unable to attain his signature on their child's birth certificate. Certainly administrative remedies, whether at the policy level or legislative level, need to incorporate the realities of non-Indigenous mothers who have parented with Indian men. Further research is required, research that includes non-Indigenous mothers of Indigenous children as a stakeholder group.

As a measure of fairness and objectivity, and to assure this chapter is comprehensive, readers will find it interesting to know that AANDC offers three administrative remedies. First, AANDC recommends that applicants for Indian status have their birth certificate amended. Second, a statutory declaration signed by the applicant's mother and biological father should be provided. Third, in the event that a biological father is uncooperative, unavailable, or deceased, it is suggested that the applicant provide a statutory declaration from the biological father's family members that affirms what they believe. These remedies fail to address many of the issues discussed by Clatworthy, Mann, and myself and as such fail to crest the horizon of the issues.

Summary and Conclusion

Despite decades of advocacy and litigation work by Indigenous women that eventually led to amendments to the *Indian Act*, under AANDC's current regime of determining Indian status registration, and as of 1985, a father must sign his child's birth certificate for his Indian status registration to be factored into the child's eligibility. Otherwise, through an unstated paternity policy, the Registrar of AANDC applies a negative assumption of paternity whereby the child may not be entitled to Indian status or, consequently, Band membership and their treaty rights. This assumption of non-Indian paternity is sex discrimination.

What is particularly disturbing about AANDC's unstated paternity policy is the way it targets Indigenous mothers and children. As I have discussed, women sometimes conceive through an abuse of power such as in situations of incest, rape, gang rape, sexual slavery, and prostitution where as such the terms "unreported," "unnamed," "unacknowledged," "unestablished," "unrecognized," and "unknown" paternity are more appropriate descriptors than the current and inadequate "unstated."

Regarding the creation of the 1985 AANDC unstated paternity policy, it is now clear to me that the remedial legislation intended to eliminate the sex discrimination was little more than an opportunity for Canada to manipulate the legislative change process into creating new and worse forms of sex discrimination. Many people may correctly argue that additional research is required in remedying AANDC's unstated paternity policy, yet it is my contention that a well-defined research methodology alone will not resolve the issues faced by Indigenous women. It is my view that the legislative silence presently codified in the *Indian Act* was manipulatively crafted by sexist and racist patriarchs as a mechanism to then create discriminatory policy at the departmental level. AANDC's unstated paternity policy is a new low for the Canadian state and is "morally reprehensible."[51] AANDC must rest on a foundation of morals rather than economics and cultural genocide.

It is precisely this unstated paternity policy that is preventing me from gaining Indian status and consequently First Nation Band membership in my kokomis's community, citizenship in the broader Anishinaabeg citizenship endeavour, and access to my treaty rights such as health care. When AANDC denies me Indian status registration it denies me important aspects of my identity as an Indigenous person and, as a result, my right to live mino-pimadiziwin as an Algonquin Anishinaabe-kwe. It is for this reason, as well as for young mothers and their babies, that I continue my effort.

Chapter 16

Ontario's History of Tampering and Re-Tampering with Birth Registration Documents

THE RITUALS AND PRACTICES ASSOCIATED WITH THE CELEBRA-
tion of motherhood and childbirth must be preserved as sacred
because fundamentally they serve to shape and guide who a child is
and where their life journey will take them, and they also serve the special
relationship between mother and child. In the context of imposed secular-
ism, the process of registering a child's birth through registration documents
has taken on enormous meaning for both mother and child. When state officials interfere with the process of recording a child's birth, through standard
operational procedures of administration, policy, and legislation—ways that
deny dignity to a mother and her child—this is more than unfortunate. The
health and well-being of mothers and children are crucially important to a
healthy society and as such they must be at the forefront of all cultural practices, especially during the process of recording the miracle of birth.

I have written in abundance about INAC's proof of paternity (PoP) policy. Succinctly, the PoP policy applies a negative presumption of paternity

when the father's information is not recorded on the long-form birth document.[1] What I mean by this is that the PoP policy assumes all unrecorded
fathers are non-Indian as defined by the *Indian Act*. The result of this policy
is that it denies Indian status to a child whose mother is registered under
section 6(2) of the *Indian Act* and assigns a lesser form of Indian status when
the mother is registered under section 6(1) of the *Indian Act*.[2] This INAC
policy was, suspiciously, created in 1985 after Canada removed the protective provisions that once existed in the *Indian Act* regarding children born of
unknown and unstated paternity. As I have explained elsewhere, this policy
also applies in situations of sexual violence such as rape and sexual slavery.
Further, it applies whether the mother is Indigenous or non-Indigenous.
Without a doubt, the creation of this policy was a step backwards in that the
stated intention of the 1985 amendment to the *Indian Act* was to remove sex
discrimination in the act. Yet sex discrimination is inherent in INAC's PoP
policy in that the policy affects mothers more than fathers, because more
often than not it is the fathers who are unknown and unstated. It is in this
way that INAC's PoP policy is contrary to the *Canadian Charter of Rights
and Freedoms*.

I could go through a lengthy process of summarizing everything previously offered about the topic of INAC's PoP policy, but my preference in
this chapter is to remain focused on a new yet related topic that requires
a discussion all its own. It is for this reason that this article will offer an
important aspect of the PoP policy and the *Indian Act* that I have not yet
addressed: administrators in the province of Ontario have tampered with
birth registration documents. It is my thought that all practices that harm
mothers and their children, or harms the relationship between mother and
child, are immoral.

My Goal and Methods

It is important for me to stress at the onset that this chapter is an entry
into understanding a topic not yet addressed in the literature. It is not a
comprehensive analysis. Indeed, more research is required. That said, a person's methods are always important to reflect on when reviewing any or all
knowledge productions as they serve to shape and guide the research and
analysis. The methods of my obtaining this knowledge and giving it back

to the broader community consist of listening to first-person accounts of birth stories; conducting a review of a sample of birth registration records; thinking critically; practising community responsibility in terms of listening to, and giving back, meaningful knowledge; interviewing an expert; and writing this chapter in an accessible form. It is also important that I qualify here that I do not offer an analysis of vital statistics acts; rather, I rely on a secondary source for this knowledge.[3] This chapter also represents a collaborative effort in the sense that after it was complete I asked stakeholders including Karen Lynn, president of the Canadian Council of Natural Mothers, as well as a person whose identity is protected if they would read it and offer their ideas, thoughts, and comments. It is important to note here that aspects of the personal stories have been changed as a mechanism to respect people's privacy.

The Ontario *Vital Statistics Act*

Here in Ontario the *Vital Statistics Act* came into being in 1869. It was not until more recently, in 1986, that the birth registration process changed from a one-name informant or parent signature requirement to a two-parent signature requirement. Confirming this, and extending the knowledge more broadly, Michelle Mann offers that today "where parents are unmarried, Vital Statistics in most jurisdictions require the father's signature on the birth form."[4] In this way, while birth registration forms before 1986 asked for the signature of one informant or parent, in its latest incarnation the form requires the signature of both mother and father.

Most people are familiar with wallet-sized birth certificates. These are a shortened extract of the information recorded on an original long-form birth registration record. They contain the person's name, date of birth, birthplace, and sex, and the certificate number; they do not include information about the parents. A long-form birth certificate, which is considered a certified copy of the original birth registration record, contains the person's full name, date of birth, birthplace, sex, and location of birth, as well as important details about the parents, such as their names, dates of birth, and birthplaces.[5]

Prior to 1986, as noted above, the *Vital Statistics Act* only required one informant or parent signature.[6] In many instances where the mother was either not married or separated she was actively prevented from recording the father's information—his name, age, place of birth, and citizenship—on her child's birth registration form. Cathy Henderson has written on the topic of tampered documents and submitted a report to the United Nations. Henderson argues that in the province of Ontario, from 1960 through 1980, "unwed father's names were illegally deleted from original birth registrations. During these decades provincial law stated that the Registrar General did *not* have the legal authority to alter information on these documents" (emphasis in original).[7]

While in the past the *Vital Statistics Act* stated that "the birth of a child of an unmarried woman shall be registered showing the surname of the mother

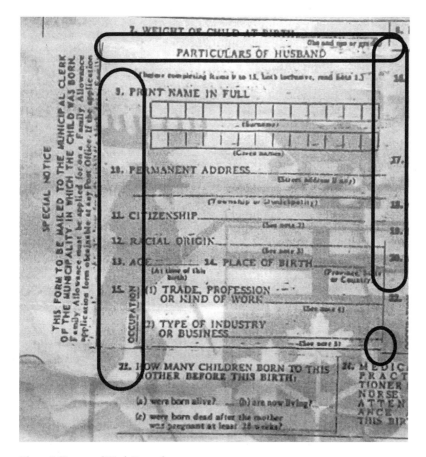

Figure 8. Tampered Birth Record

as the surname of the child, and no particulars of the father shall be given," Henderson argues that in fact there were additional provisions that further guided the process of birth registrations.[8] Henderson cites sections of the 1960 *Vital Statistics Act*:

> 3.(2) Where it is found upon examination that any registration received from a division registrar is incomplete as to the required signatures, the Registrar General shall cause the registration to be returned by registered mail to the proper division registrar in order that the signatures may be obtained. [...]

> 30.(1) If, while the registration of any birth, death or still-birth is in the possession of a division registrar, it is reported to him that an error has been made in the registration, he shall inquire into the facts and, if he is satisfied that an error has been made in the registration, he may correct the error according to the facts by a notation on the registration without any alteration being made in the registration. [...]

> 30.(3) If, after a registration has been received or made by the Registrar General, it is reported to him that an error has been made, the Registrar General shall inquire into the facts and, upon evidence satisfactory to him, supplemented by statutory declaration in the prescribed form, he may correct the error by a notation on the registration without any alteration being made in the registration.[9]

Henderson argues these clauses directed the Registrar General's responsibility to ensure birth registrations were as complete as possible, including obtaining the required signatures of unwed fathers. Further, she argues, as per the *Vital Statistics Act*, in the event that an error was made the Registrar General only had the authority to add a *notation* on the birth registration, nothing more. The deletion of fathers' names was not allowed; clearly this was not the jurisdiction of the Registrar General, argues Henderson.

Standard Procedure Prevented Mothers from Recording Fathers' Information

Genealogical research, family history research, the examination of certified original birth records, and the Oral Tradition have informed me that in some instances where an unmarried mother attempted to record the father's information on birth registration records, hospital personnel such as nurses, social workers, adoption personnel, and medical doctors actively prevented the information from being recorded. These measures consisted of orally chastising mothers and sometimes tearing up or destroying the registration document, forcing mothers to complete another form. When such efforts failed and the mother did record the father's information, another tactic relied on was a process of marking over the information to mask it. In short, the documents were tampered with. Surely this practice of interference was not in the best interest of the mother or the child. Rather, it was in the interests of the patriarchal order that continues to seek control of women and their reproductive roles and responsibilities.

Tampered Documents

In the work I do regarding INAC's PoP policy I have listened to many personal and private stories about this system of denial and disenfranchisement. People have shared with me their stories of ordering their certified copy of birth registration records, also known as their long-form birth certificates. One person stated their father's information was not on their birth record because their mother recorded herself as single. Another person explained to me that they had filled out the application form and sent it away to the Office of the Registrar General located in Thunder Bay, Ontario, including the $45 cheque.[10] Weeks later the document finally arrived in the mail. Upon its arrival they eagerly opened the envelope only to learn that their father's information was missing from their certified copy.[11] In this latter particular incident, this person's mother had recorded herself as separated.

There is more. Upon close inspection of three birth records that I personally have come across, something seemed odd or unusual in that the lines and the section numbers on the forms were misaligned, where parts of the lines were also inconsistently masked or created. Intuitively one person knew this was not right; her own reasoning informed her that official forms would never be this poorly and messily constructed. As suggested, in the work I have done helping people gain Indian status I have had the privilege of looking at several certified copies of birth registration records. I too have noticed a similar pattern of misalignment and sloppiness when the mothers are recorded as unmarried or, for that matter, separated.

One individual proceeded to tell me more of their story, which stands as a case study of what other people may be going through. Suspicious at what they were looking at when they received the certified copy of their birth certificate, and desiring to know who their father was, they contacted the Office of the Registrar General and insisted that they see their original birth registration record, instead of the certified original copy they had paid for and received. This person wanted to hold their birth record in their own hands and look at it with their own eyes, as a means of getting answers as to what was done to their original birth document. In their own words, they told me, they were determined to "get to the bottom of things."

After several weeks had passed, sometime in 2002 the Office of the Registrar General set up an appointment, and this impassioned person travelled to the Toronto office. They were "summoned to a room, told to put on white gloves, and I was handed a file folder that contained my original birth registration record." Upon opening the file, and to their shock, they discovered that their original birth record had a blank piece of white paper glued on top of the section dedicated to their father's information, thereby masking the very information their mother had inscribed and the very knowledge they sought. This realization once again horrified the individual.

Certified Original Tampered with Again

As I listened to this person's story and reflected, eventually I realized that in actual fact their birth registration record had been tampered with two times: first, when an administrator took the time to glue a blank piece of white paper on top of the father's information her mother had put on the record; and second, when the Office of the Registrar General took the time to cut out a blank version of the father section of a form and place it on top of the first white piece of paper that masked the original information. While the first time the document was tampered with was at the time of birth, the

Office of the Registrar General tampered with it a second time some time later when a copy of the certified original was requested. Based on my work and observation, this practice of tampering with documents a second time appears to be ongoing and current.

At first I was inclined to think this tampering process occurred to all birth registration records where the informant or parent who signed them was not the father, married or not married. But this is not so. From the birth registration records that I have seen, it appears that from the early 1930s through the 1960s it was the marital status of the mother that was the determining factor in whether the father's information remained intact. For example, I know of a situation in 1967 where a married woman was the signatory and the father's information remained untouched. In sum, from what I understand, if the mother was married, the father's information remained; if she was single, separated, or possibly divorced or in the process of divorce, the information would be removed.

Reflections of the President of the Canadian
Council of Natural Mothers

Not surprisingly, this past practice of removing the father's information at the time of the child's birth has huge implications for many children, especially children of adoption. In June 2009, when the province of Ontario opened 250,000 adoption records, adoptees were eager to learn who their biological parents were. Many mothers and fathers were also eager, yet anxious, to find their children. The problem, though, is that fewer than 10 percent of adoptees' birth registration records had the fathers' information filled in. Said another way, 90 percent of the birth registration records had no father information.[12] It appears that in many cases the information was removed as a result of inadequate interpretation and understanding of the rights of parents and/or subsequent hospital and social work administration practices that forbade mothers from recording who they knew the father of their babies were.

In 2015 I interviewed Karen Lynn, president of the Canadian Council of Natural Mothers. She is very familiar with this issue of birth documents being tampered with and argues that this practice of removing information has caused much heartache and anguish to both the children of adoption and the mothers and fathers who surrendered their children for adoption so the children could have better lives. It stands to reason, Lynn argues, that the information on a person's original registration of birth has huge emotional significance. She argues that this is especially true for adopted people, as it is the beginning of discovering their personal histories. Many people of adoption are devastated to find their fathers' names missing, she explains; they then turn to and blame their birth mothers, with whom they would much rather build a loving relationship of trust, instead of blaming the authorities. Further, mothers too are outraged when they learn that this important document they filled out and signed in good faith was altered without their permission or notification. Lynn argues, "This was a betrayal to both mother and child that manifests in a harmful way in what should be the beginning of a good relationship."[13]

She continues, "There was no reason for this to happen. Issues around the financial responsibility of potential fathers could be resolved through some other process, such as mothers swearing an oath of truth or fathers offering contrary evidence." She adds, "Today, the process is not much better." She continues, "While it may be true that the birth registration process changed in 1986, the father's information is still not preserved when his signature is not on the record." Furthermore, "when a father does not sign, the Registrar will not accept the document as the mother recorded the information, and the mother is instructed to issue a new record." Lynn then asks, "One has to wonder, what do they do today with the original? Do they throw them in the trash can?" She adds, "There is no reason that the record, and the information contained, cannot be accepted as is," in that today "matters related to child support payments and estates can be addressed through genetic testing or some external structure such as the court system." What is more, drawing on her experience with mothers and children who have experienced adoption, Lynn speculates that many children harmed by this practice of tampering are probably Indigenous. This places Indigenous children in double jeopardy and this is a form of cultural genocide, she argues.

How Does this Relate to Status Registration?

It is a tragedy that Ontario has denied children the right to know who their fathers are by tampering with their birth registration records. But there is more. This practice of tampering with birth documents intersects with INAC's PoP policy, because it is this policy that INAC relies on when administrating Indian status registration. It is another blow to Indigenous children whose birth documents have been tampered with because this policy assumes all unknown, unstated, and unrecognized fathers are non-Indian. In thinking further, one has to wonder, as I do, how many Indigenous children have been denied their identity and treaty rights because of an inadequate understanding of Ontario's *Vital Statistics Act* and subsequent practices that prevented mothers from recording the father's name?

International Conventions and Declarations Violated

It should come as no surprise to learn that this process of tampering with birth registration records, and, for that matter, the process of re-tampering that continues today, violates several international conventions and declarations, some particular to Indigenous Peoples. I offer a numbered list here.

1. United Nations Universal Declaration of Human Rights, adopted 1948. Article 25(2), Motherhood and childhood are entitled to special care and assistance. All children, whether born in or out of wedlock, shall enjoy the same social protection.

2. United Nations Convention on the Rights of the Child, adopted 1989. Article 8(1), States Parties undertake to respect the right of the child to preserve his or her identity, including nationality, name and family relations as recognized by law without unlawful interference; (2), Where a child is illegally deprived of some or all of the elements of his or her identity, States Parties shall provide appropriate assistance and protection, with a view to re-establishing speedily his or her identity. Article 30, In those States in which ethnic, religious or linguistic minorities or persons of indigenous origin exist, a child belonging to such a minority or who is indigenous shall not be denied the right, in community with other members of his or her group, to enjoy his or her own culture, to profess and practise his or her own religion, or to use his or her own language.

3. United Nations Declaration on the Rights of Indigenous Peoples, adopted 2007. Article 33(1), Indigenous peoples have the right to determine their own identity or membership in accordance with their customs and traditions. This does not impair the right of indigenous individuals to obtain citizenship of the States in which they live; (2), Indigenous peoples have the right to determine the structures and to select the membership of their institutions in accordance with their own procedures.

4. United Nations Convention on the Prevention and the Punishment of the Crime of Genocide, adopted 1948, includes in its definition of genocide Article 2(e), Forcibly transferring children of the group to another group.

Summary and Conclusion

I have identified that unmarried and separated mothers were actively prevented from recording the information about their child's father on birth registration records. Hospital personnel and administrators incorrectly instructed mothers to leave the information off the record. In one situation the birth registration record was tampered with, where a piece of paper was glued on top of the knowledge. In this same situation, the Office of the Registrar General tampered with a birth registration record a second time as a way of disguising the first process of tampering when a certified copy was ordered. This is morally deplorable.

It stands to reason that the process of preventing mothers from recording the father's information occurred more often with children who were placed up for adoption. This includes Indigenous children. While certainly it is a violation to deny children the knowledge of who their father is, Indigenous children face a double jeopardy when INAC assumes that in all situations where a father's signature is missing, the father is a non-Indian, whereby many children are potentially denied their treaty rights.

In terms of future direction, additional research and funding dollars are required to determine the prevalence of birth document tampering. Many questions remain: Did this happen to mothers who were divorced and widowed? Does the Office of the Registrar General continue to tamper and re-tamper with birth documents today? And are the children who request to see their original birth registration records treated with respect and dignity? In addition, how many children are denied Indian status registration as the result of the practice that denied mothers the right to record the father's information?

PART FIVE

A Talk,
a Testimonial,
and a Submission

Chapter 17

Law Society of
Upper Canada Talk

I REMEMBER WELL WHEN I HEARD THE STATEMENT OF RECONCILI-
ation on January 7, 1998, by the then Minister of Indian Affairs, Jane
Stewart.[1] When I first heard the apology, unlike many Aboriginal Peoples I distinctly remember saying to myself, "Oh my goodness, someone is
actually apologizing for what processes of colonization did to me."

At that time, my father was denied Indian status registration because he
was hit with what is known as the second-generation cut-off rule, which
denies status to Native Peoples after two generations. The Registrar applies
these new rules retroactively to the children and grandchildren of enfranchised women, which of course is a problematic practice.

In any case, I knew what I had to do and so, despite visual limitations,
I began an archival research project at the Archives of Ontario here in
Toronto, searching for my great-great-grandmother's family. My kokomis
told me a little about her; for example, she told me her name was Angeline
Jocko, that she was a black Indian, and that she had adopted a little white
boy named Moses Martel.

After years of research, I found the necessary document to have my great-great-grandmother, Angeline, established as a 6(1)c Indian and in turn her son Joseph Gagnon as a 6(2) Indian. As a result, my kokomis was upgraded to a 6(1)f Indian, as both her parents, Annie and Joseph, were now considered Indians. My father, though, was only registered as a section 6(2) Indian because we do not know who his father is or was. And as a result of his unknown paternity, I was now hit by the second-generation cut-off rule.

Interestingly, there are no provisions in the current *Indian Act* regarding how the Registrar is to address issues of unknown paternity. Rather, the Registrar simply applies a negative presumption of paternity to my unknown grandfather; that is, the Registrar makes the assumption that my grandfather is or was a white person.

In February 1995, after ten years of work, I was denied entitlement to registration. I filed a protest with Indian Affairs, and in February 1997 the Registrar informed me that my name had correctly been omitted from the Indian Register. It is now 2005. My lawyers at ALST tell me my case is heading toward discoveries in January 2006 and that it may proceed to trial in the year 2007. It has now been over twenty years and I am still waiting to have this matter resolved.

Having said all this I would like to take some time to briefly explain to you that there are huge implications to what the Canadian government has done to the identity productions of Indigenous Peoples, in terms of the contemporary treaty and self-government process, as these policies are all connected.

The Algonquin here in Ontario are in the process of trying to get back to treaty talks with the provincial and federal governments.[2] After years of being denied who we are as Algonquin, through the treaty process our identities are suddenly being affirmed via Algonquin enrolment law, a process put in place to identify us. Disturbingly, the federal and provincial governments are interpreting the large number of Algonquin who continue to sign up as representing support for the treaty process, when in fact it is more about identity affirmation. Algonquin enrolment law has become our new identity rite of passage. In this way, the Canadian state is harnessing and manipulating the history of the destruction of our cultural identities and the vulnerable position in which it left many of us.

While at university I have been learning a lot about Indigenous philosophy, culture, and values. I was more than eager to learn about my kokomis's worldview because I had become so very aware of the limitations and inadequacies of western philosophy and values, which merely root reality in the physical-ness of molecules and atoms, thus stripping the significant meaning that directs and guides people in constructive ways. I acquired this awareness through first-person experience when I was working in the environmental science field. There I was trained in, and equipped with, a lot of sophisticated tools, as all technicians and scientists are; despite this, the pollution kept coming. I discovered that water quality, Mother Earth's lifeblood, was ruled by industry and economics. Conversely, I discovered that in western culture there is little reverence or meaning for the Earth as our mother in a manner that would serve to guide people to make better decisions regarding her care.

I have learned from an Indigenous perspective that treaty relationships are about sharing land and resources; that treaty relationships are about negotiating a special relationship with other Nations; and that these relationships are sacred and must be honoured, as our relationship with the Earth must be. This differs substantially from the western perspective where negotiating a treaty with Indigenous Peoples is about land rights extinguishment and the relinquishment of Indigenous rights.

I am having difficultly bringing this knowledge to the Algonquin People and to the negotiation process for many reasons, one of which is because I am a non-Status, out-of-territory Algonquin person. Another reason is people who manipulate and confuse the contradiction I pose, in that I challenge the *Indian Act* through the court system while at the same time I advocate for equality between Status and non-Status Algonquin People in our treaty process. In short, many Algonquin cannot understand that the results of my *Charter* challenge could have national significance for many children and that as a result I cannot walk away from it simply because the Algonquin may one day have a treaty. Succinctly, many Algonquin People do not understand my need to carefully negotiate this difficult yet very real situation that I have found myself in. As a result, who I am, and the ideas I carry and continue to generate, remain marginal. In this way, the discrimination in the *Indian Act*, past and present, has implications today.

Moving full circle, as a result of the journey I have taken in terms of my continued denial of status registration combined with my insider knowledge of how the disruption of Algonquin identity productions is having huge implications on the contemporary treaty process, the meaning of Canada's Statement of Reconciliation is shifting. Unfortunately, today, and more and more as time goes on, I am beginning to view the apology delivered by Jane Stewart as a fiction created by Parliament, the very Parliament that squats on Algonquin land.

Chapter 18

House of Commons Committee Testimony

T HANK YOU FOR INVITING ME TO SPEAK TODAY ABOUT BILL S-3. I am happy to be here in my traditional territory of the Algonquin Anishinaabe. I have been working on the issue of sex discrimination in the *Indian Act* for more than thirty-two years. It was in 1945 when my great-grandmother, Annie Meness, was informed by Indian agent H. P. Ruddy that she became a white woman when she married Joseph Gagnon, who was Indigenous through his mother, Angeline Jocko. That was seventy-two years ago, yet the sex discrimination that denied my great-grandmother continues to deny my nieces and nephews today.

When the *Indian Act* was amended in 1985 to bring it in line with the *Charter*, the very provisions that protected children of unknown and unstated paternity were suspiciously removed and the *Indian Act* became silent on the matter. Subsequently, Indian and Northern Affairs Canada (INAC) then began its process of discriminating against these children at the departmental level through a proof of paternity (PoP) policy that assumed all unknown and unstated paternity situations were non-Indian men. In the process of harming Indigenous mothers and babies through this policy, INAC claimed they lacked the ability of reason and moral judgement. In INAC's defence, the Department of Justice also argued that Indigenous women would take advantage of Indian status registration rights if there was a gap in their PoP policy.

It took me twenty-two years to move through Canada's court system. In this process I was up against many barriers, such as a mother who would prefer that I not look critically at matters of paternity; a lack of funds to move the process forward through Canada's court system in a good way; INAC's deep, deep pockets of money gained through unilateral access to Indigenous land and resources; and INAC's absolute failure to disclose evidence so it could be properly adjudicated as per the rule of law. Regardless of the misery imposed, this past April the Ontario Court of Appeal's judgement came through and it was determined that I won. In short, the court determined that INAC's PoP policy that assumed all unknown and unstated paternity situations were non-Indian men was unreasonable. This process of defending against my quest for Indian status cost Canada more than $750,000,[1] yet I was told I was the mischievous one. It is now clear to me that Canada is hell-bent on eliminating Status Indians and the associated treaty rights through methods of sex discrimination and off the backs of Indigenous women and their descendants.

While lawyers view the outcome of my court case as a victory, I struggle with sharing this joy. Let me explain. I am happy that the court struck down INAC's PoP policy. I am happy with the clauses that my legal representatives Emilie Lahaie and Mary Eberts put forward as well as the evolution of the clauses established in consultation with Minister Carolyn Bennett's office. One of the clauses directs INAC to accept circumstantial evidence regarding situations of unknown or unstated parentage; the other clause clarifies that in situations of an unknown or unstated parent, such as in situations of rape, there is to be no presumption that the said parent would not have been entitled to be registered.[2]

That said, I am not happy that the judges stated I was only entitled to 6(2) Indian status. This is wrong. I was born pre-1985 and therefore I should be entitled to 6(1)a Indian status. My great-grandmother's brother's descendants are all entitled to be registered under 6(1)a. With this so-called court remedy of granting me 6(2) status I am only entitled to being "less than" because of my matrilineal ancestry. Indigenous women have worked hard to resolve the sex discrimination in the *Indian Act*: Mary Two-Axe Earley, Jeannette Corbiere Lavell, Yvonne Bédard, Sandra Lovelace Nicholas, Sharon Donna McIvor—together we took what we thought was the right path.

The Liberal government came into power on the platform of reconciliation and respecting the nation-to-nation relationship. If this government moves forward with the "6(1)a All the Way!" remedy, as I hope, a remedy that addresses all the sex discrimination in the *Indian Act*, Prime Minister Justin Trudeau, Minister Carolyn Bennett, and the rest of Canada will truly have something to celebrate. Otherwise, Canada will remain stained. Again, it took me twenty-two years to move through Canada's court system, and in the end the so-called remedy offered is nothing but a new form of sex discrimination. This is not fair and is out of line with Canada's *Charter*. Canada can do better than this.

I have listened to some of the guest testimonies and the questions the committee is asking. The first thing I want to clarify is that nation-to-nation consultations do not take place when within the Indigenous Nations the descendants of Indian women are not equal to the descendants of Indian men. INAC will never accomplish true nation-to-nation discussions when consulting with Nations where the descendants of Indian women are missing from the conversation.

INAC claims it cannot move forward with the "6(1)a All the Way!" remedy, and thereby remove all the sex discrimination, because of the claimed need to consult on a nation-to-nation basis. At the same time, INAC prevents First Nations from welcoming their members through imposing fiscal restraints that are not rooted in genuinely valuing what is nation-to-nation, such as sharing the land and resources in an equal way and in such a way that the Indigenous Nations are able to embrace matrilineal descendants. On the one hand, Canada is saying it cannot resolve all of the sex discrimination in the *Indian Act* because it must respect the nation-to-nation relationship, yet on the other hand, Canada does not really respect the Indigenous Nations' need to enter into what are genuine nation-to-nation discussions.

The second thing I want to clarify is that yes, it is correct that many First Nation bands, such as my kokomis's, conflate Indian status with First Nation Band membership. This practice is being argued by INAC as its excuse not to resolve all the sex discrimination, as there is a need for First Nations to be consulted. We need to keep in mind that First Nation Band membership codes are within the jurisdiction of First Nations, not INAC. My point being, INAC presents a poor argument—i.e., that, in many situations, Indian status registration equals First Nation Band membership—as the rationale not to resolve all the sex discrimination. That said, and regardless, the goal we are discussing today is the need for Canada to resolve all the sex discrimination in law, not in First Nation membership codes.

Third, Canada's failure to resolve the "matrilineal-descent sex discrimination" actually establishes a colonial and patriarchal foundation for the land claim and self-government process in that the descendants of Indigenous women are marginalized and thus vulnerable in the process. Genuinely respecting the nation-to-nation relationship would abolish the sex discrimination inherent in the 6(1)a–6(1)c hierarchy.

Fourth, in fact contrary to the claim of the need to respect the nation-to-nation relationship, Canada is not doing that at all. In the Algonquin land claim and self-government process we are only being offered a mere 1.3 percent of our traditional territory and a one-time $300 million buyout.[3] Please stop using the need to respect the nation-to-nation relationship as the reason not to resolve the matter of matrilineal-descent sex discrimination. There is so much wrong here.

The fifth thing I want to speak to is the argument that it would be irresponsible for Canada to implement the "6(1)a All the Way!" remedy without further analysis. It is my position that this claimed place of potential irresponsibility is actually an excuse that has been carefully constructed through decades of intentional and strategic deception and manoeuvring rooted in the need for Canada to eliminate Indians. The Canadian government has been completely aware of Indigenous women's efforts to remove sex discrimination from the *Indian Act*. This effort is not new. Not at all. Canada has had decades as well as the deep pockets required to accommodate the research needed to draft legislation that would remove all the sex discrimination and bring about *Charter* compliance. Instead, what Canada has done is placed its time, dollars, and effort into crafting legislative amendments that ignore, confound, disguise, and for that matter craft silent forms of sex discrimination, as we learn from *Gehl v Canada*. In this process INAC has in fact crafted new forms of sex discrimination instead of ensuring the *Indian Act* is *Charter* compliant. It is my position that Canada's claim that it would be irresponsible to move forward without further analysis and consultation is more about disrespecting what is genuinely a nation-to-nation relationship. And it is the complete manipulation of the agency of Indigenous women— Indigenous women who are already burdened.

Sixth, I ask members of this committee to support the amended version of Bill S-3 as it is crucial both to upholding the human rights of Indigenous women and their descendants and to finally putting Indian women and their descendants born prior to April 17, 1985, on the same footing as Indian men and their descendants born prior to April 17, 1985. Please stand with Indigenous women's calls for *Charter* compliance and for equality.

Chapter 19

Inter-American Commission on Human Rights Submission

R EGARDING: THE FEMINIST ALLIANCE FOR INTERNATIONAL
Action's (FAFIA) hearing with the Inter-American Commission on
Human Rights (IACHR) regarding sex discrimination in the *Indian
Act* of Canada.

My name is Lynn Gehl. I am an Algonquin Anishinaabe and I was born
and reside in what is now called Canada. In 1985, when the *Indian Act* was
amended to address the long-standing sex discrimination against Indian
women who married non-Indian men, new forms of sex discrimination
were passed on to their descendants. The discrimination results from the
way reinstated Indian women and their descendants born before 1985 are
ascribed a lesser form of Indian status—6(1)c and 6(2), respectively—yet
Indian men and their descendants born before 1985 are ascribed a stronger
form of Indian status: 6(1)a. What results from this difference is that Canada
affords Indian men the right to pass on Indian status to an additional generation in a way that reinstated Indian women cannot.

Sharon Donna McIvor has taken this very issue to court, wherein Canada
appealed her victory to the British Columbia Court of Appeal, which then

greatly narrowed the remedy offered by the lower court. What has resulted is that descendants born pre-1951, and descendants born post-1951, continue to be discriminated against, albeit in different yet significant ways.

In addition to this, in 1985 a brand-new form of sex discrimination was created whereby INAC made the assumption that all unknown/unstated fathers on birth certificates were non-Indian men. This resulted in the loss of Indian status for many Indigenous children and grandchildren. This new assumption was imposed on pre-1985 births even though prior to the 1985 amendment to the *Indian Act*, there was a provision that protected children in this situation. This new form of discrimination was how I was denied Indian status when I first applied in 1994. After thirty-three years, which included twenty-two years of litigation, in April 2017 I was successful at challenging this INAC paternity assumption when the Ontario Court of Appeal ruled in my favour, arguing it was unreasonable. While I won my case, I lost at the same time when I was hit with Canada's practice of providing me an inferior form of Indian status, 6(2), because, like Sharon, my Indigenous ancestry comes from my line of grandmothers rather than my grandfathers. Said another way, if my ancestry came through my grandfathers I would be a 6(1)a Indian, as I was born before 1985.

Like many people, I was hopeful that Bill s-3, An Act to Amend the *Indian Act* (the elimination of sex-based discrimination), which is currently before Canadian Parliament and will soon become law, would resolve the sex discrimination that Sharon and her descendants, Indigenous Peoples in her situation, and me and people in my situation continue to face. Alternatively said, I was hopeful Canada would take a proactive approach in remedying all the sex discrimination and finally bring the *Indian Act* in line with Canada's *Charter*.

Unfortunately, Prime Minister Justin Trudeau, along with Minister of Indian Affairs Carolyn Bennett, Minister of Justice Jody Wilson-Raybould, and Minister of Status of Women Maryam Monsef removed the very remedy clauses that Canada's Senate had put forward. In exchange, Canada has offered a two-stage consultation process with First Nation Chiefs to remedy the issue. Yet Canada refuses to meet First Nations on fair and moral grounds regarding the concomitant need and the Chiefs' call to adjust land and resource distribution to accommodate the women. In this way Canada manipulates the Chiefs' concerns as the rationale behind perpetuating the sex discrimination. Further, Indigenous women's rights are not something that requires consultation. Not at all. Rights are rights. An additional problem with Canada's position is that a two-stage approach was promised in 2010 and nothing resulted from it.

Indigenous women have been living under this regime of sex discrimination in the *Indian Act* for more than a century. Many have taken this very issue through Canada's court system, yet we are unable to gain the remedy we seek: to live free from sex discrimination. Indian women and their descendants must be entitled to the same rights as Indian men and their descendants. Canada's ongoing sex discrimination bleeds into and shapes our process of self-government, the land claim process, and our membership and citizenship codes, and it is for this reason that we are seeking protection and support from the IACHR.

PART SIX

Bill S-3

Chapter 20

Understanding "6(1)a All the Way!"

I T SEEMS THAT THERE ARE PEOPLE WHO ARE STRUGGLING IN understanding "6(1)a All the Way!" By "people" I mean members of Parliament, senators, community people, settler Canadians, and journalists. Knowledge is foremost a relationship and so you may have to read this a few times to move the awareness to understanding, to knowledge, to wisdom. It is said that knowledge moves through four levels.

The first thing learners need to know is that it was in 1985 that Parliament passed Bill C-31 to bring the *Indian Act* in line with the *Charter*. It failed. This is when the second-generation cut-off rule was invented. Read on...

The second-generation cut-off rule is a process where after two generations of parenting with non-Status people, second-generation descendants are not entitled to be registered as Status Indians. It is a process where a family lineage is, first, bumped down a level to 6(2) status and, second, bumped out to being non-Status. The problem is in the way this rule is applied differently to the descendants of men versus the descendants of women who were once enfranchised and then reinstated in 1985. Read on...

In 1985 Indian men, their wives, and their descendants (born before 1985) were all registered as 6(1)a Indians, while reinstated Indigenous women were registered as 6(1)c Indians. Here lies the issue: there is a difference between the 6(1)a and 6(1)c categories in that while the second-generation cut-off rule is applied to men and their descendants *after* 1985, it is applied backwards, or retroactively, to Indian women and their descendants born *before* 1985. Figure 9 may help with understanding the difference in the way the second-generation cut-off rule is applied in a way that is sex discrimination. The "6(1)a All the Way!" amendment that many women, and our allies, are calling for is not intended to address the second-generation cut-off rule post-1985. Rather, it is intended to address the way in which it is applied faster, and also retroactively, to Indian women reinstated in 1985 and their descendants. Another way to say this is that we are calling for 6(1)a to be applied *all the way*—to all reinstated women and their descendants in a way that is equal to Indian men and their descendants. It is that simple yet that hard to understand. Take some time and think, as it is the best way to establish a relationship with the knowledge.

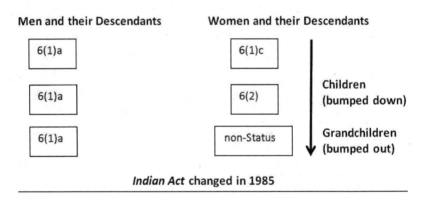

Figure 9. Understanding "6(1)a All the Way!"; © Lynn Gehl

Chapter 21

Carolyn Bennett's
"2 Million" New Indians

THE *INDIAN ACT* WAS AMENDED IN 1985 TO BRING IT IN LINE with the *Charter*. While this created 114,000 new or reinstated Indians, it did not resolve all the sex discrimination in the *Indian Act*. Worse, the 1985 amendment created a new form of sex discrimination when INAC discriminated against children of unknown and unstated paternity through its unstated paternity policy. This policy made the assumption that if no father's signature was on a child's birth registration form then he was non-Indian, which meant many children were deemed non-Status and thus not entitled to their treaty rights. This policy applied in situations of sexual violence such as rape and incest and, further, in situations where young girls did not even have the legal right to consent to sex. This newly invented policy was diabolical.

Bill s-3, "6(1)a All the Way!," and Bennett's 2 Million Indians

While the Senate Committee on Aboriginal Peoples, after listening to experts such a Sharon Donna McIvor and myself, put forward a version of

Bill s-3, An Act to Amend the *Indian Act*, that would resolve all the sex-based inequities through the inclusion of the "6(1)a All the Way!" clauses, INAC Minister Carolyn Bennett, flip-flopping on her previous position, urged members of Parliament to vote against it. Bennett then put forward a version of the bill that would perpetuate sex discrimination.

Obfuscating the process, Bennett said the "6(1)a All the Way!" clause would result in two million new Indians. This number was rooted not in a demographic analysis but rather in what appears to me as a need for her to fear-monger. It is my suggestion that the number is more likely 60,000 to 100,000.[1] Pam Palmater estimates 200,000.[2]

2010: McIvor Creates 45,000 Indians

Sharon Donna McIvor took the issue—that of Indigenous men and their descendants born before 1985 being ascribed the strongest form of Indian status, 6(1)a, yet Indigenous women and their descendants born before 1985 being ascribed lesser forms of Indian status, 6(1)c or 6(2)—to court in British Columbia. Relying on this comparison Sharon won her case. It was a victory. INAC appealed the decision to the British Columbia Court of Appeal, where the court ruled that some of the sex discrimination in the *Indian Act* was justified. The justification was that the matter was an issue of matrilineal descent. Then the court relied on the 1951 double-mother clause imposed on the descendants of Indian men as the comparator group to narrow down the remedy. This was a terrible moment for Indigenous women.

Sharon wants 6(1)a for all her descendants born before 1985 rather than what she, her son, and her grandchildren gained: 6(1)c, 6(1)c.1, and 6(2), respectively.[3] The SCC refused to hear her appeal and so Sharon is now at the international level. Regardless, through Bill C-3 the *Indian Act* was amended and 45,000 people became registered Status Indians.

2015: *Descheneaux* Creates 35,000 Indians

Stéphane Descheneaux was unable to pass on Status to his descendants because he was only registered as a 6(2) Indian. This was the result of his matrilineal descent, meaning it was his grandmother and not his grandfather who was Indian. This is known as the "cousins issue," in that

Stéphane's second cousin born through the patrilineal line was entitled to 6(1)a status.

Susan Yantha, as a girl child born out of wedlock pre-1985, was only registered as a 6(2) Indian, which meant she could not pass on Status to her daughter Tammy, whereas her hypothetical brother born out of wedlock would be entitled to 6(1)a status. This is known as the "siblings issue."

When the Quebec court judge ruled on these cases before her, she was clear that there exists a need to eliminate the sex discrimination. It has been said that the resolution of the cousins and siblings issues will create between 28,000 and 35,000 Indians. It is the Descheneaux case that resulted in Bill S-3, which is currently before Parliament.

2017: *Gehl* Case Affects 100,000 Births

As stated, the issue of unknown and unstated paternity is a form of sex discrimination invented in 1985. I was denied status due to an unknown paternal grandfather. It took me more than thirty years to move through my family oral history, archival research, and the litigation process. In April 2017 Ontario's highest court ruled that this sex discrimination was unreasonable and I was granted Indian status. But I was granted the lesser form of status. This is why I am invested in making sure the "6(1)a All the Way!" clauses remain a part of Bill S-3.

My court case was heard while Bill S-3 was moving through Parliament so the required remedy will be included in Bill S-3. Parliamentarians are not debating this. Demographers Stewart Clatworthy and James S. Frideres agree that the estimated number of births affected by INAC's unstated paternity policy as of 2004 totalled over 60,000.[4] While the majority of these people were relegated the lesser form of 6(2) status, 15,000 were actually denied status. Through the *Gehl* clauses now codified in Bill S-3 these 45,000 people will be entitled to 6(1) status which means all their children will also be entitled; and 15,000 will be newly entitled as 6(2). As we think about Clatworthy's and Frideres's numbers we need to keep in mind that they represent births up to 2004. As of 2017 the numbers will be higher. I suggest 77,000 people may be entitled to 6(1) status and 25,000 people may be entitled to 6(2) status. It is said the government recently commissioned Clatworthy to determine the number of people who would be entitled to

Indian status through the "6(1)a All the Way!" clauses. Hopefully parliamentarians step up and remove all the discrimination Indigenous women and their descendants are dealing with.

Chapter 22

Valuing Discourse

Senators Discuss Indian and Northern Affairs
Canada's "Unstated Paternity" Policy

W HEN MEMBERS OF PARLIAMENT AND SENATORS BORROW,
assimilate, or adopt gender-neutral language such as "unstated
parentage" or "unnamed parent" when the discrimination is anything but, they potentially approve legislation that harms mothers and babies.
Prior to 1985 the *Indian Act* protected Indian mothers' children when
their father's signature was not recorded on their birth certificate, in that
those children were considered to be Indian. When the *Indian Act* was
amended in 1985 this protection was removed. What resulted was that the
Registrar of INAC gained more control when processing applications in situations of unknown, unacknowledged, unrecognized, unnamed, and unstated
paternity. It was at this moment, when power was placed more firmly in the
hands of administrators than in the legislation, where INAC was able to more
easily apply its goal: to eliminate the Indian problem—the new low being
that mothers and babies became the target.

At first there was no written policy, but eventually INAC posted its "unstated paternity" policy online. While the name of the policy itself is an issue, in that it clearly blames mothers, the policy advises affected people to have their birth certificate amended or to obtain a statutory declaration signed by both parents; another option offered is a statutory declaration from the biological father's family members. The problem is that these options do not capture the lived reality of conception and birthing, nor the failure of documents to understand the lived reality of abusive situations. For example, INAC's policy does not account for situations of rape where a mother does not know the identity of the father (best known as the offender); situations of domestic violence where a mother needs to protect herself and her child; or situations where a father refuses to acknowledge the child.

It is important to pay attention to the process of naming because oftentimes power is inherent. The words people rely on shape the way people think and therefore have the potential to shape remedies, if needed. Of course, this process in which word use shapes our thinking includes elected members of the House of Commons and appointed senators who make up the legislative branch of the government of Canada. My point is that while INAC names its policy "unstated paternity," it is best to understand the situation from within the lived reality of mothers where "unknown paternity," "unrecognized paternity," "unacknowledged paternity," and "unnamed paternity" are more appropriate word choices.

As many know, recently INAC tabled Bill S-3, An Act to amend the *Indian Act.* This bill was in response to a 2015 Quebec court decision by Justice Masse in the case involving Stéphane Descheneaux and Susan and Tammy Yantha.[1] Although she was embarrassed about the lack of consultation with interested parties in the development of the bill, the Minister of INAC, Carolyn Bennett, moved it forward.

From late November through early December 2016, interested parties had the opportunity to speak to members of the House of Commons Standing Committee on Indigenous and Northern Affairs, as well as to the Standing Senate Committee on Aboriginal Peoples. Many of the parties, including Descheneaux, Sharon Donna McIvor, the Women's Legal Education and Action Fund (LEAF), and the Quebec Native Women (QNW), were unhappy because of the lack of proper consultation, a result of which was that the bill failed to address all the sex discrimination in the *Indian Act.*

As it stands today, INAC has been granted an extension so proper consultations and reconsideration of the content of the bill can occur.[2] Regardless, I noticed something rather peculiar as I listened to these House and Senate discussions specifically regarding word choice when discussing the issue of unknown and unstated paternity. As many know, I have been working on this very issue now for over thirty-one years.

Perplexed and concerned with the word-shifting process, as I was, I opted to conduct an analysis of the language used by interested parties, the assistant deputy minister, the counsel for the Department of Justice (DoJ), the Minister of INAC, and senators when talking about the issue of unknown and unstated paternity.

When speaking in the House of Commons, interested parties relied on the terms "unstated paternity," "so-called unstated paternity," "unknown paternity," and "unacknowledged paternity." This language correctly names the issue. Minister Bennett also relied on this language during these discussions.

When speaking to the Senate Standing Committee, INAC Assistant Deputy Minister Joëlle Montminy relied on the term "undisclosed and unknown paternity," and the lawyer for the DoJ, Martin Reiher, relied on "unknown parent," adding "which is usually an unknown father." Bravo! Like Minister Bennett, they used language that closely represents the lived reality of Indigenous women—but this changed. Pay particular attention here to my analysis of the discourse and how the language use shifts.

During these same Senate discussions, interested parties, some of whom I mentioned above, used the terms "unknown parents," "unstated paternity," and "other reasons for not identifying the father," but one senator, an important and potential ally, relied on *"unknown parent."* This to me marked the beginning of the unfortunate language shift. Again, a few days later during these same Senate discussions, Montminy and Bennett—now, in my opinion, more cognizant of their goal—began to rely on *"unstated paternity"* and *"parenthood"* and *"unnamed parent."* Unfortunately, the same senator continued using *"unknown parentage."*

In sum, and my point is, the shift in language use during these important discussions, from "unstated and unknown paternity" to the gender-neutral language of "unknown parentage" and "unnamed parent," was first introduced by the Minister and Assistant Deputy Minister of INAC, both of whom are guided by the goal of eliminating Status Indians. The danger of naming without critical thought is that it begins to shape the thinking of Members of Parliament and senators, potentially preventing them from understanding the sex discrimination that harms mothers and babies. It is really sad when women, mothers, and potential allies adopt the oppressor's language, as happened during these discussions.

We must not allow the very people and organizations, such as INAC, who hold power over others, to name reality in a way that is misleading and inadequate in regard to the lived reality of oppressed people. I have come to know that sometimes gender-neutral language is just more of the same; more specifically, sometimes gender-neutral language is disguised patriarchy.

PART SEVEN

Dishonouring Wenonah's Jurisdiction

Chapter 23

My Last Chapter

I Am Only a Woman

The two-parent rule contained in the Indian Act *combined with
proof of paternity requirements arguably constitutes discrimination
against unmarried First Nations women and their children.*

—Michelle Mann,
"Disproportionate and Unjustifiable"

I
N THE 1971 JEANNETTE CORBIERE LAVELL CASE, YORK COUNTY
Court in Toronto determined that Corbiere Lavell had rights equal to
all other married Canadian women and thus she lost, meaning the court
ruled against her. Corbiere Lavell appealed this decision to the Federal
Court of Appeal, where the judges determined that different rights did in
fact exist between men and women who married non-Status Indian Peoples
and that this was indeed a violation of the Canadian Bill of Rights. Canada
appealed this decision and, in 1973, Yvonne Bédard's case was joined
with the Corbiere Lavell case; the Supreme Court of Canada (SCC) heard
both cases and determined that these Indigenous women were not being

discriminated against. The reason, Patricia Monture-Angus argues, was that the Canadian Bill of Rights only protected them from discrimination *before* the law when they sought equality *under* the law.[1]

Sharon Donna McIvor offers the same understanding: in 1971 Corbiere Lavell lost her case at the trial level, then won at the Federal Court of Appeal level, and then, when Canada appealed, the SCC restored the trial judge's decision to a formal equality approach that the Canadian Bill of Rights offers. At the trial level, the judge compared married Indian women to married Canadian women, arguing that Corbiere Lavell had equality of status with married Canadian women. McIvor explains, "Under this logic, a woman derives her status from her husband, and, thus, if an Indian woman marries a man not registered under the *Indian Act*, she gains his Canadian status and loses her Indian status and band membership."[2] The barrier here was the comparator group on which the court relied, meaning comparing married Indian women to married Indian men would have produced a different result. In doing this, the SCC adopted a narrow, procedural notion of equality *before* the law. In sum, and again, the Canadian Bill of Rights was too narrow a framework to ensure the protection of human rights.[3]

Collectively, Monture-Angus and McIvor argue that the failure of the Canadian Bill of Rights shaped the lobbying efforts regarding the need for the entrenchment of women's rights in Canada's 1982 *Charter of Rights and Freedoms*. As a result of this lobbying effort, both equality before the law and equality under the law are now protected in section 15 of the *Charter*. Monture-Angus further stresses that, in the end, Canada's failure to protect Indigenous women's rights has resulted in better protection for all women who live in Canada.

As I have shown earlier, I worked for a long time addressing INAC's unknown and thus unstated paternity policy, whereby a person whose father's signature is not on their birth certificate, or whose ancestor's father did not sign an ancestor's birth certificate, was either denied the right to Indian status registration or relegated to the weaker form, by which they are unable to pass on registration in their own right.[4] While I knew the 1985 version of the *Indian Act* was silent on the issue of unknown and thus unstated fathers, I had no idea if INAC had a written policy, a standard operating practice, or a directive to guide, determine, and administrate issues of paternity. Rather, in my process of being denied registration I simply named INAC's practice and inherent assumption whereby my unknown and thus unstated grandfather was deemed non-Indian as "INAC's unknown and unstated paternity" policy. In naming my reality I created the ability to talk about it with others. As I look at this issue now I realize that I should have called it "INAC's unknown and *thus* unstated paternity" policy all along, versus "INAC's unknown and unstated paternity" policy, as it more clearly expresses that my situation was different from a "known yet unstated paternity." Don't let these two ways to talk about the issue confuse you. That said, INAC's practice of denial resulting from paternity issues is also referred to as INAC's negative presumption of paternity, meaning it is assumed the father is a non-Indian man.

Prior to 1985 Indian registration followed down the father line, where white (or, best to say, non-Indian) women whom they married became registered, as were their children; in contrast, Indian women who married non-Indian men were no longer considered Indian and lost entitlement through a process called enfranchisement, and their children were also denied. In 1985 INAC reinstated these enfranchised Indian women and their descendants, but with a weaker form of entitlement, either section 6(1)c or 6(2), while Indian men, their wives, and their descendants born before 1985 where granted the strongest form of entitlement: 6(1)a. In doing this, Canada immediately imposed on these reinstated women and their descendants the second-generation cut-off rule, which Canada invented in 1985, whereas the second-generation cut-off rule is only applied to men and their descendants post-1985.

As a reminder for readers who do not know the details of the second-generation cut-off rule, it is the practice whereby after two generations of parenting with non-Indians, as defined by the *Indian Act*, the right to Indian status registration ceases. In more colloquial terms, the second-generation cut-off rule is a "bump, bump, and you are a non-Status" process of elimination. Or as Alexandra McLean suggested—during a lunch conversation with Mary Eberts, Senator Lillian Eva Dyck, and Senator Sandra Lovelace Nicholas in the parliamentary dining room—a useful comparison that may help people understand is that it is much like passing on Canadian citizenship abroad. If, for example, you move to Britain, your children will be entitled to Canadian citizenship, but your grandchildren will not. In terms of the *Indian Act*, it is worth repeating that while the second-generation cut-off rule was invented in 1985 and immediately applied to the descendants of reinstated 6(1)c women, through the invention of section 6(1)a it is only applied to men and their descendants born after 1985. This difference is referred to as the 6(1)a–6(1)c hierarchy. Yet another way to understand this is: It was in 1985 when INAC brought in the two-parent rule. This means Indian registration is no longer determined solely through the father line; rather, it is now determined through the combination of both parents' right to registration. Again, while the two-parent rule applies to all births post 1985, for the reinstated women and their descendants it applies immediately in a retroactive sense. And no, it is not rational; it is sex discrimination.

With that repeated and repeated, INAC's unwritten, unknown, and thus unstated paternity practice/policy was invented following the 1985 amendment to the *Indian Act*, and it was applied to my 1994 application for Indian registration, where as a result I was denied entitlement. Immediately I felt this was a form of sex discrimination because, after all, section 15 of the *Charter* states, "Every individual is equal before and under the law and has the right to the equal protection and equal benefit of the law without discrimination and, in particular, without discrimination based on race, national or ethnic origin, colour, religion, sex, age or mental or physical disability."[5]

Within section 15, race, national or ethnic origin, colour, religion, sex, age, and mental or physical disability are referred to as "enumerated grounds" where the addition of the words "in particular" implies there are other ways people may be discriminated against. These other ways are best referred to as "analogous grounds," but it is the court that determines if they are analogous to the enumerated terms. That is, the question becomes, is the discrimination imposed on me on an enumerated or an analogous ground? I was sure it was discrimination based on sex, in that if my kokomis were my grandfather I would be entitled to 6(1)a registration. However, judges make these decisions based on their training, precedent, and the arguments and evidence that lawyers present. The problem is that justice is very much a function of worldview, power, and economics, and I was in trouble against them because I had no power and no access to a pot of money.

Before I proceed, it is important that I remind readers where the unknown and thus unstated paternity in my lineage is located. I was born in May 1962; my father, Rodney, was born in May 1935; and my kokomis, Viola, was born in May 1911. I do not know who my paternal grandfather was.

For clarity, my paternal grandfather is the man who fathered my father. Whoever this man was, he is an ancestor of mine whom I have never known. He is unknown and *thus* unstated on my father's birth certificate. Because my great-grandmother and kokomis were no longer considered Indians as defined by the *Indian Act*, my father and I were also denied Indian status. As a result, we were denied our treaty rights that included medical, dental, and education rights, as well as our right to live in our ancestral First Nation community. There is so much I can say about this, such as I am sure my own mother's life would have been less miserable and less stressful if she had had these health and education rights for her and her children. Indeed, Canada was and remains a wiindigo, and pathologically rotten to the core, for what it has done to so many fathers, mothers, and children.

Drawing from my family oral history, I learned that it was in the late 1920s or early 1930s that my great-grandmother Annie Jane Meness (born January 1891) was escorted out of her community, then called the Golden Lake Indian Reserve, now Pikwàkanagàn First Nation, by the RCMP. This happened after it was determined that her husband, Joseph Gagnon Jr., was considered a white man when in fact his mother, Angeline Jocko (born 1865), was an Indian from the Lake of Two Mountains. His father, though, Joseph Gagnon Sr., was a French man. It was in 1945 when Annie Jane wanted to know if she was considered to be an Indian and so she wrote government officials. Within a few weeks she was told by Indian agent H. P. Ruddy that when she married Joseph Gagnon Jr., a "white man," she "became a white woman."

I have written previously about my effort to become a registered Indian. The sources are multiple and have been placed online, and many are now gathered here in this book, as I have worked hard to ensure community people are aware of INAC's unknown and thus unstated paternity policy. I seek now to write what I hope will be my last chapter on this life-giving yet paradoxically life-sucking effort. Before I proceed, though, it is important for me to discuss my methods and theoretical frameworks that combine to form my methodological approach because they tell the story of where this knowledge production emerges from and what my limitations in telling my story are. We all have gifts and we all have limitations.

Revisiting Methods and Methodology

Regardless of what some people may think, or are unaware of, positivism no longer lives or holds the privileged and powerful position it once did. It is no longer accepted that white able-bodied heterosexual historians, judges, lawyers, and scientists tell the truth and nothing but the truth through the methodology of legal positivism and their inherent methods, such as facts, artifacts, physical matter, evidence, objectivity, and quantitative analysis. All knowledge-producing and truthing systems and their inherent theories (methodologies) and practices (methods) rest on a set of assumptions and beliefs. Truth is no longer considered to be some exterior universal fact that we are able to obtain through some pure and objective way or form. Furthermore, not only do humans rely on both conscious and subconscious lenses, power plays a huge role in how it shapes knowledge productions and the subsequent societal structures we build. For example, it is now well known and accepted that historical artifacts and documents were constructed through bias and skewed through a colonial lens and the assumptions inherent in the Doctrine of Discovery with the agenda of usurping Indigenous land and resources; further, we know that judges are biased through the Doctrine of Discovery and, as a result, Canadian law has become the jurisdictional framework that denies Indigenous jurisdiction and rights. What is more, today there is also the call for knowledge producers to examine their positionality and subconscious motivations because they too shape knowledge productions. For these very reasons, in any knowledge production such as this one, it is always important to flesh out one's methods and methodology.

Having completed an undergraduate degree in cultural anthropology, a master's in Canadian and Native studies, and a doctorate in Indigenous studies, I have spent a lot of time reading, thinking, and discussing Indigenous knowledge philosophy and the inherent and numerous ways of knowing and being, also known as methods, such as storytelling and learning by doing. I have always felt that through my graduate educational training I had a strong grasp of these methods, and I was proud that I learned how to read and think well enough to move through the complex conceptual thought needed to understand. This was no small feat. Although I have a strong grasp of them, I have always used Indigenous methods in combination with western methods, such as relying on lengthy literature reviews and on western scholars and scholarship, to justify or sanction my work as a worthy contribution.

Regardless of how confident I was about relying on Indigenous methods in combination with others' methods, it was not until I began to write this last chapter that I was faced with the reality of having to move deeper into embracing my ancestral ways of knowing. I had to put aside all of the rhetoric and processes of comparing Indigenous methods with other ways of knowing; I had to walk away from bolstering my knowledge through adding western ways of knowing; I realized that if I did not push aside the need for what is called "objectivity," the need for a comprehensive literature review, the need for copious referencing, and quoting expert knowledge holders, I would never be able to do what was needed to complete this very task. As an example, publishing my doctoral dissertation was a process laden with people and academics who lacked an appreciation of Indigenous ways of knowing and being. The reviewers of my manuscript in effect wanted to colonize my work, or they tried to, so much so that after a few years I had to walk away from the first publisher I worked with. Eventually I turned to Fernwood Publishing. In 2014, four years after completing my doctoral program, I successfully converted my dissertation to book form.[6]

What I am getting at is that the Indigenous methods that have moved my effort forward to do this work have been a heavy burden; as a result, forcing myself to rely on western methods in combination with Indigenous methods was presenting a barrier in completing the task of this final chapter of my *Charter* challenge. As one can imagine, I have been, and continue to be, way too immersed in the deep rabbit hole of this effort. The process has monopolized my life, my thinking, my heart, and all I do for more than thirty years. I am exhausted and, to tell the truth, damn well sick of it. When I reflect on my need to move into the final writing and dissemination of this work, I realize Creator has already given me the tools I need to tell my story.

Having qualified this, I will add that while doing this work I have read some, not all, of the court documents this process has produced, including my affidavit, my SoC, the factum of the plaintiff, the factum of the appellant, and the two court judgements. For the most part the methods I relied on in completing this task consisted of family oral history, experiential knowledge, subjectivity, memory, emotional knowledge, rationality, deep introspection, reading over my personal notes and timeline, talking with others who helped me along the way, and finally writing in a storytelling approach in terms of the dissemination of this knowledge in this final chapter.

In my thinking about methods and methodology I am able to delineate them. While it is true that Indigenous theory is inherent in Indigenous methods, I prefer to be explicit about what theory or theories I think and perceive through and about what framework motivates my thinking and agency forward. That said, it is foremost an Indigenist framework that guides my thinking and agency. What I mean by this is that situated at the core of all my works are the needs of Indigenous mothers and children, Indigenous Peoples, and Indigenous issues. Within an Indigenist framework, Indigenous Peoples come first. We are deserving of more from Canada; after all, it is our Land that the invention of Canada, and its citizenry, squats on and continues to usurp. In adding to this, this particular work also emerges from an anticolonial framework. While I may be reading and learning from what are known as primary source materials, those being court judgements, I am well aware of the reality that these so-called primary source materials emerged through a colonial lens such as the assumption of the Doctrine of Discovery where Canada's—or, in this situation, judges'—power has too much control in shaping how people think about Indigenous women, our children, and our rights and jurisdiction.

Still further, when I think more deeply about what has motivated me in this work of challenging the sex discrimination in the *Indian Act*, Cindy Blackstock's "moral courage" resonates. Blackstock argues when it comes to caring for vulnerable people and children, there is a need to step into moral bravery. Moral courage involves standing up for the right thing even in the face of negative repercussion. It is moral courage, she continues, that is needed when blowing the whistle on long-standing rights violations perpetrated by powerful institutions and individuals.[7] In this work I have moved forward through moral bravery, not only in dealing with the powerful DoJ and with Canada's deep pockets but also in terms of dealing with oppressive patriarchs and matriarchs within Indigenous circles who argue that my effort at challenging the *Indian Act* emerges from a pitiful colonial mindset. While I may be only a woman and thus pitiful, as I have stated before I am fully aware that Indigenous rights to land and resources are much broader than what the *Indian Act* narrowly defines and imposes. A quick review of my book *The Truth the Wampum Tells* illustrates this. While I will admit I am concerned that people will narrowly slot all my work within the sex discrimination in the *Indian Act*, I move forward, and continue to move forward, with the moral courage that moves through my heart. Indigenous mothers and children are more important than what some people may say and think about me and my work and more important than the human ego.

In this lifelong work I also moved forward with moral bravery in the sense that, early on, an older sibling tried to steal this work from me. They tried to have the court case placed in their name versus mine, despite the fact that I did all the oral history and I alone completed all the archival research. Despite my incredible disappointment in this betrayal, I had to be brave and prevent it from happening in the best way I could. I had hoped that this person's interest in my work was genuine rather than rooted in their ego and greed. Realizing a family member is not someone who can be trusted is difficult to deal with. I am pretty sure that my spirit left my body when I was dealing with this awful situation. Talk about gut-wrenching and spirit-leaving.

What is more, I also had to move forward with moral bravery in terms of members of my larger family. My mother, because of her own issues with patriarchy, sexism, and colonization, completely loathed this work, and she undermined me as I moved along. Making it worse, I was isolated in knowing how she was undermining me because, after all, it was me she was undermining not other family members, and thus I was more attuned to what she was doing. Through deep and lengthy introspection I realize my mother's issues with my work on the *Indian Act* had to do with her hatred for the man who biologically fathered her children, as well as her fear that I was getting too close to a family secret she was working hard to hide. Within the context of me being undermined, a few of my siblings actually seemed to enjoy what our mother was doing, and one of them would manipulatively encourage my mother's hatred of me. I am not sure what this was about but I think it is hard to love eight children in a way where competition for mother love is not played out. Jealousy is a strong emotion and a strong subconscious urge. We all know this. Within this context of obfuscation and nonsense I realized I had to be strong and move forward. Needless to say, my mother and I were estranged for many years. As a matter of fact I made the tough decision to completely walk away from all the destructive family dynamics that colonization manifested. Fortunately, or maybe unfortunately, I had a sibling who had taken this very same path years before me, and so I just followed their footsteps in moving outside my mother's neurosis that patriarchy and colonization had imposed on her and within her body. The reasoning I relied on was that I had a lot of work to do and could not be thrown into constant chaos and emotional sabotage at home. Years later a sibling implied that my estrangement from the family was my mother's doing. This line of thinking was a sure indication of continued ignorance and assumptions about who I was, and an insult to my thinking and my agency. I left because I had work to do and the context was unbearably pitiful. Indeed, humans are pitiful, myself included.

Lastly, in terms of my positionality it is important for me to remind the reader that within this work I am an Algonquin Anishinaabe-kwe, a plaintiff, and for the most part a non-paying client of Aboriginal Legal Services of Toronto (ALST). I am not a lawyer, nor have I been trained in law.

Respect for Natural Law

It is also important for me to stress here that the reality of *not* knowing who a father is falls in line with natural law. It must be remembered that monogamy is an assumption versus a rule, meaning women, like men, can and will continue to have more than one sexual partner. While a woman's partners come and go, it is She who does Creator's work, conceiving and nurturing life, and it is She who opens the Eastern Doorway giving birth.

It is also important to stress that as a result of issues of oppressive power in society, and men's greater physical strength over women, many children are born through horrible acts of sexual violence such as incest, molestation, rape, gang rape, and sexual slavery. And there is the rare reality that some women are not aware they are pregnant until they go into labour. What is more, there is a history where unmarried women were prevented from documenting who a child's father was and a history where officials tampered with birth documents (see chapter 16 in this book). My point here is that in doing this work I in no way stand in judgement of women. And while I do, in fact, judge men who abuse children and women—as well as Canada, INAC, the DoJ, and the women and men hired to uphold and defend laws and policies that perpetuate harm—my primary goal is and has always been to stand up for vulnerable people such as my kokomis, my father, and me. I do not judge natural law and where women and mothers are situated within it; rather, I value it and defend it. Natural law predates pitiful human law. For example, I know I am only a woman, but I also know women have a special relationship with Creator in the work we do opening the Eastern Doorway.

Telling My Story

Discrimination is unacceptable in a democratic society because it epitomizes the worst effects of the denial of equality, and discrimination reinforced by law is particularly repugnant. The worst oppression will result from discriminatory measures having the force of law. It is against this evil that s.15 provides a guarantee.
—Andrews v Law Society of British Columbia, 1989

The first time I contacted INAC regarding becoming registered as a Status Indian, asking for an application form and some details about the process, was in February 1990. From there, proving that my kokomis was entitled through her mother was not very difficult at all. All I needed was her extended birth certificate that clearly stated who her mother and father were: Annie Jane Meness and Joseph Gagnon Jr. Then from their marriage record I was able to link Annie Jane with her father, Frank Meness. Frank remained a member of Golden Lake Indian Reserve, meaning he was never enfranchised into white society, like his daughter was for marrying out, and as such his name remained recorded in the historical Indian Register. According to my personal files it was in July 1990 when I received the letter from INAC stating that my great-grandmother Annie and my kokomis were now deemed entitled to be registered under section 6(1)c and section 6(2), respectively. As I have explained ad nauseam, these are weaker forms of status registration that place limits on their ability to pass it on. Section 6(1) a is the strongest form of Indian status registration.

Through the practice of registering and imposing on my great-grandmother Annie and my kokomis weaker forms of registration, my kokomis could not pass status entitlement to my father. Working within the INAC rules, this meant that I had to prove my kokomis's father, Joseph Gagnon Jr., was also entitled through his mother, Angeline Jocko, who was my great-great-grandmother. This requirement forced me to move into archival research, specifically searches of Ontario's vital statistics records. This effort was no small feat, especially for someone who struggles with reading text and print materials because of a vision disability. Essentially, the process involved searching hundred-year-old birth, marriage, and death records held at the Archives of Ontario, then located in downtown Toronto, the city where I was born and was living at the time.[8] Again, I was in search of how my kokomis was also entitled to Indian registration through her father and his mother, Angeline Jocko, whose year of birth was 1865. In taking on this task I had to learn the science of genealogy, as well as library archival science and the minute details of INAC's requirements for Indian registration, meaning how the Registrar of INAC was using the new 1985 *Indian Act* rules of entitlement. Because, and as stated, historically Indian registration travelled only down the father line, I went in search of records for the men in Angeline's family to learn who her father, my great-great-great-grandfather, and her male siblings were. I had far to go.

Through the Oral Tradition, my kokomis told me the name of Angeline's brother, John Jocko, and his son, Paul Lee Jocko, Angeline's nephew. After months and months and months of researching, eventually I found a delayed birth document for Paul, who was born August 20, 1882. It turns out Angeline was present during his birth, and it was she who signed the document dated December 1934. My introspections and approach were correct to seek out male family members. Immediately I knew I had found the needle in a gigantic stack of straw. In November 1994 an uncle submitted this newly found birth record to INAC along with three Indian status registration applications for me, him, and another uncle. These uncles were/are my father's half-brothers. Sadly, by this time my father had already passed on.

It turns out Paul Lee Jocko was also recorded in the Indian Register and his delayed birth document linked Angeline to her brother John. Therefore, she too was now entitled to registration, as a reinstated woman, as a 6(1)c Indian—again, a weaker form than the strongest 6(1)a that men and their descendants born before 1985 gained in 1985. Through Angeline's entitlement, it was in February 1995 when my kokomis was upgraded from a 6(2) to a 6(1)f Indian, a form of status registration that means she had two parents who were entitled to be registered. This upgrade also meant my father, although posthumously, and my uncles were now entitled to 6(2) registration. I, though, continued to be denied. Miserably, although I had done most of the work, I was denied. Talk about bittersweet. By now five years had passed since INAC first registered my kokomis, and it was now ten years after the *Indian Act* had been amended to bring it in line with the *Charter*.

While it was an incredible accomplishment that my father's and his brothers' entitlement was established, the weaker form of status registration

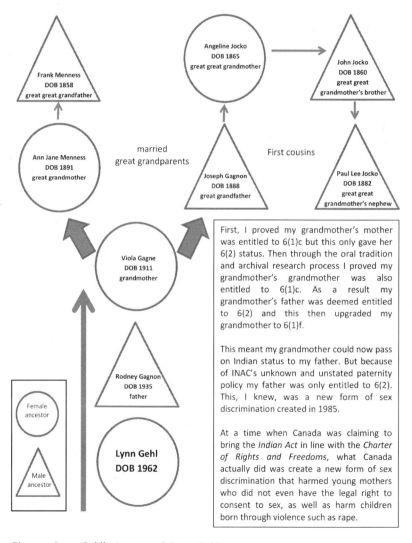

First, I proved my grandmother's mother was entitled to 6(1)c but this only gave her 6(2) status. Then through the oral tradition and archival research process I proved my grandmother's grandmother was also entitled to 6(1)c. As a result my grandmother's father was deemed entitled to 6(2) and this then upgraded my grandmother to 6(1)f.

This meant my grandmother could now pass on Indian status to my father. But because of INAC's unknown and unstated paternity policy my father was only entitled to 6(2). This, I knew, was a new form of sex discrimination created in 1985.

At a time when Canada was claiming to bring the *Indian Act* in line with the *Charter of Rights and Freedoms*, what Canada actually did was create a new form of sex discrimination that harmed young mothers who did not even have the legal right to consent to sex, as well as harm children born through violence such as rape.

Figure 10. Lynn Gehl's Ancestry; © Lynn Gehl

meant that my father could not in his own right pass registration entitlement on to me. To me this was sex discrimination: First, because if my Indian ancestry had flowed through the male line, my ancestors all the way through to me would be registered under 6(1)a. It is this very sex discrimination that I began to think about challenging. And second, it was sex discrimination because INAC's unknown and thus unstated paternity policy harmed women and their descendants. The problem was that I did not have the resources to cover legal representation nor the time for a lengthy protracted legal challenge. Regardless, it was around December 1993 when I first found the courage to contact ALST, to ask if they would be interested in managing my file moving forward. This was a gigantic step for me, because I was wrestling with so much that colonization had imposed on me, such as my poor reading skills that were pretty much nonexistent, my many questions of the existential kind, and the issue of my identity. I also felt isolated in my knowledge. And, of course, I was being undermined by family members.

In February 1995, after INAC denied me registration, I wrote a letter to the Department. At the time, and even though I could barely write, I made the argument that discrimination based on sex was contrary to the *Charter*. I informed INAC that I knew that if my Indian lineage had come down the male line I would be entitled to registration. Eventually I turned more concretely to ALST and made an appointment with them asking for help. A sibling tagged along with me during this face-to-face meeting. The executive director, Kimberly Murray, was welcoming, greeting me by asking something like "What took you so long?" I am not sure what she meant by this question, but I think she asked because the *Indian Act* had been amended almost ten years earlier. Kimberly did not know about the oral and archival research I'd had to complete to get there or my poor reading skills. Thankfully she agreed to take on the effort and took over my protest attempt.

In March 1995, as per the *Indian Act*, ALST formally protested INAC's decision of denial, and in February 1997 we were informed that my name had been correctly omitted from the Indian Register. In May of 1997, ALST submitted a second-stage protest arguing that, as per the common-law duty of fairness, the Registrar must reach its decision with fairness and, further, that INAC's decision was contrary to the *Charter*. ALST argued that my father and I were entitled to be registered under section 6(1)a.

In April 1998 INAC informed us that the burden of proof of my entitlement resided with me, meaning it was my responsibility to provide the information regarding who my paternal grandfather was.[9] This INAC letter stated that the *Indian Act* now determines entitlement through both parents, also known as the two-parent rule, and it would be contrary to the *Indian Act* and also unreasonable to assume that my unknown and thus unstated grandfather was entitled to registration. With this, INAC stood firm that I was correctly omitted from the Indian Register. The Department also argued that it did not violate my section 35 constitutional rights or my section 15 *Charter* rights because when the *Indian Act* was amended it was examined to make sure it was in line with the *Charter*. Of course, what makes no sense is that the two-parent rule—whereby children of unknown and thus unstated paternity are either denied entitlement or relegated the weaker from of entitlement— is indeed sex discrimination. By this time, four years had passed since my application was submitted to INAC. It was in May 1997 when ALST filed a notice of constitutional question. I was told that this is a necessary step in the process of moving forward through the court system.

It was around this time that I began university as an undergraduate student. I ached to learn. I quickly realized that there was no way I could attend university full time but rather had to go at a much slower turtle pace. At this time my reading and writing skills only existed at the public-school level. As a result, I began with one course; then, once successful, I took two courses from September through April and one course in the summer. During this time I realized my vocabulary was hugely narrow and I needed to work on it. Throughout my undergraduate degree I carried an electronic dictionary in my bag at all times and made a very conscious effort to look up every word that I heard uttered or read that I did not understand. The effort was worth it in that my first university essay, titled "The Queen and I," was published in a feminist journal (and is included here). This publication helped me gain scholarships and awards to pay for additional university courses. I had always wished I could read and write, and I was happy I was learning. Of course my partner, Nik, helped me.

Oftentimes I have reflected on my complete ignorance in moving forward with my *Charter* challenge. As I have suggested, there were numerous issues: coming out of the poverty, violence, and neglect of my childhood imposed by colonization and patriarchy; scavenging for love; my ignorance about processes of colonization such as the treaty and land claim process; my need to find answers to larger existential issues; the deep rabbit hole I was in learning how to read and write; and then the process of completing undergraduate and, later, master's and doctoral degrees.[10] My cognition was in overdrive all the time in a way that was more than super-saturated. In short, I was overwhelmed all the time.

Of course, as I moved along in my process of learning and thinking, my feet were beginning to find a little bit of solid ground to stand on. I was no longer sinking to my knees, waist, and at times up to my neck. To offer an example of my ignorance, at one point early on in the litigation process I remember being brave enough to ask Kimberly who INAC's lawyers were. She laughed pretty hard and said something like the largest law firm in Canada. Recently I have come to know that the Department of Justice has more than 4,600 staff members and lawyers with an annual budget of $662 million.[11] Yup, she was right. This story embarrasses me a lot, but I can't care about this too much. All too often I wished for the comfort of a mommy's or daddy's coattail that I could ride on, as it would make my life and work easier and I would also have a support system.

Shortly after the second INAC denial letter came in 1998, ALST filed a statutory appeal under the *Indian Act*. This, I think, would have taken the Registrar's dismissal of my protest directly to the Ontario Superior Court, but I really don't know. However, for some reason, maybe a strategic reason on behalf of ALST that I am ignorant about, this statutory appeal was held in abeyance while Kimberly took my case in another direction: a constitutional/*Charter* challenge.[12] What many people do not know is that ALST submitted my first statement of claim (SoC) in May 2001 as *Gehl v Her Majesty the Queen* (*Gehl v Canada*, as it became known). In this SoC we challenged the Registrar's presumption of non-Indian paternity when paternity is unknown and thus unstated.[13] I was informed that my challenge was based on section 35 of the Constitution and section 15 of the *Charter*. Kimberly asked for damages, arguing that as a result of the defendant's bad faith I had suffered and continued to suffer. I had also been denied my cultural identity. The damages were set at $1.2 million. The DoJ argued that we had to challenge section 14.2(4) of the *Indian Act*, which eliminated the damages through section 24 of the *Charter*. ALST disagreed because the *Charter* challenge was with respect to a government administrative practice, not an exact statutory provision of the *Indian Act*, whereas section 14.2(4) referred to protest processes internal to the *Indian Act*.[14]

In August 1999 Kimberly applied for funds from the Court Challenges Program of Canada (CCPC) as well as from INAC's Test Case Funding Program. In September we were informed that INAC had denied us test-case funding because Canada does not fund section 15 *Charter* challenges to the status provisions of the *Indian Act*. Looking at this now I realize how bad this INAC position is, and again we were challenging the Registrar's practice, not the *Indian Act*. In December the CCPC also refused us test-case funding because the program only provides one-time funding for cases that are similar. It seems some other similar case had already been funded by it. Despite this, the CCPC instructed ALST to reapply specifically under the issue of INAC's unknown and unstated paternity policy of denial. In February 2000 CCPC approved $50,000 in funding. Although Kimberly had jumped through the hoops to obtain this funding, it was in my name, meaning I was responsible for signing the invoices and keeping track of the process. This makes sense, in that as the plaintiff I was the only constant. The ALST lawyers changed more than a few times.

In October 2001 the DoJ motioned to strike our initial SoC because, according to the Department, there was no cause of action, meaning it was not possible to address an administrator's decision and practice under the *Charter*. What this meant was that the DoJ's lawyers were challenging the way ALST framed our argument at the level of practice and policy rather than law. The DoJ was of the thought that we should not focus on the Registrar's assumption and practice of denial. Kimberly was of a different mind, in that, after all, the 1985 *Indian Act* was completely silent on the matter of what to do in the situation of an unknown and thus unstated father, and so there was nothing to challenge in the legislation itself; thus, Kimberly correctly directed her argument at INAC's practice and policy. In November 2001 we were in the Ontario Superior Court to hear the DoJ's motion to strike. At the time Kimberly and Jonathan Rudin represented me. In offering moral support, my university friend Georgina Varga tagged along and observed the proceedings, and my partner, Nik, was there too. Unfortunately, Justice Katherine Swinton, an employee of Canada's judicial arm and court system, agreed with the DoJ and the SoC was struck. Swinton also argued that the damages to be awarded to me were without merit.

It is important that I stress here that Kimberly was not alone in her understanding of how to frame the legal arguments. Michelle Mann addresses the issue of unknown and unstated paternity in her work, explaining that the INAC PoP policy is an internal Department policy and not codified within the *Indian Act*.[15] Pamela Palmater agrees, arguing there is no legal basis to assume that an unknown and unstated father is a non-Indian. Palmater further argues that PoP is a policy choice made by Canada (INAC) to reduce the number of Indians over time.[16] My point here is that there is no need to blame my lawyer; rather, we need to keep in mind that the DoJ and the court system belong to colonial Canada. What is more, when I reflect deeply on this it is my view that Canada carefully crafted this silence in law on unknown and thus unstated paternity in order to manipulate at the practice and policy level.[17]

In September 2002 ALST appealed to the Court of Appeal for Ontario but unfortunately this court upheld the lower court decision, meaning we lost. While our SoC was struck we were given leave, meaning permission, to refile our claim as a challenge to section 6, the registration provisions of the *Indian Act*, rather than a challenge to the presumption and practice of the Registrar. Moving quickly, in October 2002 Kimberly filed the second SoC, arguing that both my section 35 Constitution Aboriginal rights and my section 15 *Charter* equality rights were infringed upon. In terms of the *Charter* rights, we were arguing that the registration requirements in section 6 of the *Indian Act* were a violation based on the enumerated grounds of race, sex, and marital status. At the time I did not understand this shift from policy to law. My cognition was oversaturated and remained that way for a long time. I understand more today.

At the time of the second SoC I was also informed that my case was assigned to be case managed, meaning it was selected to have senior master judges oversee it. This, I understood, would serve to provide guidance through the legal system. According to the government, "Case management is a system designed to reduce unnecessary delay and cost, facilitate early and fair settlements, and bring cases promptly to a just conclusion."[18] This made me happy because by now eighteen years had passed since the *Indian Act* was amended, and eight years had passed since I had first submitted my application for Indian registration. By this time, in 2002, I had completed my undergraduate degree and, shortly after, Nik and I had relocated to Peterborough, Ontario, because I was accepted into a two-year master's program on full scholarship. As a non-Status person I could not rely on treaty rights to help me cover education and medical expenses. My topic was the spiritual implications of essentialized discourses of identity. It would be an understatement for me to say I was overwhelmed at every turn and too old to slow down.

As readers can determine, a section 35 Constitution/section 15 *Charter* rights challenge has many elements. From my perspective, there seemed to be a lot of discussion about how the process would unfold. As discussed, beginning in November 2002 my case was managed by Master Ronald Dash. Dash recommended that my court case be compartmentalized, meaning we should separate the section 15 *Charter* equality issue from the section 35 Constitution Aboriginal rights issue. ALST was considering this.

In 2004 I finished my master's degree and moved immediately into a doctoral program, again on full scholarship. Again, as a non-Status person I did not rely on treaty rights to help me cover the expense of my education. My topic shifted from identity to the Algonquin land claim process. Busy as I was learning about Canada's genocide of Indigenous Nations through the land claim process, I was informed via email that during the production period, between January and March 2006, ALST received more than 7,000 documents from the DoJ, the legal representatives of INAC (Canada, really). Apparently this is a common strategy of delay and denial known as a document dump, meant to overwhelm the plaintiff's lawyer.

In the spring of 2006 ALST and the DoJ met with Justice Archie Campbell, who suggested we move forward with filing a motion to determine a legal issue, that being to address whether section 6 of the *Indian Act* is a violation of section 15 of the *Charter*. In doing this, the Constitution rights issue would be held in abeyance, meaning it would be set aside for the time being. Around this time I was also told that my case was proceeding by way of an action with the request for damages. I was also informed my case was no longer a *Charter* challenge. Rather, it was now a personal injury claim for breach of my *Charter* rights. To be truthful, it was all over my head. Like many plaintiffs I trusted my lawyers' training and suggestions.

It was soon after this time when ALST spoke more concretely to the DoJ about switching my *Charter* case from an action to an application, meaning we would proceed by way of application yet with an SoC, and through legal arguments, affidavit evidence, and expert reports.[19] In May 2006 all parties agreed to this shift, and here Justice Campbell began managing my *Charter* challenge; he gave us leave to schedule a summary judgement motion (SJM) and leave to rely on both affidavit evidence and witness testimony evidence. The SJM was set for ten days in June of 2007 and a timeline of how this would all unfold was established. For some reason this date came and went. Maybe this was a good thing as I was entirely overwhelmed with graduate school, reading, thinking, and learning. I will always remember the day a professor chuckled at me when I read a hundred-page article he had incorrectly assigned. In all directions it was more than a miserable time, but unlike another student in the doctoral program who was being coddled like a child, at least by this time I could read and write.

Shortly thereafter, ALST completed their affidavits: mine in November 2006 and that of the Chief of Pikwàkanagàn First Nation, Kirby Whiteduck, soon after.[20] I do remember reading mine and making a few changes. Throughout March and April 2007 the DoJ provided six affidavits from INAC employees: Alan Tallman, Indian Registrar; Linda McLenachan, protest and appeals officer; Marion Amos, protest and appeals officer; Catalina LaForce, junior information analyst; John Paul Fournier, senior capital adviser; and Bonnie Tolstoy, director of benefit management, Non-Insured Health Benefits Directive of Health Canada.

The DoJ's cross-examination of Chief Whiteduck's affidavit took place on September 14, 2007, one day before mine. I was cross-examined by senior DoJ lawyers Dale L. Yurka, Gail E. Sinclair, and Catherine Phillips. This was just a few days after I had submitted the first draft of my doctoral dissertation on the Algonquin land claim process.[21] Kimberly, and ALST staff lawyers Mandy Eason and Lori Mishibinijima, met Nik and me for lunch that day in downtown Toronto; she told me later that she had been concerned at how overwhelmed I appeared to be. I think I was more relieved to have been able to submit a draft of my dissertation, as it completely took over my cognition. And if I remember correctly, the DoJ wanted to cross-examine me when my mind was focused on writing my dissertation. I had the cross-examination delayed. It was almost as though the DoJ was following me, seeking to get me when I was overwhelmed as its strategy to defeat me. Possibly needless to say, writing my dissertation was as miserable as my court case.

Drawing from my memory, after the DoJ lawyer completed her cross-examination of my affidavit, Kimberly was quick to ask me, "Lynn did you ask your grandmother who your father's father was?" I remember my response was quick. I said something to the effect of, "No, I did not, because first of all that is not a question a granddaughter asks her grandmother and second, the end result was my father had no father." My point here being that whoever the man was, he was no father. I said something to the effect that being a father was a social process, not a biological process. Once the cross-examination was over, Kimberly made a point of telling me that as a witness I was the DoJ's worst nightmare because of my ability to respond to their questions in such a solid way. It seems in my learning journey I had learned what I had sought out to learn. I am happy I did not let Kimberly and the rest of the ALST team down that day.

During this time, in March of 2007, Justice Edward Belobaba was assigned to hear the SJM on the *Charter* issue. He decided he wanted to keep the motion hearing even more streamlined, suggesting that we not call viva voce (oral) witness testimony, meaning he wanted to avoid oral testimonies and have the case move forward by way of affidavit and cross-examination only. This meant I would not have to testify and this was completely fine with me. By this time I just wanted the bloody process over with.

Along the way one thing I did that proved helpful to me in terms of writing this case history—or, better said, my story—is that I asked Kimberly if I could get a summary of how the case was unfolding. In June 2007 ALST staff lawyer Amy Britton-Cox followed through, offering me a case history from 1994 through 2007. Here I was reminded that the court date scheduled for June 2007 had come and gone. Another good and helpful thing occurred in 2009, when ALST hired Amanda Driscoll as a staff lawyer. I am so grateful for Amanda. She heard me in my frustration and served this court case in such a big way. I was having such a hard time with the process.

Throughout, I had little choice but to trust my lawyers; my *Charter* challenge was case managed, after all. As we moved along, both my SoC and the DoJ's statement of defence (SoD) were amended several times. The last time my SoC was amended was in September 2010 and, again, to tell the truth I cannot speak about the exact details of why and how it was amended. At this time I was also trying to end the misery of my doctoral process. I was navigating two streams of sexism and patriarchy and the power that these two wiindigos, Canada's court system and the university system, unleash. I was both an overwhelmed doctoral candidate and an overwhelmed plaintiff. I was like a helpless eel being chopped up by a hydroelectric dam. I do know, though, that somewhere along the process my case became *Gehl v Attorney General of Canada* and so I bid farewell to the Queen.

Unfortunately, Kimberly left ALST in April 2010, to work on the Truth and Reconciliation Commission of Canada (TRC), after which there was a structural change within ALST and a few changes in lawyers associated with my *Charter* challenge. Mandy Eason managed my file for a short while until she too left, following Kimberly to the TRC. Then one of the new ALST legal directors who followed Mandy's departure actually wanted to fire me as a client because, it seems, I was annoying her with questions and concerns about my case not moving forward. This was more than a miserable time for me. From my perspective as the plaintiff, the case seemed to be sitting dormant. It was difficult because Kimberly took with her the memory of the case. Unfortunately, I did not have the sense to suggest a case management meeting. It was completely my fault, I think, but maybe ALST realized the case was bigger than me. I knew it was bigger than me.

By this time in 2010 it had been sixteen years since I had first applied for Indian status registration and twenty-five years since the *Indian Act* had been amended in 1985. My eyes are emotional and when no one was looking they cried rivers big enough for a migration of eels. I just wanted it over. I wanted jurisdiction of my cognition and agency. I wanted the chatter in the back of my mind, which damn well travelled with me everywhere I went, to become as silent as the *Indian Act* was on the paternity issue I was challenging. I ached and wanted to walk away from the process the same way the ALST lawyers and staff were able to. Through their departure I was both disenfranchised and full of envy that they could walk away from *Gehl v Canada*. Yet regardless of what I wanted to do, I was in too deep. There were many young Indigenous mothers and children who were being harmed by INAC's unknown and thus unstated paternity policy and—because of the deep pockets of the DoJ, pilfered from Indigenous land and resources, no less—could not afford a lengthy court case such as the one that was sucking the life out of me. So I very miserably soldiered forward and was crapped on in every direction I turned.

Keep in mind that I was not a paying client of ALST. If I had been wealthy it is my thought that I would have had more power in moving the case forward, because I would have been able to hire people to help my process. I say this without intending to slight ALST. Most of us know by now that laws and law reform are for the rich. As suggested, eventually Amanda Driscoll, sensing my frustration in the lack of progress, suggested that we have a teleconference twice per month. I was happy and cried but I responded that once per month should be a good structure to move the case forward.

Fortunately, in May 2011 ALST hired Christa Big Canoe as the legal advocacy director, and she moved my *Charter* challenge forward. Actually I am not sure my case would have moved forward if not for Amanda's suggestion and Christa's effort. Eventually Amanda too moved on to a new job, leaving ALST and me behind. I was sad and jealous of her freedom. Regardless, the monthly teleconference meetings that she had put in place continued. I was always ready for these monthly teleconference meetings with questions and pencil in hand. The problem was that the process of communicating via telephone was incredibly frustrating and difficult. The sound was poor, especially when other speakers at the other end of the telephone line chimed in. I could not hear them, let alone process issues around my case that were being discussed. Many of these meetings ended with me not feeling as though I knew what I needed to know.

What is more, after I completed the misery of my doctoral defence and leaving the power structures inherent, I began to work with a behavioural optometrist with the goal of learning about and improving my vision. Behavioural optometry, or vision therapy, is a relatively new and costly practice in Canada. It relies on the science and process of neurogenesis. It involves a series of in-office and in-home practices encouraging the intentional creation of new neural pathways to better serve, in my case, the goal of achieving binocular vision. During this process I had to purchase special and expensive lenses for my glasses, which cost over $1,000. They should have been covered by my treaty rights, but I continued to be denied Indian status registration. I did this vision-training work for two years, and at one point travelled to the United States for treatment. During this time, with my reading skills greatly improved, I also made great efforts at reading the journal literature on vision training. Some people would call this research but I don't, as it was more about my life, much like the matter of INAC's unknown and thus unstated paternity policy. Through this practice and reading the literature, I learned a lot about my vision, and a lot about behavioural optometry, and while I value it as a science and practice for some people, after a few years of reading, practising, and deep thinking I decided it was best for me to quit. I could not afford it and I became doubtful that I was a candidate for vision training. As can be determined, an intersectional framework of structural oppression was being lived out.

Again, drawing from my positionality as a plaintiff and client, the process of receiving the expert reports seemed to go on forever. The DoJ relied on Stewart Clatworthy and ALST relied on James S. Frideres as their expert witnesses.[22] ALST received Clatworthy's expert report in December 2007; more than two years later, in March 2010, ALST received a revised version. Then almost a year later, in January 2011, Frideres submitted his expert report and response to Clatworthy, yet for some reason it was not until November 2011, ten months later, that Frideres stated he was in need of Clatworthy's method or formula of determining the number of births born of unknown and unstated paternity so he could properly evaluate them and offer his expertise. In April 2013 ALST received yet another revised version of the Clatworthy expert report, and the issue of Clatworthy's method of analysis remained outstanding.[23]

In terms of additional expert reports, ALST commissioned one from Michelle Mann.[24] Mann's report addressed the administrative difficulties mothers encounter when trying to obtain fathers' signatures, such as when a mother is flown out of her community to give birth. Mann also addressed substantive issues. She explained there are situations where a mother decides not to name the father, or the father refuses to acknowledge paternity. Mann identified a number of such situations, including where the mother and father have an unstable relationship; where concerns about confidentiality exist in small communities; and where a mother has concerns about child custody and access. Further, the pregnancy may be the result of sexual violence and abuse, such as incest, rape, or gang rape, where the mother is unwilling or unable to identify the father.[25] Lacking morals, the DoJ opposed this expert report; as a result, it was not submitted within the book of authorities. Both ALST experts, Frideres and Mann, were paid for their work through the CCPC funds Kimberly had secured in 2000. I am grateful to both Kimberly and the CCPC.

I distinctly remember journaling the number of times I asked ALST about the completion of the expert reports and our request for Clatworthy's method of analysis. It was in November 2011 that the DoJ suggested a conference between the experts, known as "hot tubbing," so they could narrow down the issues. After six consecutive months of no progress I told ALST that I no longer wanted to wait, that six months of my asking for the reports was long enough. Remember, it had been years since the first report came in. I am not sure why ALST and I did not request a case management conference with the master judge watching over my *Charter* challenge. Eventually, in September 2013, an arrangement was made whereby the experts narrowed down the issues and submitted a joint statement. In sum, this expert report process, for whatever reasons, went on from 2007 through 2013. Looking at it now, at the time of writing this chapter, this length of time seems outrageous, but this is what happened. I think the deep pockets of the DoJ, staff turnover at ALST, and my inability to navigate my responsibility because I was overburdened collectively caused this. It was clear I was not wealthy enough to get this case done.

While I thought the decision had already been made to avoid viva voce witnesses, it continually arose in my discussions with ALST. We discussed it several times in 2012 and again in 2014. ALST decided they preferred to have Mann offer oral testimony, which in the end did not happen because the DoJ argued against it, as the Department did not want the sociological and cultural arguments that led to situations of unknown and unstated paternity that she put forward heard. Then there was the decision to have the expert witnesses, Clatworthy and Frideres, offer oral testimony, but this was cancelled in 2014 when it was decided that a joint expert report would be submitted.

While all this was happening, eventually I realized I had to take on a public persona regarding my *Charter* challenge. Truthfully, my preference was not to, but I had to be brave because the issue of INAC's unknown and thus unstated paternity policy was without public currency and thus was not gaining the public's attention. I felt that community members needed to be aware of the issue. This thinking was my motivation in creating a personal website (www.lynngehl.com), a Facebook group, and a formal strategy: my National Strategy to Raise Awareness on Unknown and Unstated Paternity and the *Indian Act* (NSRAUUP). Many Indigenous Peoples were now using social media as a means of staying informed about what was going on at a national level. I had to move in this direction and get on social media, something I had avoided in part because, owing to my vision, I am terrible at reading and interpreting cryptic text messages. Regardless, I will always remember when I sent out an email in September 2010 letting people know what I was taking on, Kimberly responded with "Lynn you rock!" This statement was affirming and cleared any doubts I had about taking on a public persona and about my strategy. I ran my NSRAUUP campaign with no funding or resources. Just me.

Although I was already writing publicly on Indigenous issues in *Anishinabek News*, it was under the banner of NSRAUUP that I began to write and publish in more abundance in various other venues, including *rabble. ca*, *Briarpatch*, *Canadian Dimension*, *Journey Magazine*, and my personal blog, *Blackface Blogging*. I also published in Indigenous and mothering-related journals such as *First Peoples Child & Family Review*. I created posters, infographics, and short videos for easier circulation because, again, there was the need for me to reach community people, particularly Indigenous mothers.[26] What is more, with encouragement from my friend Lana Ray, in October 2013 I initiated an online petition that served well in terms of disseminating updates about my *Charter* challenge.[27] Through the duration of this petition, now closed, I gathered over five thousand signatures.[28] Again, my primary goal with NSRAUUP was to raise awareness about INAC's PoP policy and INAC's policy/practice that assumes all unknown and unstated fathers were non-Indian men, even in the context of sexual violence, where as a result many children were losing entitlement to registration.

Miserably, on November 1, 2012, ALST was notified that my court case had been ordered dismissed due to delay, with costs. ALST submitted a motion to set this order aside. The grounds for the motion were that dismissal would deny me access to justice and that the plaintiff and defendant were making efforts in good faith to determine a mutually agreeable date for the SJM. On November 26 the court heard the motion and, on reading the joint submissions, set aside the order to dismiss. Then the court ordered the parties to appear before the scheduling motions court to set a hearing date. This was an unhappy experience for me and I was fed up, but I had no power. Since the court has more power and influence, maybe this was a good thing. The hearing date was set for May 26, 27, and 28, 2014. I felt that all of the lawyers who were being paid to do their jobs needed to move on. By this time I had such loathing for the DoJ and, of course, Canada.

Mclvor and Descheneaux

One index that might be taken as a measure of
disorganization is the rate of illegitimacy.
—H.A.C. Cairns, S.M. Jamieson, and K. Lysyk,
A Survey of the Contemporary Indians of Canada (see Table 2)

It is important for me to take some time to talk about two additional court cases that are related to and that shaped my effort. As stated, when the *Indian Act* was amended in 1985 to bring it in line with the *Charter*, it was celebrated because it reinstated Indian women once enfranchised for marrying non-Indians. Many of these women were now grandmothers and great-grandmothers, and sadly many, such as my great-grandmother Annie, had already passed through the Western Doorway and on to the spirit world. Despite the celebrations, and as I have argued, it was quickly realized that the children, grandchildren, and great-grandchildren (born before 1985) of the now reinstated Indian women were treated as less than the descendants born before 1985 who had a male Indian lineage. Things were not equal between men and women and between their descendants. As discussed, the inequality is rooted in what is known as the 6(1)a–6(1)c hierarchy. It is that simple, yet it is also that complex. While Status Indian men and their descendants born before 1985 are all registered under section 6(1)a, the reinstated women were registered under section 6(1)c. Through this difference, the pre-1985 descendants of reinstated women are impacted by the second-generation cut-off rule earlier than the descendants of Indian men.

Fortunately, powerhouse—and s/hero to many people—Sharon Donna Mclvor, who is legally trained in law at both the bachelor and master's level, took this sex discrimination inherent in the 6(1)a–6(1)c hierarchy to court. Sharon's case was heard in the British Columbia Supreme Court, where she won. Justice Ross ruled there was the need to eliminate all the discrimination in the *Indian Act*. The DoJ (Canada) on behalf of its client INAC (Canada) appealed the decision in the Court of Appeal for British Columbia, where Justice Harvey Groberman narrowed the broader legal remedy through the poor reasoning that "matrilineal discrimination" was not sex discrimination.[29] By relying on the double-mother clause as the comparator group, a legal remedy was offered for Sharon's son, Charles Jacob Grismer. While

Sharon remained a 6(1)c Indian, her son gained a new *subcategory* of 6(1)c.[30] In making this decision, lawyer Mary Eberts, of the Law Office of Mary Eberts (LOME), was of the thought that Justice Groberman's ability to reason "seems to be at war with himself in his discussion."[31] Somewhere along the way I learned, and it is relevant to my court case, that both of Sharon's parents were born out of wedlock.[32]

In opposition to the Court of Appeal decision in *McIvor*, the Marche AMUN protest was organized while Bill C-3, the supposed remediation for the *McIvor* case, was moving through Parliament. Working with Michèle Audette, I did some work in the background where, drawing on my knowledge of cultural politics and hegemony, I birthed the slogan "6(1)a All the Way!" While I participated in the protest, I did not pay attention to the parliamentary discussions, or the Senate and House of Commons testimonies because this was again during the time I was tied up in a PhD program. Despite the community protests and expert oral and written submissions, in 2011 the *Indian Act* was amended, again leaving much sex discrimination intact. At the time Canada made the argument that the broader issues of sex discrimination would be addressed in a two-stage consultation process. Apparently this was the same excuse Canada provided in 1985 but that consultation process was a bust. Nothing changed.

In 2015, because Canada had refused to address all of the sex discrimination as mandated by the lower court in *McIvor*, the case of Stéphane Descheneaux, Susan Yantha, and Tammy Yantha was heard in the Superior Court of Quebec. The issues addressed in this case were the "cousins issue" and the "siblings issue." The cousins issue pertained to the fact that, through the 6(1)a–6(1)c hierarchy and the unequal application of the second-generation cut-off rule, children descended from Indian men were registered under 6(1)a while the children descended from Indian women were only registered as 6(2); thus, sex discrimination caused first cousins to be registered differently and unequally. The siblings issue had to do with the differential way that an Indian man's children born out of wedlock were registered: a male child was registered as 6(1)a, but a female child was registered as 6(2). Again, they were registered differently and unequally. As I have said, 6(2) is a weaker form of registration entitlement.

Like McIvor, Descheneaux, Yantha, and Yantha won their case. What is more, once again a judge, Justice Masse, argued for *all* the sex

Band	Unwed Mother as % of All Mothers
Skidegate	90
Caughnawaga	2.0
Walpole Island	113
Sheshaht	5.3
Lorette	Nil
Squamish	10.1
Tyendinaga	5.0
Six Nations	9.1
Curve Lake	12.2
Mistassini	1.1
Masset	24.4
Dog Rib Rae	14.3
Port Simpson	16.1
Kamloops	22.8
Sarcee	13.2
Fort William	13.6
Williams Lake	27.5
Moose Factory	10.3
Fort Alexander	n/a
River Desert	10.7
St. Mary's	11.4
Attawapiskat	11.0
Pointe Bleue	1.2
Tobique	9.5
Pikangikum	4.6
Shubenacadie	15.7
Oak River	5.7
Rupert House	7.2
Cold Lake	83
Fort St. John	35.5
Deer Lake, Ont.	2.3
The Pas	8.4
James Smith	7.8
Peguis	12.5
Big Cove	6.4
Piapot	9.5

Table 2. Unwed Mothers in Cairns, Jamieson, and Lysyk, 1966

discrimination to be addressed versus only the cases that make it to the courtroom.[33] Because Prime Minister Justin Trudeau promised a change in his relationship with Indigenous Peoples, INAC and the DoJ did not appeal this court decision.

Interestingly, what once again emerged within the Descheneaux, Yantha, and Yantha lineages, as with McIvor, was the situation(s) of children being born out of wedlock or born of unknown and thus unstated paternity. I am less sure about the exact details, but I am not too concerned about this because my lack of knowing does not take away from the story. Also, it would be counterproductive for me to clog your cognition with details that are not crucial. With this qualified, it is important to know that Mary Eberts was acting as co-counsel in the *Descheneaux* case and she was present on January 8, 2015, when INAC employee Linda McLenachan testified as a witness. This testimony was significant to my case.

In sum, *McIvor* addressed the 6(1)a–6(1)c hierarchy, but the legal remedy was narrowed, and despite protests and expert submissions Parliament accepted the narrow remedy under the pretense that consultations were needed. Through *McIvor* the *Indian Act* was amended in 2011 as failed remedial legislation. The *Descheneaux* case addressed the cousins and the siblings issues. My court case, yet to be heard at this point, was attempting to challenge INAC's unknown and thus unstated paternity policy. While the *McIvor* legal remedy and the *Descheneaux* case resulted in a finite number of new registrants—meaning a particular set and number of people are now entitled to registration: 45,000 and 28,000 to 35,000, respectively—the issue I was raising involved an unknown and potentially immeasurable number of people because it is women who open the Eastern Doorway as they give birth while there will always be situations of unknown and thus unstated fathers.

Returning to My Story

The previous 1970 incarnation of the Indian Act provided that the child of a registered mother was entitled to registration unless the child's father was proven non-registered by the First Nation.
—Michelle Mann, "Disproportionate and Unjustifiable"

While some Canadians shield the Canadian government from culpability for the residential school fiasco by improperly suggesting that the people of the period did not know any better, there can be no reasonable doubt that the current Canadian government knows better.
—Cindy Blackstock, "The Complainant"

Prior to 1985, although it shifted over time, there were provisions in the *Indian Act* that protected children who were born out of wedlock and who were of unknown and thus unstated paternity. Drawing from my reading and thinking, I rely on Larry Gilbert's summary of INAC's rules about matters of paternity.[34] Gilbert was once the Registrar of INAC and so I do see his work as an authority. From 1927 through September 4, 1951, section 12 of the *Indian Act* stated that any illegitimate child of a man or woman, who also shared in Band funds, was considered a member of the Band. From September 4, 1951, through August 13, 1956, the criteria shifted slightly in that the Registrar had to be satisfied that the father was not an Indian before a child was omitted from the Indian Register. The criteria shifted again from August 14, 1956, through April 16, 1985, where illegitimate children were automatically added to the Indian Register and then the Band members had twelve months to protest; only if a protest was successful—meaning the Registrar determined the child had a non-Indian father—was the child's name removed from the register.[35] In sum, issues of paternity were regulated by legislation, versus an internal policy or practices, and although the inclusive process was once narrowed, the criteria was re-expanded to include children regardless of non-paternity disclosure unless a successful protest was made. This legislated process of inclusion remained in place until 1985 when Canada amended the *Indian Act* to bring it in line with the *Charter*. Of course, as I have been arguing, this was not what happened.

As I was doing this work, and doing my best to keep up with the demands on who I was, in 2012 I noticed that INAC had posted online, and thus publicly, its guidelines regarding what it called "unstated paternity." I captured this online INAC document, "Unstated Paternity on Birth Certificate: Quick facts on documentation required," through the use of my computer's snipping tool and it is reproduced here (see Table 3). You will notice that the policy contains no provisions that effectively address situations of unknown and thus unstated paternity, past or current. Nor, for that matter, were there provisions that effectively addressed situations of sexual violence, where men are not known or cannot be named owing to issues of a mother's and child's safety. What this online INAC policy offered was the option of alternative documentation when a known father is not stated on a child's birth certificate: a birth certificate amended to include the father's name; a statutory document signed by both the mother and the father; or a statutory document from the biological father's immediate family members affirming their belief of the father's identity. As can be determined, INAC's silence—or refusal to accept the reality that there are times when a woman does not know who the father of a child is, resulting from situations of sexual violence—is asinine to say the least. In reading this online policy, I felt that INAC was willfully ignorant to the reality of many women and children and, further, that this ignorance was intentional as it served INAC's mandate of getting rid of the "Indian problem." I felt this perpetuated patriarchy's need to control women's bodies—actually, to control their vaginas not only through rape and sexual abuse but also in terms of the babies they birthed. I was disgusted and remain so today.

While this was the unstated paternity policy that I and other community members were able to access online, during the production period of my court case INAC disclosed an internal draft PoP policy marked in capital letters as "DRAFT FOR DISCUSSION PURPOSES ONLY" dated June 17, 2003.

I✦I Government Gouvernement
of Canada du Canada

Canadä

Indigenous and Northern Affairs Canada

INAC > Indian status > Unstated Paternity on Birth Certificate: Quick Facts on documentation required

Unstated Paternity on Birth Certificate: Quick Facts on documentation required

- The Indian Registrar is responsible for determining entitlement to registration for all individuals who are applying for Indian Status.
- The 1985 amendments to the *Indian Act* provide that a person's entitlement to registration is determined on the basis of his or her parents' respective entitlements to registration.
- A person's birth certificate listing his or her parents' is the primary document provided with an application for registration as evidence of parentage.
- The Office of the Indian Registrar understands there are situations where an applicant's father may not be listed.
- In order to assist applicants whose birth certificate does not contain their father's name, the Office of the Indian Registrar has outlined alternative documentation that is accepted to support an application for Indian status.
- In situations where an applicant's father is not listed on the birth certificate, but the applicant asserts that his or her biological father is in fact entitled to be registered as an Indian, the Office of the Indian Registrar may request that such an applicant have his or her birth certificate amended so that both parents' names are listed on it.
- If amending a birth certificate is not an option, the Registrar may accept other evidence in support of an application for registration as the Registrar sees fit. For example, the applicant might provide statutory declarations signed by the applicant's mother and biological father affirming the identity of the applicant's father.
- If a statutory declaration cannot be obtained from the biological father (e.g., because the father is uncooperative, unavailable, or deceased), the applicant might provide statutory declarations from the biological father's immediate family members (e.g., the applicant's grandparents, aunts or uncles) affirming their belief of the identity of the applicant's biological father.
- For more information contact AANDC's Public Enquiries Contact Centre.
  E-mail: Infopubs@aadnc-aandc.gc.ca
  Phone (toll-free): 1-800-567-9604
  TTY (toll-free): 1-866-553-0554

Date modified: 2012-04-12

Table 3. 2012 Indigenous and Northern Affairs Canada's Online Unstated Paternity Policy

This draft PoP policy also listed alternative options that the Registrar could/would rely on when paternity is not disclosed: amended vital statistic records, meaning an amended birth certificate; court orders declaring paternity; statutory declarations; DNA evidence via court order; and finally, the option of an oral hearing with the Registrar of INAC, including a face-to-face conversation or a telephone hearing. While this draft PoP policy adds the options of DNA evidence via a court order and an oral hearing with the Registrar, this criteria set did not accommodate for situations of an unknown and thus unstated paternity. Furthermore, nothing in this draft PoP policy outlined what steps the Registrar could/would offer in terms of births long past, such as in my case where I do not know who my paternal grandfather was. To me there was a silent yet screaming gap in INAC's PoP policy, both the public online version and the internal written draft version, just as there was in the *Indian Act*. I must clearly state to readers of this book that this PoP policy remained in draft form long after the *Indian Act* was amended in 1985. This means that this so-called written draft policy, which my legal team received in 2003, was at the time eighteen years old—possibly, I think, as a measure to avoid public knowledge of its very existence. There was so much wrong here. Again, the online version did not appear until 2012. It seems this was a secret policy.

Eventually the SJM date was set for late May 2014; however, in April 2014, again from my positionality as a plaintiff and client of ALST because that is all I know, for some unclear reason, other than an administrative glitch, I learned that this date had been lost. It was rescheduled for October 20 through 22, 2014. Around this time the DoJ began making arguments to delay the process, arguing that ALST did not file a notice of constitutional question, which Kimberly did in May 1997. Also, I heard via telephone that the DoJ lawyers were making what is known as *res judicata* arguments, claiming the issue had already been argued and decided in 2001 and 2002. Remember, back then the Court of Appeal for Ontario did grant us leave to reframe our *Charter* argument and refile our SoC.

The task and steps that needed to be completed prior to the SJM hearing were crunched, meaning our timetable had to be adjusted. The DoJ was scheduled to complete the joint motion record (JMR) on June 15 so ALST could review it before completing our factum. While the JMR consists of all materials relied on in a case, such as the collection of affidavits and expert reports, a factum is a concise record of arguments relied on in a case. Our factum was due to be completed and filed on June 30. However, for some reason the JMR was late; it was completed on June 30. This meant ALST could not meet the deadline to complete and file our factum. As a result, ALST received a two-week extension, to July 15, which in turn adjusted the DoJ's due date for their factum completion to September 30. ALST met their new deadline but the DoJ did not, requesting an extension to file on October 14. ALST agreed to an extension but only to October 8 because Christa felt she needed at least two weeks to prepare. On October 3 the DoJ filed a motion with the court to delay the hearing, apparently due to an illness. ALST's position was that we did not want an adjournment. The judge did not adjourn the hearing date and instructed the DoJ to provide its factum by 2:00 p.m. on October 10. At this point I did not trust the process at all. Keep in mind that as a plaintiff I was hearing things secondhand. Sadly, I had no faith in anyone.

ALST's factum of the plaintiff spelled out the legal arguments in support of my case, as factums do. Again, our position was that section 6 of the *Indian Act* discriminated against me based on race, sex, and marital status. As ALST was instructed to do by the Court of Appeal for Ontario, we framed our argument against the *Indian Act* as a section 15 *Charter* violation. Of course, the factum addressed the matter of INAC's draft PoP policy disclosed during the production period. ALST argued, on my behalf, that through this policy when a child is born and the father is unable to or does not sign the birth certificate, the assumption made by the Registrar of INAC that the father is a non-Indian person. It was argued that the policy is best thought of as an *assumption of non-Indian paternity*. Said another way, ALST argued that the policy instructs the Office of the Registrar to assume the applicant's father is non-Indian when a father's signature is not present on the long-form birth certificate. My factum spelled out the following relief:

(i) A declaration that section 6 of the 1985 Act violates section 15(1) of the *Charter* insofar as it discriminates against applicants for registration entitlement who were born out of wedlock or whose ancestors were born out of wedlock; and (ii) A declaration that section 6 of the 1985 Act violates section 150 [*sic*; section 15] of the *Charter* insofar as it discriminates against applicants for registration entitlement who do not know their or their ancestors' paternity;

(iii) A declaration that section 6 of the 1985 Act be interrupted [*sic*; interpreted] and applied in a manner that does not disadvantage individuals or descendants of individuals whose paternity is unknown; (iv) Costs of this motion on a solicitor and client basis; and (v) Such further and other relief as this Honourable Court may deem just.[36]

Ontario Superior Court Ruling

[T]he lengthy and costly process that the litigants had to engage in for the purpose of effecting incremental changes to the Indian Act in both Gehl and Descheneaux shows how burdensome and ineffective Charter challenges can be.
—Elysa Darling and Drew Lafond, "Barring Claims against Discriminatory Legislation"

Finally, on October 20, 21, and 22, 2014, my *Charter* case made its way into the Ontario Superior Court. Christa Big Canoe and Caitlyn Kasper, both of ALST, represented me.

While I do not offer an analysis of the DoJ's SoD, some of the oral arguments that the DoJ uttered were disturbing. Drawing from my memory and notes taken at the time,[37] such arguments consisted of the following: the matter was about unknowable paternity, which is neither an enumerated nor an analogous ground as per the *Charter*; men and women are treated equally in the application process and therefore no discrimination exists in the process; it was my grandmother's discrimination, not mine; if anything it was my father who suffered the indignity, not me; it was not my historical disadvantage, but my father's; this case is about my need to provide evidence of paternity as per INAC's PoP policy requirements and not a section 15 *Charter* violation of the *Indian Act*; my situation is unique and thus a remedy is not required; the injustice is reasonably justified; Canadian citizenship for generations abroad is lost after two generations; the good for all outweighs the negative for the few in the same situation; and—and this is horrible, most insulting, and disturbing—the DoJ argued that Canada risks "mischief if there is a gap in the policy," meaning if the lack of a signature is permitted in the registration process, women would take advantage of this policy gap. The DoJ also argued that despite a five-year period between my application for registration and my grandmother's death, I did not ask her who my grandfather was. Apparently I was mischievous. That is what they were implying. It is important for me to note here that all of the DoJ lawyers were women.

Regardless of these pitiful DoJ arguments, made by women no less, some of presiding Justice Stewart's oral comments were hopeful. For example, she commented on the broader implications of the case, adding that it was not just about money, and she asked the question, "What happens when the man is unknown versus known and unstated?" Regardless, the judgement came out in June 2015: I lost. Stewart's ruling sided with the DoJ's argument that my denial of registration was the result of unknowable paternity and not the enumerated grounds of race, sex, and marital status, pointing out that unknowable paternity was not an analogous ground as per section 15 of the *Charter*.[38]

Obviously there is a tight relationship between unknown paternity, sex, and marriage. This relationship, according to Stewart, did not qualify as a *Charter* violation, meaning the *Indian Act* was not discriminatory. Stewart's judgement further stated that my INAC application for registration was treated in the same way as applications that men submitted; in other words, my application and a male's application are processed through INAC's administration in an equal way.[39] Through this reasoning of the administration of my application as equal versus reasoning of what was inherently wrong with the *Indian Act*, Stewart atomized me from my grandmother and father and the reality that my denial for entitlement was a result of my grandmother's experience. I struggle with this because substantive equality, one would think, includes the effects of sex discrimination on a woman's children and grandchildren.[40] For those who are not aware, substantive equality encompasses what is inherent within the law or policy, whereas formal equality is more of a thin surface analysis of the law and its administration.[41] My right to live free from discrimination has to include an understanding of how I was treated as a result of my kokomis's sex discrimination. Her sex discrimination was also my father's sex discrimination and also my sex discrimination. I also think my right to live free from sex discrimination has to mean more than the equal administration of my application. The judge, in my opinion, reasoned poorly. But then maybe it was not reason she used; maybe it was all about colonial power and genocide.

Fortunately, ALST determined there were three errors of law in Stewart's judgement, the result being that we could move forward to the Court of Appeal for Ontario. These errors were as follows: (1) Applying the post-1985 rules of the *Indian Act* regarding unknown paternity to a situation arising before 1985 is an incorrect retroactive application of the two-parent rule. (2) The Registrar's PoP policy infringes my rights under section 15 of the *Charter* when the policy's attendant requirement of known paternity goes beyond the plain language of the statute. (3) The policy is ultra vires of the statute, meaning it goes beyond the authority of the *Indian Act.*

Shortly after the Ontario Superior Court judgement was released on June 2, 2015, sometime in July ALST learned from Mary Eberts about the existence of new evidence that very much pertained to my *Charter* challenge. Mary learned of the existence of this evidence as co-counsel in the *Descheneaux* case, when DoJ witness Linda McLenachan, again an INAC employee, was cross-examined on January 8, 2015.[42] This date was after my Ontario Superior Court date but before my judgement was released. In her testimony McLenachan spoke about an internal INAC post-*McIvor* policy shift the Registrar used to govern situations of unknown and thus unstated paternity. Actually, there were two internal policy directives created after the *McIvor* case in 2011.

ALST and LOME ordered McLenachan's testimony transcripts from the *Descheneaux* case on August 11, 2015, and received them on September 4. Upon receipt, greater clarity was obtained. On September 23 my legal team requested from the DoJ information about the two INAC post-*McIvor* directives. The DoJ, however, produced nothing. On October 1, Mary Eberts officially came on board as lead counsel in my *Charter* case. Then on January 7, 2016, LOME and ALST requested the policy directives again. On that same day, actually at the very end of the business day, the DoJ sent us a directive titled "Memorandum Deeming 6(1)c omitted 'illegitimate child' deceased before September 4, 1951 and deeming 6(1)a or 6(1)c 'illegitimate child' alive on or after September 4, 1951." It was date-stamped January 10, 2012. Following a review of this directive, LOME and ALST made a request for additional information regarding the implementation of the policy at the Indian Register level and for any other additional related policies. On January 22, 2016, the DoJ sent us a document titled "Memorandum Deeming non-Indian paternity 6(1)c omitted." It was date-stamped June 13,

2011. Apparently these two policy directives became known as the "post-*McIvor* 1" and "post-*McIvor* 2" policy directives, sometimes collectively called the "post-*McIvor* policy."

Disturbingly, these post-*McIvor* policy directives state clearly that the Registrar of INAC did not have the power to deem non-Indian paternity in any situation: "the power of the Registrar to deem non-Indian paternity was not carried over in the 1985 *Indian Act* amendments."[43] What is more, and also disturbing, the Department also stated, "We will not be taking any action to seek out, and then investigate or rectify past decisions at this time."[44] What this means is INAC had no intention of reopening closed files to reconsider applicants who had been denied Indian registration through INAC's 1985 practice and policy; this includes cases where there is an ancestor with an unknown and/or unstated paternity born before 1985 in an applicant's lineage, such as in my situation where I did not know who my paternal grandfather was. In other words, the Registrar was applying the assumption of non-Indian paternity to births after 1985 as well as retroactively to births such as my father's, even though it did not have the legislative authority to do so.

Worthy of repeating, and said in another way, the 2011 directive explicitly stated that in fact INAC did not have the authority to deem an unknown and/or unstated father as non-Indian. In pre-1985 contexts, if a successful protest was made a child could be denied registration; yet post-1985 INAC did not even have this authority because this clause was removed and the *Indian Act* was silent on what to do in the situation of an unknown and/or unstated paternity. This is huge in that this 2011 policy directive stated clearly that the Eastern Doorway was morally open in all situations of unknown and thus unstated paternity. INAC had no authority to deny any child where the father was not known or named! And what is more, INAC had no authority to protest. The 2012 directive provided further clarity on how this applied to pre- and post-1951 births: while some will be entitled to 6(1)a, others will be entitled to 6(1)c. Once again we see here the nonsense of the 6(1)a–6(1)c hierarchy. Of course, when I learned about this post-*McIvor* policy directive I had a lot to think through and about. Years later I am still coming to understand what INAC and the DoJ—again, really Canada—did to me.

What this post-*McIvor* policy directive told me is that Canada was perpetuating its colonial policy of genocide and was now targeting mothers and babies. The other thing I thought about was why the DoJ put me through the unnecessary litigation of my *Charter* challenge. One would think the DoJ would want to dispense of the *Gehl v Canada* case. Then maybe, I thought, it was because, as many people think, the DoJ is an industry that employs many settler Canadians as high-priced lawyers. After all, it was through an access to information request dated November 2018, which my partner, Nik, took on, that I learned the DoJ (Canada) billed its client INAC (Canada) a total of $1,031,338.89 to defend its unknown and thus unstated paternity policy and litigate my court case. I remember one night asking Nik to explain to me how much a million dollars is. "The cost of two or three starter homes," he responded.

Then I thought maybe the DoJ could not dispense of my *Charter* challenge and register me as an Indian because it would be too risky in that registering me would send a clear message that INAC's assumption of non-Indian paternity was invalid and had no authority via the legislation.[45] Certainly I would let people know through my NSRAUUP initiative, my online petition, and my community writing. No matter how I tried to rationalize and understand how I had been abused, eventually I thought to myself, were not INAC and the DoJ obligated to disclose this evidence of the post-*McIvor* policy directive to ALST? I also wondered if the failure to disclose was a violation of the rule of law.

Moreover, I still cannot help but wonder what the outcome would have been if this evidence had been properly disclosed and adjudicated when I was in the Ontario Superior Court in October 2014. Would Justice Stewart have made a different decision if the post-*McIvor* policy directive was produced, as rules of law dictated the evidence should have been? Would she have then seen my unknown paternity as an analogous ground as per the *Charter*?

If you can believe it, the DoJ actually argued in correspondence with ALST and LOME that this evidence was not relevant to my case. It is my position that it was not up to the DoJ to make this decision; the evidence should have been disclosed and properly adjudicated by the judge. My legal team thought so too. I, of course, was curious to see what the Court of Appeal for Ontario judges would do in the presence of this evidence. The problem was that we had received this evidence too late to properly meet the deadline of submitting our factum of appeal. Our factum was due January 8, 2016—the same day the DoJ/INAC sent us the post-*McIvor* policy directive.

This meant we needed an extension, which then again caused a cascade of shifts in the schedule leading up to the Court of Appeal date. Of course the DoJ knew ALST and LOME had a deadline of January 8 to submit my factum of appeal; regardless, the Department stalled and delayed. I understand full well now that the law is more about power than morals and truth.

While this nonsense was happening, there was a discussion of the various options we could take regarding the appeal. The word "interlocutory" moved through my email as this matter was discussed. ALST and LOME were considering the possibility of bringing a motion forward on the abuse of the process, or bringing the matter before a judge. After all, the post-*McIvor* policy directives were only disclosed to us in 2016 after we asked for them, yet they were created in 2011 and 2012. Apparently there was also the option of filing a motion to strike the DoJ's SoD, because the DoJ had not disclosed the evidence beforehand. I was told that if we won on this motion to strike, INAC would have little choice but to grant me registration, and further, I would be entitled to very large damages because I had been made to undergo a lengthy litigation process when the answer had been sitting in the DoJ files. ALST and LOME opted to take the matter of new evidence to the Court of Appeal for Ontario.

On February 8, 2016, ALST staff lawyer Emilie Lahaie informed me that the new deadline for ALST and LOME to submit our factum of the appellant was May 13, while the DoJ now had until July 29 to submit its response. This new timetable was agreed on to give ample time for ALST and LOME to write to the court requesting case management oversight as well as time to produce our factum that would address the matter of the new evidence. On March 17 we were informed that our request for case management oversight was denied. However, Chief Justice Strathy did advise that we should file a notice of motion seeking leave to file further evidence. We were told the motion would be heard and argued at the time of the appeal.

Then on May 13, I was told that we would not meet our deadline for our factum of appeal. Apparently, I was told, an order from Justice Stewart was missing and so the timeline was extended. One month later, on June 13, we submitted our factum, but now because of our delay the DoJ's new deadline to submit its response shifted two months to September 16. Then, on August 9, I was informed that the DoJ had requested an extension to submit its factum and materials to November 4, leaving the December 20 court date intact. ALST offered October 14 as the better option versus having to contend with a motion and potential change of court date; the DoJ agreed to submit the materials on October 14. I will always wonder if I should have said to cancel the court date.

In August of 2016 we then learned that the DoJ's legal counsel and senior lawyers, Yurka and Sinclair, were no longer representing INAC in my appeal. It is my opinion that this shift was a strategy that prevented them from answering to their failure to produce the post-*McIvor* policy evidence. On September 12, Emilie Lahaie completed the needed motion and affidavit of new evidence.

Moving tangentially for a moment, during the time between court dates I had a conversation with Mary where I was telling her that many Indigenous women have told me their stories about the sexual violence that led to their pregnancies and the birth of their children. I told Mary it was such a heartfelt burden to listen to these stories. Some of the mothers were so young, less than sixteen years old when the rape or incest took place. Of course, these young mothers don't have the ability to address INAC's PoP policy, let alone deal with the DoJ. In agreement, Mary lamented that it is indeed deplorable that young girls who do not even have the right to consent to sex are then faced with the discrimination of INAC's paternity policy. Mary's quick mind is impressive.

It is my understanding that an intervener is an organization that represents the special interests of people who may be affected by the outcome of a particular case and can side with either the plaintiff or the defendant.[46] Intervener status is granted by the court at the court's discretion. Women's Legal Education and Action Fund (LEAF), represented by lawyers Renée Pelletier and Krista Nerland from Olthuis Kleer Townshend LLP, applied for and gained intervener status in my case.[47] This meant they too submitted a factum, which LEAF filed on October 24. On December 20, the case was heard at the Court of Appeal for Ontario, Ontario's highest court.

Court of Appeal Factums: Mine, LEAF's, and the DoJ's

*It is readily apparent that this entire case proceeded on a
false basis due to the Registrar's deliberate silence.*
—*Gehl v Canada*, Factum of the Appellant, 2016, at para 117

As suggested, but worthy of repeating, in preparing my notice of appeal my legal team argued that the Ontario Superior Court of Justice erred in law in three ways: it was incorrect to apply INAC's post-1985 PoP policy to my father's pre-1985 birth; the PoP policy infringes my rights under section 15 of the *Charter* because the requirement of known paternity goes beyond the plain language of the *Indian Act*; and the PoP policy goes beyond the authority of the *Indian Act*. My factum of appeal also argued that the 1985 *Indian Act* was a breach of section 15 of the *Charter* because it denied me equal benefit of the law on the basis of race, gender, and marital status, specifically because the PoP policy weighs more heavily on women than on men because in most cases it is apparent who the mother of a child is but not so readily apparent in many cases who the child's father is. Furthermore, there are important reasons why a mother may not wish, or be able, to put the name of the child's father on the record, as in cases of abuse, rape, or incest.

My factum outlined the important aspects of the *Indian Act* that pertained to my case. While entitlement once passed through the male line, one exception was that an Indian woman could pass on status to her child if the child's paternity was not, through a protest process, established to be non-Indian. Again, what I am getting at here is that at one time there was the option for someone in the community to protest the addition of a child. In the event that the protest was successful INAC would deem the child a non-Indian. In 1985, when the *Indian Act* was amended to bring it in line with section 15 of the *Charter*, it was said that the reasons for the amendments were to remove sex discrimination and to restore entitlement to those who had lost it as a result of sex discrimination. In 1985 INAC then introduced the PoP policy that requires that the identity of the child's father be revealed for registration entitlement purposes, imposing administrative requirements of what kinds of proof were acceptable. This PoP policy permitted no exceptions; disclosure of the father's name was required, even in situations of rape or incest, if the child was to obtain entitlement. In sum, the difference between the old system and the post-1985 PoP policy is that after 1985 the onus was placed on the mother to produce proof that the father was registered or registrable, whereas before 1985 the onus was on the party challenging the child's entitlement.

My factum also explained that during the review of my application, the Office of the Registrar assigned my father, Rodney Gagnon, registration pursuant to section 6(2). In doing this the Registrar applied to him and his circumstances the post-1985 PoP rules, under which unknown or unstated paternity means that the person will be considered to have only one Indian parent,[48] yet my father was born in 1935. The alternative to applying the post-1985 rules should have been applying the legislation applicable at the time of his birth. Under that legislation, my father would have received full status from his mother, Mary Viola Bernadette Gagnon.

As a reminder, section 15(1) of the *Charter* provides that in Canada all people are equal before and under the law, that all people have the right to equal protection and benefit of the law without discrimination based on race, national or ethnic origin, colour, religion, sex, age, or mental or physical disability. My factum further argued that, while for some time a mirror comparator analysis was relied on in determining discrimination, today substantive equality is determined by a two-part test: first, does the law create a distinction based on an enumerated or analogous ground; and second, does the distinction create a disadvantage by perpetuating prejudice or stereotype. That said, within the *Charter*, section 1 comes before all else. It states that *Charter* rights are subject to "reasonable limits prescribed by law as can be demonstrably justified in a free and democratic society." Regardless, in my factum it was argued that INAC's PoP policy failed to meet what is known as a section 1 save. Among the reasons argued were that the PoP policy is not rationally connected to the purpose of removing sex discrimination from the *Indian Act* and that the PoP policy treats men and women the same even though, as we know, they are differently situated in terms of the ability to identify the parent of the child.

My factum further argued that in contrast to the earlier Canadian Bill of Rights, which only addressed the right of the individual to *equality before the law* and the *protection of the law*, the *Charter* also guarantees *equality under the law* and the *equal benefit of the law*. It is stated that this specific language was intentionally chosen to remedy the limitations under the Canadian Bill of Rights.[49] Within my factum it was also argued that the PoP policy, and its application to my father's circumstances, violated the guarantee of *equality before the law* and *equal benefit of the law* without discrimination on the basis of sex. My lawyers argued that the *Charter* applies to the PoP policy, even though it is an administrative requirement and not created by the *Indian Act* itself, in that it is law for the purposes of section 15 of the

Charter. They further argued that the two-parent rule is an example of a situation where the same treatment does not result in equal treatment. The same statutory treatment for Indian men and women produces substantive inequality for Indian women because the life circumstances of Indian women differ from those of Indian men. In this way the impact of a law, it was argued, rather than the written words of the law, is the source of the inequality. Thus, the two-parent rule is a violation of the substantive equality rights of Status Indian women: their right to *equality under the law* and to the *equal benefit of the law* are withheld or compromised by this statutory rule. The right to transmit Indian status to a child has been acknowledged as a benefit of the law.

Within the factum my legal representatives noted that McLenachan had testified on cross-examination that the Registrar of INAC applies the old "illegitimacy" (meaning born out of wedlock) provisions of the *Indian Act* to persons born before 1985. Thus, the Registrar should have applied to my father the "illegitimacy" rules in effect at the time of his birth, instead of the 1985 PoP policy. They argued that restoring Indian women once enfranchised, yet not allowing them the full benefit, is only an exercise in formal equality. They explained that men and their children born out of wedlock before 1985 do not have the PoP policy applied to them and that the retroactive application of the PoP policy to historical situations was contraindicated. In this way, they argued, the PoP policy and its application to my father are not reasonable limits on my rights as per section 1 of the *Charter* and not justified in a free and democratic society.

Regarding the implications of the new evidence, my legal representatives argued that the DoJ had not produced the post-*McIvor* policy directives. They argued that at no time before January 7, 2016, did the DoJ acknowledge the existence of these policy directives, which required that cases of children born out of wedlock before 1985 be assessed according to the former statutory rules. They further explained that the British Columbia Supreme Court in *McIvor v Canada* found that "the power of the Registrar to deem non-Indian paternity was not carried over in the 1985 *Indian Act* amendments. This means that the Registrar does not have the power to deem non-Indian paternity even when he/she are satisfied that the applicant's father was non-Indian."[50] They further argued that although these 2011 and 2012 policy directives were not in effect when I applied for registration and was denied registration, they did come into effect during the course of my litigation, and they are applicable to the determination of my father's entitlement and thus mine.[51]

My factum offered that the 2011 post-*McIvor* policy directive states, "We will not be taking any action to seek out and then investigate or rectify past decisions at this time"; and the 2012 policy states, "Although the registration category determination for 'illegitimate children' provided in this directive varies from previous approaches, the Office of the Indian Registrar will not be revisiting closed files."[52] INAC's intent was to only apply the second directive to future applications, meaning after 2012. My legal team of LOME and ALST called this "the Secretive Policy Change," and what resulted was that my entire court case proceeded on a false basis because of INAC's deliberate silence and the refusal of INAC and the DoJ to disclose evidence that would have had an outcome at the lower court level.

Section 15 violations require comparator group analysis to illustrate how a particular group of people are denied a benefit that a comparable group of people have access to. The comparator group offered in my father's situation was the "illegitimate" children who were registered prior to 1985 and who maintain their status after 1985 if there is no evidence declaring the child not to be entitled to registration. Applying the PoP policy retroactively to some but not all situations creates a disparity between two groups of people who should have equal rights. What is more, my legal representatives argued that applying the PoP policy to my father and not the post-*McIvor* policy also fails to meet the remedial purpose and intention of the 1985 legislation. The post-*McIvor* policy is a clear admission that the Registrar of INAC did not have the authority to omit "illegitimate" children from entitlement. Lastly, it was argued that it is both illogical and unconstitutional to retroactively apply a reinstatement that acknowledges a woman was entitled to be registered regardless of her marriage, yet not retroactively apply the post-*McIvor* polices to the child she birthed out of wedlock before 1985. Finally, of course, the factum outlined the relief sought by me, the appellant:

i. A declaration under s.52 of the *Constitution Act, 1982* that the two-parent rule in section 6 of the *Indian Act* of 1985 and the Proof of Paternity policy formulated by the Registrar are contrary to the *Charter*, and a further declaration that the Proof of Paternity policy not be applied to determination of the registrability of Dr. Gehl's father Rodney Gagnon.

ii. A declaration that Dr. Gehl's father Rodney Gagnon is entitled to be registered under s.6(1)(a) of the *1985 Act*, and that she is therefore entitled to be registered under s.6 of the *1985 Act*.

iii. Her costs of this matter on a substantial indemnity basis.

iv. Such further and other relief as this Honourable Court may deem just.[53]

LEAF's factum focused on the absolute unknown paternity issue, and it began by explaining that through the PoP policy when a woman cannot prove the Indian status of the father, by default he is presumed to be without status. Through this process the PoP policy removes the presumption of Indian paternity that existed pre-1985. LEAF also argued that the registration provisions of section 6 of the *Indian Act*, as implemented through INAC's PoP policy, is contrary to the *Charter*. Offering a substantive equality analysis, they argued that it is women, and especially unmarried women, who have children of unknown and thus unstated paternity. They stressed that there are times when paternity cannot be known and stated, and that this represented a distinction based on sex and marital status. LEAF further argued that Justice Stewart had rested her position on "unknowable paternity" as a non-analogous ground and the position that the impugned provisions treat all applications in the same way. In doing this, LEAF argued, she failed to value the relationship between paternity, sex, and marriage and took a formal approach to equity—the antithesis of the substantive equality approach required under section 15(1) of the *Charter*.

Then LEAF argued that, collectively, section 6 of the *Indian Act* and the PoP policy fail to account for the lived reality of registered Indian women. LEAF further argued that the PoP policy could be remedied without striking down section 6 through providing registration entitlement for children when paternity cannot be established. LEAF continued that, in the event that the court determines the PoP policy is consistent with section 6, then section 6 must be struck down.

The DoJ factum restressed that we had lost at the Ontario Superior Court level because of an "unknowable paternity" rather than an enumerated or analogous ground as set out in the *Charter*. The DoJ also argued that INAC's PoP policy on its face was gender neutral[54] and that any differential treatment did not constitute substantive discrimination; rather, it was in line with section 15 of the *Charter*. The DoJ also argued that section 15 *Charter* rights are personal to an individual. My discrimination was too remote because it came from my father and grandmother. I was discriminated against based not on sex but on my lineage. The DoJ further argued that the 1985 amendments to the *Indian Act* were not designed to entirely undo the past. The Department proceeded to argue that if there was discrimination based on an enumerated or analogous ground it was a reasonable limit under section 1 of the *Charter*.

In its factum the DoJ also argued that the Registrar is obligated to rely on the *Indian Act* when determining if a person is entitled to be registered, whereas INAC developed its PoP policy to respond to situations in which a father is not named. The DoJ argued that INAC's PoP policy is flexible to the point of considering oral testimony and circumstantial evidence in situations of *unstated paternity* or when a mother is unwilling to identify the father or obtain his consent. The DoJ argued that through reviewing circumstantial evidence, decisions could be made based on a balance of probabilities that the father was entitled to registration. Then the DoJ proceeded to argue that I offered no evidence of who the man was, and as a result, the Registrar had no choice but to deny me registration; the Registrar could not assume my unknown and thus unstated grandfather was entitled to registration in the absence of any evidence because to do so would mean the PoP policy did not guide the interpretation of the *Indian Act* but, rather, contradicted it. Remember here, as I have said, I have no idea who my grandfather was. This man was unknown and thus unstated, versus known and unstated. I did, though, in my affidavit provide some details about the circumstances of my father's early life.

The DoJ factum addressed the post-*McIvor* directives that the DoJ had failed to disclose. It was argued that they were irrelevant because they only applied in situations of 6(1)a and to illegitimate children born before 1985 and in situations when there was no evidence the child was once omitted from the register. According to the DoJ's interpretation, these post-*McIvor* policy directives did not apply in situations of 6(1)c. The DoJ also argued that the difference in treatment between the descendants of 6(1)a–6(1)c had to do with the need for Canada to preserve the pre-existing rights people have even if they were the result of a discriminatory scheme. To me these arguments are all nonsense, made to perpetuate Canada's genocide.

The Court of Appeal for Ontario relies on three judges to hear cases. My case was heard on one day, December 16, 2016. Both Mary Eberts and Christa Big Canoe made oral arguments on my behalf. So did LEAF's fist-pumping representatives, Renée Pelletier and Krista Nerland, who, as stated, made oral arguments more focused on unknown paternity. One thing that struck me about the DoJ's oral arguments was that their draft PoP policy was now adopted by the Registrar as a formal policy. This took thirty-one years! The other thing that struck me was the age of the DoJ lawyers. They were not senior lawyers of Sinclair's and Yurka's age and experience. Oppressors do that: they rely on younger people and also on persons with disabilities, to manipulate an outcome that they want. The latter is sometimes referred to as "disability porn."

I was fortunate in the sense that many community people filled the gallery and benches of the courtroom, with many more standing in the back. Supportive friends such as Alice Olsen Williams, Lynne Porter, Laurie Siblock, Pam Heart, and Sheila Nabigon-Howlett from the Kawartha Truth and Reconciliation Support Group also attended, as did Peterborough community people Roy Brady, Dorothy Boddy, and even Margaret Slavin. My friend Monica Vida and, of course, Nik were also there listening and observing.

There was another familiar face in the gallery. Actually, she was sitting on a bench adjacent to me. At first I could not place her face and so I found myself staring at her. Although it took me a while to decipher who she was, I eventually realized it was the DoJ's senior lawyer Dale L. Yurka, who had worked on the *Gehl* case for years but was since removed or excused. I can only assume she was curious enough to come and listen, or maybe her employer, the DoJ, mandated her to be there. She seemed like such a "nice" lady sitting there. Through my life journey, struggling with colonization and genocide, I have come to understand that "nice" people scare me.

The sitting judges were Justices Robert J. Sharpe, Peter D. Lauwers, and Bradley Miller. I also found that Sharpe was especially kind with the new and younger DoJ lawyers. In this way the DoJ played a good strategy when switching their lawyers.

Court of Appeal for Ontario Judgement

Canada focused on how to better craft a policy with the same goal *of Indigenous land denial, rather than a genuine process of learning and subsequent policy adjustment that respected and preserved the land rights of Indigenous nations.*
—Lynn Gehl, *The Truth That Wampum Tells*

The *Gehl v Canada* Court of Appeal judgement was released on April 20, 2017.[55] I won. I also lost. Taking the lead, maybe because he was the more senior, Justice Sharpe began his analysis by reviewing the procedural history of my court case, commenting that the action had lain dormant for a lengthy period. Sharpe was also of the thought that after the INAC Registrar's dismissal, my case should have moved forward by way of a statutory appeal, noting that for some reason it had moved in the direction of seeking *Charter* and declaratory relief, and where eventually we sought to resolve the matter via SJM. I found this discussion frustrating because first, as I have said, I am not trained in understanding the legal system and thus cannot even decipher if this is a reasonable analysis, and second, because my *Charter* case was managed by several master judges. Surely, I thought, my lawyers and the master judges, through their legal training and work, held knowledge about how my case should proceed through the court. Then he offered, "While her action was framed as a constitutional challenge, during the argument of this appeal it became clear that Dr. Gehl does not press her challenge to the constitutional validity of s. 6(1)(f) or the 'two-parent' rule. Dr. Gehl does, however, challenge the adequacy and reasonableness of the Policy. Her central submission is that, on the evidence she has presented and on a proper application of s. 6(1)(f), it is unreasonable to deny her status."[56]

Justice Sharpe moved on, offering many interesting comments: for example, stating that removing the word "illegitimacy" from the text of the *Indian Act* did not mean Canada removed the practice of "illegitimacy." He stated that the administrative process of determining registration was gender neutral. Then he moved into administrative law and what it offers, as opposed to *Charter* law, to render his decision, stating that INAC's PoP policy was administrative rather than legislative in nature, where the Registrar must be guided by *Charter* values in making a decision—meaning, the Registrar should have balanced *Charter* values with the statutory objective—adding that the decision should be reasonable. If not, the decision would be vulnerable to review. Further, he reasoned, the PoP policy had no statutory force, and it did not consider substantive equality issues. He also stated that I could not rely on the pre-1985 presumption of paternity approach, because it was repealed in 1985, yet the 1985 amendment did not replace the former presumption of paternity approach with a presumption of non-Indian paternity; that the evidentiary requirement burden in the PoP policy failed to take into account and reflect the equality-enhancing and remedial purposes of the 1985 amendment to the *Indian Act*; and finally, that the PoP policy was therefore unreasonable. Within his analysis I like these paragraphs:

> [A] woman may have good reason for her reluctance or inability to disclose the identity of her child's father. The child may be the product of a relationship the mother is reluctant or unable to disclose. The pregnancy may be the result of a relationship with a man the mother is fearful of identifying, for example, a relative, or the spouse or partner of a friend or family member. The pregnancy may be the product of abuse, rape or incest. The mother may have had multiple sexual partners.
>
> [...] [T]he Policy falls well short of what is required to address the circumstances that I have just described making proof of paternity problematic for many women. This failure perpetuates the long history of disadvantage suffered by Indigenous women. As Parliament itself recognized in 1985, the historic practice of stripping and denying Indigenous women of status represented a significant disadvantage that was inconsistent with the *Charter's* promise of equality.[57]

Justices Lauwers and Miller were also of the position that I had allowed the action to languish for many years and argued that this case should have been advanced by way of the statutory appeal, held in abeyance, from the Registrar's dismissal of my protest. They also argued a shift with this statement: "The radical change in the [*sic*] Dr. Gehl's position before this court is that she has effectively abandoned her challenge to the constitutional validity of s. 6(1)(f) of the *Indian Act* or the '2-parent' rule. Instead, she challenges the Registrar's Policy and the Registrar's decision."[58] As a plaintiff I really did not know I had done this.

Then, relying on the principles of administrative law, Lauwers and Miller were of the thought that there was a need to stay away from reasoning through *Charter* values. They further stated that the Registrar had imposed an impossible burden on me to name an unknown and unknowable person as a precondition for my entitlement. In this way, the PoP policy operated in an exclusionary manner; circumstantial evidence existed to imply that more likely than not my paternal grandfather was an Indian, with no evidence to the contrary; the PoP policy is unreasonable because it is at odds with the purpose of section 6 of the *Indian Act*, which is to provide for the registration of persons who are entitled; and the PoP policy denies the benefit of registration solely because of an inability to satisfy an unreasonable evidentiary demand that is not mandated by the *Indian Act*. The following are two additional clauses that I like in the judgement. The Registrar of INAC acted "in an exclusionary manner to deny registration and status to an entitled individual who cannot identify a relevant ancestor by *name*. It is the demand for evidence of specific identity when, in some circumstances, only circumstantial evidence of Indian status of an ancestor whose actual identity is not known (and is not knowable) is available."[59] And, "The demand for evidence of a specific identity is unreasonable because it is a demand for evidence which is not only superfluous, but now, through the passage of time, unobtainable in this instance."[60]

In summary, the Court of Appeal judgement stated that the INAC Registrar had operated in an unreasonable and exclusionary way when there is the need to be reasonable and inclusionary. The PoP policy failed to take into account evidence of the kind that I submitted about who my unknown and thus unstated paternal grandfather might have been. They stated that the demand for the actual identity of a father in situations when only circumstantial evidence of his identity is available is unreasonable. In the absence of evidence of who a father is or was, the default reasoning of the Registrar cannot be that he was a non-Indian man. Sometimes the absolute truth—or, better said, the absolute known—is not available. It was the Court of Appeal's decision that it is sufficient for applicants to provide "evidence capable of giving rise to the inference that an unknown father may have had status, which constitutes sufficient proof of paternity for the purposes of the legislation, in the absence of any evidence to the contrary."[61] The decision also stated that going back to the pre-1985 protection for "illegitimate" children is not required. For the court it was clear that the post-1985 *Indian Act* did not replace the former presumption of paternity with a presumption of non-paternity.

Regarding the statutory appeal that was held in abeyance, although collectively the court stated that my case could have and should have been advanced by way of my statutory appeal from the Registrar's dismissal of my protest, it was agreed that the case should not be sent back to the administrative decision maker, because there was only one possible outcome. However, this was not a correct statement, in that, as I have discussed, there are different Indian registration categories. Regardless of all my time and effort, these employees of Canada's legal system opted to make the decision regarding what form of Indian registration I was entitled to, and they decided on 6(2), thereby imposing on me more sex discrimination. This discrimination is similar to that in Sharon Donna McIvor's case, in that the women in my ancestral lineage remained as 6(1)c instead of 6(1)a. If my kokomis, great-grandmother, and great-great-grandmother were men they would all be entitled to 6(1)a and so would I. This would also mean my nieces and nephews would be entitled to Indian registration. Yet through this ruling I continued to be impacted by sex discrimination in the *Indian Act*. Just lovely!

Within a few weeks of the Court of Appeal for Ontario hearing on January 25, 2017, Christa Big Canoe took a two-year leave from ALST. She went to work with the National Inquiry into Missing and Murdered Indigenous Women and Girls.

The Senate and the House of Commons

As discussed, on August 3, 2015, Descheneaux, Yantha, and Yantha won their case. In September 2015, under Prime Minister Stephen Harper, the Conservatives appealed this decision, but in February 2016, after Justin Trudeau was voted in as prime minister—on a platform of reconciliation and the need to respect the nation-to-nation relationship with Indigenous Peoples—this appeal was dropped.[62] During the summer of 2016 the Liberal government began talking about a two-stage approach to resolving the broader sex discrimination in the *Indian Act*. In the first stage they would address the court-identified sex discrimination, while the broader issues inherent in the 6(1)a–6(1)c hierarchy would be taken up a consultation process with Indigenous communities. Indigenous experts, including Sharon Donna McIvor and me, thought this was nonsense because the same approach had been argued in 1985 and 2011.

At the time of the *Descheneaux* ruling, Justice Masse gave Canada eighteen months to remedy the *Indian Act*, which meant the legislative fix was required by February 3, 2017. Because the Senate was less busy than the House of Commons, Bill S-3, An Act to Amend the *Indian Act* (elimination of sex-based inequities in registration), began there. The first reading in the broader Senate took place on October 25, 2016; the second reading took place on November 17. The bill was then referred to the Standing Senate Committee on Aboriginal Peoples (APPA), to hear expert oral testimony and written submissions for further discussion. On November 22, I watched online as Stéphane Descheneaux, Tammy Yantha, and legal counsel David Schultz offered their oral submission to the APPA committee. They were not happy about the approach Canada took in moving Bill S-3 forward. They argued that neither INAC nor the DoJ had consulted with them when drafting the bill that was sitting in front of the APPA Senate members.[63] At the time I was struck upon learning that it is the DoJ who drafts the legislation. To me this seems like the fox taking care of the hen house. I was learning too much to cognitively process everything. I can be a slow processor. I also remember learning at this time that Chief Rick O'Bomsawin, of the Abénakis of Odanak First Nation, was a client of David Schultz, Marie-Eve Dumont, and Mary Eberts, the lawyers who had represented Descheneaux, Yantha, and Yantha. I was envious and wished for this kind of support from a Chief.

On November 30, during her oral submission to the APPA committee, Carolyn Bennett, the Minister of INAC, said she was embarrassed that INAC and the DoJ had failed to consult with the plaintiffs and legal representatives on the bill before drafting it. As a result, in December the APPA committee, chaired by Senator Lillian Eva Dyck, refused to pass the bill in its current form on to third reading. Then, in January 2017 Justice Masse granted Canada six additional months to accommodate proper consultations with the experts. This extended the deadline for the completion of Bill S-3 to July 2017.

On April 20, 2017, the judgement for my case was released, and on May 16, I was thrust into offering oral and written testimony to the APPA committee. I really needed more time to rest, think, and cognitively process the judgement—a judgement where I both won and lost—and my feelings about how INAC and the DoJ had suppressed evidence that was pertinent to my court case. I also had a hard time understanding the judicial reasoning and shift in the case that came out of the Court of Appeal for Ontario, that being the shift from *Charter* law and the *Indian Act* to administrative law and INAC's PoP policy. It was not until the day before my oral submission to the APPA committee and after listening to Shelagh Day and Pamela Palmater talk that I was able to more fully understand some things. Mary Eberts and ALST staff lawyer Emilie Lahaie also offered oral submissions to the APPA committee. And Nik reluctantly answered a question posed to him by Senator Murray Sinclair. Sinclair asked Nik for his comments on the situation, to which Nik responded with something to the effect that he was not very proud of Canada and not very proud of what Canada was doing to his partner, meaning me. During my testimony I told the Senate members that while I had defeated INAC's non-Indian paternity policy assumption in situations of unknown and thus unstated paternity, I was not happy with the new sex discrimination imposed on me. Like Sharon, I argued I should be entitled to 6(1)a registration because I was born before 1985. Through collective effort Bill S-3 was eventually amended to include the "6(1)a All the Way!" clauses that would address all the issues inherent in the 6(1)a–6(1)c hierarchy, and the *Gehl* clauses regarding unknown and unstated paternity were added as well.

On May 17, the clause-by-clause reading took place in the APPA committee where Senator Sinclair was to read in his version of the *Gehl* clauses, yet in his fluster of activity and thought he forgot the second *Gehl* clause.[64] It was also during this time when I noticed senators beginning to rely on the language of unknown "parentage" versus unknown "paternity." This alarmed me because I worried that it was gender-neutral discourse that masked women's experiences. Within this clause-by-clause discussion Senator Marilou McPhedran was a strong proponent of the "6(1)a All the Way!" legal remedy, acknowledging that I was not happy with the designation of 6(2) registration. While almost all of the senators, some through the body language of a closed fist pump, accepted the "6(1)a All the Way!" clauses put forward, Senator Sinclair voted against it. To me Senator Sinclair's behaviour was bizarre to say the least. In watching the discussions at home and online, he seemed to think that the experts—McIvor, Palmater, Eberts, me—were unaware of what we wanted. Our goal was to achieve equality between the descendants of Indian men born before 1985 and the descendants of Indian women born before 1985, but I think Sinclair mistakenly thought our goal was the complete elimination of the second-generation cut-off rule. There was an in-camera break, after which the meeting came online again, showing he had voted against the "6(1)a All the Way!" clauses. In the end, though, it all turned out well: on June 1, 2017 Bill s-3 was read for the third time to the larger Senate members and was passed unilaterally, meaning Sinclair included, with the "6(1)a All the Way!" clauses intact. It seems that with the help of non-Indigenous senator allies, Sinclair came on board and was now supporting Bill s-3 with the "6(1)a All the Way!" clauses intact. Moreover, it was during this third reading that a friendly amendment was made, adding the second *Gehl* clause. It was picked up off the floor. I was relieved. I mean, I had worked so hard. The prospect of human error was not a pleasant experience.

With the third reading complete in the Senate the process shifted to the House of Commons for the bill's first reading on June 2, 2017. Then, due to time constraints, it was referred to the House of Commons Standing Committee on Indigenous and Northern Affairs (INAN) for discussion and expert oral and written submissions. During this time Mary Eberts called me and suggested I ask to be invited to speak, and I did. I was invited to speak on June 8 with Viviane Michel and Cynthia Smith of the QNW. Sharon Donna McIvor and Pamela Palmater also testified on the same day. After the experts testified on the importance of leaving the "6(1)a All the Way!" clauses intact, Bennett testified, arguing that Canada was not willing to move forward with the broader remedy clause intact because preliminary estimates are not reliable, yet she further blurted out that it is estimated that 80,000 to 2,000,000 individuals are potentially entitled through the clause. Many felt, and continue to feel to this day, that these numbers were a fear-mongering tactic, but really this did not matter because an economic rationale is no excuse for denying Indigenous women and their descendants their human rights. It was an interesting gathering of women, as Senator Sandra Lovelace Nicholas and Jeannette Corbiere Lavell arrived as well to listen to the oral submissions and discussions. Sharon, Sandra, Jeannette, and I held a press conference, organized by Senator McPhedran, stressing the need for Canada to remedy all the sex discrimination in the *Indian Act*. The only woman missing that day was Yvonne Bédard, but she was always on my mind. The bill was read a second time in the House of Commons on June 13.

On June 16, INAN reported on the matter in the House of Commons. It was argued they could not include the "6(1)a All the Way!" legal remedy because of the need to consult with First Nations bands and other special interest groups.[65] Of course this was a ridiculous position in that, again, second-stage consultations were promised in 1985 and 2011 and yet nothing came of them. But what is more, a right is a right. You do not consult on rights, let alone with First Nations who will argue they need more resources to accept new members. It was obvious to me that Canada was using exaggerated numbers, and for the most part male leadership, to obfuscate the issue of equality for Indigenous women and their descendants. It was becoming clear that Indigenous women were going to have to yet again face the perpetuation of sex discrimination even though the experts had yet again called for it to end. Again and again, repetition was failing us.

Then, on June 21—Aboriginal Day, of all days—the third reading took place in the House of Commons, where members of Parliament voted on the gutted version of Bill s-3. Miserably, the Liberal caucus unanimously voted to pass this version. This included the prime minister's entire so-called feminist cabinet. Minister of Justice Jody Wilson-Raybould and Minister of Indigenous and Northern Affairs Carolyn Bennett reneged on their previous positions, where they had advocated for a broader remedy. What is more, and even worse, the Minister for the Status of Women, Maryam Monsef, also voted for this gutted version of Bill s-3 that perpetuated sex discrimination against Indigenous women.[66] Whipping women into submission is hardly feminist. Then the House of Commons rose for the summer.[67] Then, after all this lengthy and intensive lobbying, and the call for Canada to remove all the sex discrimination in the *Indian Act* that went beyond narrow interpretations of court remedies that would once again fail to resolve all the issues, on June 22 the government representative in the Senate, Senator Peter Harder, stayed the debate on Bill s-3, An Act to Amend the *Indian Act*, punting the issue off to the fall and leaving Bill s-3 to do a limbo dance over the summer.

After Parliament reconvened in the fall, on November 9 Senator Lillian Eva Dyck conceded to the House of Commons version of Bill s-3. The concession was that Canada's position was not about *if* they would address the broader remedy called for and that the experts and the Senate were asking for, but rather about *when* they would address the remedy. As a result, the bill included the "6(1)a All the Way!" provisions that would eliminate all the sex discrimination against women and their pre-1985 descendants, and *once Canada agreed to them* no new legislation would be needed; all that would be required would be an order-in-council that proclaimed them as law. At this time Senator Dyck also argued that the Senate had exhausted all its power, meaning the senators had used all the tools they had in their toolbox. She further argued that Bill s-3 was not perfect, but if we tinkered around with it any more we could stand to lose this important gain. She stated, "I really suggest that the pressure be put on members of Parliament by groups like FAFIA, by Pamela Palmater, Sharon McIvor, Shelagh Day and the others. They need to take action because they have the power at the moment and we do not. So I would say let us pass this motion."[68]

In summary, Indigenous women and our allies rallied strong and hard— both the members of the Senate and the experts, including me, political icon Jeannette Corbiere Lavell, QNW president Viviane Michel, and ally Mary Eberts. Through our collective effort the legal remedy for the broader remedy contained within the "6(1)a All the Way!" clauses that could eliminate the 6(1)a–6(1)c hierarchy was written into Bill s-3, yet at the time not accepted as law. In the end, Bill s-3 gained royal assent on December 12, 2017. The beginning of the two-stage consultation process was announced on June 12, 2018. A requirement of Bill s-3 was a report on these consultations by June 12, 2019.

Credible Evidence, *Gehl* Clauses, and the *Gehl* Numbers

The Court of Appeal for Ontario determined that INAC can no longer default to assuming unknown and unstated fathers are non-Indian. Rather, INAC has to be reasonable and inclusive and look at all the credible evidence that surrounds the child's birth. This was my victory, and the *Gehl* clauses were birthed, which served to address some of the limitations in INAC's PoP.

Since the legislation came into force, some people have contacted me asking questions such as, "What was the relevant or credible evidence associated with your application?" While not determinative in all situations of unknown and thus unstated paternity, hopefully this list of items I extracted from the 2017 *Gehl v Canada* judgement is useful:

- My great-grandparents lived in the Golden Lake Reserve community.
- My grandmother lived in the Golden Lake Reserve community.
- My father was born in the Golden Lake Reserve community as was recorded on his registration of birth.
- My father was accepted by the Golden Lake Reserve community.
- My father lived in the Golden Lake Reserve community.
- My father's godfather was a prominent Elder from the Golden Lake Reserve community.
- There is no evidence that my father was excluded from the Golden Lake Reserve community.

While LOME and ALST had their own ideas and thoughts regarding the *Gehl* clauses that should be included in Bill S-3, Senator Murray Sinclair, a member of the APPA committee, crafted his own and it is these that ended up in the amended *Indian Act*. Mary Eberts and I would have preferred to review these clauses, but we did not have the opportunity. Instead, the first time we had the chance to hear and thus think about them was during the clause-by-clause session on May 17. Section 5 of the *Indian Act* was amended with the following two subsections:

Unknown or unstated parentage: (6) If a parent, grandparent or other ancestor of a person in respect of whom an application is made is unknown—or is unstated on a birth certificate that, if the parent, grandparent or other ancestor were named on it, would help to establish the person's entitlement to be registered—the Registrar shall, without being required to establish the identity of that parent, grandparent or other ancestor, determine, after considering all of the relevant evidence, whether that parent, grandparent or other ancestor is, was or would have been entitled to be registered.

In making the determination, the Registrar shall rely on any credible evidence that is presented by the applicant in support of the
application or that the Registrar otherwise has knowledge of and
shall draw from it every reasonable inference in favour of the person in respect of whom the application is made.

No presumption: (7) For greater certainty, if the identity of a parent, grandparent or other ancestor of an applicant is unknown or
unstated on a birth certificate, there is no presumption that this
parent, grandparent or other ancestor is not, was not or would not
have been entitled to be registered.[69]

In reviewing these clauses you will see that there is a shift in language from
unknown and unstated *paternity* to unknown or unstated *parentage*. This
shift broadens the issue to situations of an unknown and unstated mother,
grandmother, or great-grandmother. In adding this language Sinclair may
have made a good move. This language shift also broadens these clauses to
situations of unstated paternity when the man is known yet not listed because
of sexual violence and abuse. Keep in mind here that my case was about an
unknown and thus unstated paternity. Through the phrase "without being
required to establish the identity" these clauses also state that the parent does
not need to be named. Further, these clauses direct the INAC Registrar to rely
on *credible evidence* instead of insisting the parent be explicitly named on the
birth certificate or other documents such as an affidavit. The second clause
offers interpretive clarity on the first clause: that there is to be no presumption that the relative was not an Indian. While some people may think this
means no presumption of who the parent is or was in all cases, this is not so.
Through discussion with my lawyers I have come to realize that some credible evidence is required. This means the unknown or unstated parentage
clause only serves some situations where there is an unknown parent with
evidence of who the person may be or have been. In situations of a complete
unknown—such as in cases of rape by a complete stranger, gang rape by
strangers, or a situation when the victim is raped while she is unconscious—
these clauses fall well short.[70] The issue of absolute unknowns remains a
statutory shortcoming. It is for this reason that some people have suggested
the *Gehl* litigation outcome only modified INAC's PoP.

Regardless, in their joint expert report Clatworthy and Frideres agreed that the estimated number of births affected by INAC's unstated paternity policy, as of 2004, totalled over 60,000. While the majority of these people were relegated the lesser form of 6(2) status, 15,000 people were actually denied status. It is my thinking that through the *Gehl* clauses, now codified in the *Indian Act*, those relegated to 6(2) status, possibly 45,000 people (that is, 60,000 minus 15,000), could now be entitled to 6(1) status and 15,000 people could now be newly entitled to 6(2) status.[71]

What is more, we need to keep in mind that the Clatworthy and Frideres numbers only represent births up to 2004. As of 2017 the numbers would be much higher. Through extrapolating the Clatworthy and Frideres estimated numbers forward to 2017, it is my calculation that 77,000 people may be entitled to 6(1) status and as many as 25,000 people may be newly entitled to 6(2) status. What this means is that more than 100,000 births could be affected by the *Gehl* court victory. Moreover, these 77,000 individuals now entitled to 6(1) Indian status are also now entitled to pass on status to their children.

In sum, through the *Gehl* court victory a large number of section 6(2) people are now entitled to section 6(1) status, the stronger form of Indian status, where they will be able to pass on status to their children. Based on these newly entitled 6(1) individuals each having two children, and adding this number to the 25,000 now entitled to 6(2) status, through *Gehl* we could potentially see 179,000 new registrants. Furthermore, the number of new registrants will continue to change over time because the *Gehl* clauses prevent INAC from applying the assumption that all unknown and unstated fathers are non-Indian as defined by the *Indian Act*. My point here is that there is no finite known number that the *Gehl* clauses will protect from INAC's genocidal practice of eliminating registered Indians through a policy that targets Indigenous mothers and babies. Thus, even if it is true that my litigation served to only modify INAC's proof of paternity policy, these numbers are meaningful, especially, one would think, to Indigenous mothers and babies.

Honoured on Equality Day

Six months after the changes became law, on Equality Day, April 17, 2018, Senator Marilou McPhedran invited Sharon, Jeannette, and me into the Senate chamber gallery as she wanted to honour our efforts. At this time

I asked the good senator to include Yvonne Bédard, and she did. It would not be right to disenfranchise Yvonne. I relied on a new friend, Pamela Schreiner, as my escort because Nik had other responsibilities, and she made sure I arrived on time for the 2:00 p.m. introduction. The weather was bad and we barely made it in time, moving quickly through the two stages of security. Once we were seated in the gallery, and after other business had been addressed, McPhedran spoke:

> I rise today to pay tribute to six Indigenous women who have made their mark on Canada's history. These leaders made a name for themselves in Canada and internationally by speaking out against injustices in the *Indian Act*, some of which are still present today. These six Indigenous women, recognized today in the chamber, continue to advocate, stand up and fight for the rights of Indigenous women and their descendants under Canadian law. Senators, today is Equality Day, recognizing the significance of Canada's Constitution Act 1982 being brought home 36 years ago today, with its entrenched *Charter of Rights and Freedoms*. Through their perseverance and tenacious strength, the Indigenous Famous Six teach us how to uphold the truth and undo injustices perpetrated by some of our laws to this day. Some of us have asked why we named them the Famous Six. Well, colleagues, this is based on words of the visionary Famous Five feminists in the Persons Case that opened the Senate to women, honoured by the statues erected on Parliament Hill just metres away from our Senate entrance. The Indigenous Famous Six represent the movement for Indigenous women's equality using the law, starting in the 1970s with Ms. Jeannette Corbiere Lavell and Ms. Yvonne Bédard and Senator Sandra Lovelace Nicholas, and into the 1980s, 1990s and now, Dr. Sharon McIvor, Dr. Lynn Gehl and Senator Lillian Dyck.[72]

McPhedran continued, stating that this was a historic day because it brought together strong and devoted women to fight for justice and equality, not only for Indigenous women but for all Canadians. Then she invited all of the senators to room 160-S, where she co-hosted, along with Senators Serge Joyal, Kim Pate, Yvonne Boyer, and other members of Parliament, a "Famous Indigenous Six Celebration" reception. She asked the senators to join with Her Excellency Rosemary McCarney, the Canadian ambassador to the United Nations in Geneva. Ambassador McCarney, McPhedran continued, demonstrated leadership to promote peace and women's rights at the United Nations in Geneva and was a strong advocate in Canada for women and girls and their rights, as well as an ally to the Indigenous Famous Six women.[73]

Unfortunately, the bad weather prevented Jeannette from making it to the Senate gallery on time. We met up with her later in Senator McPhedran's office, where I had the incredible honour of introducing Jeannette to Yvonne Bédard; up until that time the two women had never met. It was a joyful time for me. Sharon was there, as was Mary. Unfortunately, Senator Dyck was out of the country at the time and so we missed her presence.

Summary and Closing Comments

*Lastly, Lynn understands all too well that children denied
mother love fail to become fully human. She argues it is
deplorable that Canada's policies, inherent in the Indian Act
past and present, continue to interfere with mother love.*
—Melodie McCullough, "A Biography of Lynn Gehl"

In the end, in my court case the court did not consider unstated and thus unknown paternity to be a *Charter* violation based on sex, race, and marital status, but rather determined that it was unreasonable through adminis-trative law. I had to listen and read carefully to understand how Canada was thinking and arguing against it being a *Charter* violation. Through this process I learned firsthand, and the hard way, about the limitations of the *Charter* in protecting my rights as an Indigenous woman. Although the *Charter* now codifies equality beyond formal equality, such as the adminis-tration of the law to be inclusive of substantive equality or what is inherent in the law, I learned that *Charter* rights are only individual rights. When making their arguments, DoJ lawyers atomized me from my parents and my ancestral lineage and thus the sex discrimination I faced. The DoJ argued that it was not my sex discrimination that I faced but rather it was my grand-mother's and my father's sex discrimination. That is, Canada argued that the *Charter* does not protect me from the sex discrimination that my grand-mother and my father experienced, which I inherited. Said another way, according to Canada, the sex discrimination was theirs (my kokomis's and father's), not mine.

This was a hard lesson for me, as I had thought the *Charter* was about protecting me both before and under, or what is inherent in, the law, more so than protecting me before the law and the mere administration of the law. I thought the *Charter* test would rely on more than a formal equality approach to human rights; that the *Charter* took a deeper substantive equality approach to human rights; and that the *Charter* was an improvement over the Canadian Bill of Rights in its protection before the law and under the law, versus just before the law. I was wrong—so completely wrong. Through *Gehl v Canada* I have learned that what is under the law remains limited or framed within my rights as an individual, as a single person, not my rights as I inherit them from my grandmother and my father. This, I think, is how the *Charter* failed to protect me: *Charter* rights are personal. While the *Charter* may protect substantive equality rights, this is limited to who we are only as individuals. The test for substantive equality violations does not move beyond what is a personal right. The test was too narrow to protect me from the genocide inherent in sex discrimination in the *Indian Act* that Canada imposed on my female ancestors. The *Charter* failed me, Canada's legal system failed me, humans failed me.

In ending this long discussion it is important for me to restate what exactly I accomplished in taking on this issue of INAC's unknown and unstated paternity policy. Succinctly, in 1985 INAC began the practice of assuming that all unknown fathers, who were thus also unstated, were non-Indian men. I called this INAC's unknown and unstated paternity policy, intending to stress absolute unknown paternity that is thus unstated. At the time, early on, I did not articulate or mean situations of paternity known yet unstated resulting from issues such as incest, or when a man refuses to sign his child's birth certificate. Regardless, without a doubt the creation of this INAC policy was diabolical in that it targeted young mothers, many of whom did not even have the legal right to consent to sex.

Eventually INAC posted online their unstated paternity policy for situations where a father is known yet for some reason his name and signature are not on the child's birth certificate. This INAC policy was inadequate in addressing the inherent issues, in that it only offered and encouraged mothers to amend the child's birth document or obtain statutory documents from the father's family members. The problem with this policy was that it did not address situations of absolute "unknown paternity and thus unstated paternity" such as in my case, where I did not know who my paternal grandfather was. Clearly, "unknown and thus unstated paternity" results in different issues than "known yet unstated paternity." While I lost at the lower court level because it was determined that unknowable paternity is not an enumerated or analogous ground as per section 15 of the *Charter*, I won at the appeal level when the court determined that through administrative law INAC was both unreasonable and exclusionary to my situation. It further ruled that in situations of "unknown and thus unstated paternity" INAC must consider circumstantial evidence around the child's birth.

I do realize a fine hair has been split here, and so I will say it in another way. While INAC had a policy to deal with "known yet unstated" fathers, through my court case INAC must now accept the reality that sometimes fathers are unknown and deal with it in a respectful and dignified way. In these situations, through the *Gehl* ruling, all credible evidence must be considered and INAC must not assume, in the presence of credible evidence, that the man is not entitled to registration as an Indian. *This is what I accomplished*. That said, within this accomplishment there is a huge caveat that I need to be clear about. In situations of a "complete unknown paternity," such as in cases of rape by a stranger, the *Gehl* clauses may very well fall short, and this issue of absolute "complete unknown paternity" remains a statutory shortcoming.

What is disturbing about my litigation process is that it was completely unnecessary and an abuse both of me and of Canada's court system. Fortunately, colonial genocide socialized me to be familiar with abuse. After the 2010 *McIvor* decision, in 2011 and 2012 INAC developed two small policy directives stating that in the event of an unknown and unstated paternity, INAC did *not* have the authority to determine a negative presumption of paternity, even where a successful protest was made, because the protest option was also removed from the *Indian Act*. Regardless of this reality, when I applied for registration in 1994, INAC denied me entitlement and then put me through twenty-two years of unnecessary litigation. These post-*McIvor* policy directives were discussed during the 2015 *Descheneaux* trial and fleshed out further in my court case as we were heading toward the Court of Appeal for Ontario.[74] It is clear to me that INAC and the DoJ failed to disclose these directives, breaking the rule of law in the process. Regardless, the Court of Appeal judges relied on administrative law to adjudicate my case, ignoring the new evidence. Then, to add to matters, these highly paid thinkers again failed to reason well and determined I was only entitled to 6(2) registration. I was completely abused by the wiindigo that is Canada's legal system. The wiindigo is the worst thing a human can do to another human being—in this case, the worst thing a human system can impose on mothers and their babies.

Of course, I have reflected on this process of abuse and failure to disclose evidence and have realized that what Canada did in 1985, either intentionally or mistakenly, was to open the Eastern Doorway wide, meaning all children of unknown and unstated paternity were entitled if their mother was entitled because INAC had no authority to deny them even in the event of a successful protest, an option that was repealed in 1985. The *Indian Act* was silent on this very matter; again, the post-*McIvor* directives were clear that INAC had no authority to deny these children. Despite this, at the level of internal departmental practice the INAC Registrar *was* denying these children and subsequently their descendants, including me. INAC employees abused their power and hid their intentions, their practices, and Canada's policy from public scrutiny. Then, what Canada's lawyers and policymakers did was manipulate me and my litigation process to narrow the Eastern Doorway they had left open. This is annoying, to say the least, in that, again, I was put through twenty-two years of unnecessary litigation. Regardless, I came along, did the work, found a string of lawyers who thought it was an important challenge, unfolded my National Strategy to Raise Awareness on Unknown and Unstated Paternity, and blew up INAC's secret for all to see. Through *Gehl v Canada*, INAC has been forced to reconcile with the reality that it is women who open the Eastern Doorway, forced to reconcile with Creator's law, and forced to reconcile with the truth of it. Creator's law will always trump human laws that pitiful patriarchs create, pitiful laws that women employees of the DoJ and politicians enforce. In harming Indigenous mothers and children, DoJ lawyers and Canadian politicians lack the morals needed to remind them that they are only human. This is what wiindigos do: devour morality, and teach women to follow men who are less than them.

What is more, I have come to think that Kimberly Murray, past executive director of ALST, was correct in 2001 when she framed the legal arguments as a section 15 *Charter* and section 35 Constitution violation against the Registrar's *practice and internal Department policy* of denying children of unknown and unstated paternity because, again, the *Indian Act* itself was silent on the matter. Regardless, this SoC was struck and the Court of Appeal for Ontario upheld this decision where we were *instructed to challenge* the *Indian Act* legislation. Yet, when we were in front of the Court of Appeal for Ontario again, some fifteen years later, the judges ruled at the *policy level*, albeit through administrative law and not *Charter* law, as we had initially framed our legal position. Many master judges watched and directed the *Gehl v Canada* challenge forward, yet apparently we took the wrong path. Or did we? I don't think I will ever know. But I suspect it was all about power as opposed to what was right.

Regardless, I am grateful that ALST took me on as a client even though changes in staff made the process more difficult. It was also harder owing to the fact that I did not have the funds to pay for this effort, as this made it harder for me to ask for the time I needed to understand the process. While some people may be tempted to blame my lawyers and me for the delay and dismissal, critical theory reminds us that financial barriers sit at the very core of challenging structural oppression. Potential critics need to remember, as Kimberly told me all those years ago, that I was up against the largest law firm in Canada, with a staff of 4,600 and a budget of over $600 million. Through its deep pockets, pilfered from my ancestral land, Canada spent over $1 million defending its horrid position in *Gehl v Canada*. My resources were crumbs in comparison.

Five months after the Court of Appeal for Ontario judgement, on September 29, 2017, ALST received a letter on my behalf. This INAC letter referred to my original protest letter dated March 16, 1995, in which I protested the omission of my name from the Indian Register. This new letter stated that, as a result of my section 14.3 appeal and the judgement flowing from that, I was now registered as an Indian in accordance with subsection 6(2) of the *Indian Act*. By this time, twenty-three years had passed since I had submitted my application to INAC. In November of 2017, I sent away for an application for First Nation Band membership with Pikwàkanagàn First Nation. I quickly filled it out and sent it in, and on December 13, 2017, the membership clerk informed me via a letter that I now met the criteria for Band membership.

It was on January 30, 1945, that my great-grandmother Annie Jane Meness was told she was no longer an Indian; seventy-two years later, I became an Indian. In November 1999 my kokomis died a registered Indian. In November 1988 my father died when I was in the early stages of this work. He died a homeless person, killed by a train in the city of Toronto. This is what happens when racism, sexism, and genocide converge and create barriers that prevent women from loving their children, and when racism, sexism, and genocide converge and take away the network of immediate family, extended family, and community relationships that once existed and that helped mothers and children move forward in a good way. I will always blame Canada and the men and women of the DoJ, the members of Parliament, and the prime ministers whose bent morals allow them to defend the genocide of Indigenous Peoples.

My mother passed in April 2014. On her deathbed she divulged that one of her children, a sibling of mine, had a different father. By this time, this was no surprise to me. I had been able to figure this out through reflection on past miserable events. When I think about it now, a glorious wrench would have been tossed into this effort had it been me who had a different biological father than my siblings, pointing out how pitiful human-made laws are.

I have come to understand this court process as a complete debacle, but I won anyway. While I was the only constant addressing the abusive power of Canada's judicial branch of Parliament, the *Gehl* judgement was also an ending for Nikolaus K. Gehl, Kimberly Murray, Amanda Driscoll, Christa Big Canoe, Emilie Lahaie, Mary Eberts, and so many other people who worked on *Gehl v Canada*. On April 20, 2017, Senator Murray Sinclair posted the following statement online:

> Congratulations are due to Dr. Lynn Gehl for her successful challenge of the Indian Registrar's refusal to allow her to be registered under the *Indian Act*. The refusal was based on the fact that because Lynn could not prove who her paternal grandfather was or that he was entitled to be registered she could not be registered. The Court of Appeal for Ontario found that requiring her to prove the unprovable (the name of her ancestor) was unreasonable and that there was circumstantial evidence showing that he was "likely" an Indian and a member of the community. On that basis she had established all she could or needed to, and it

was unreasonable of the Registrar to demand more. The majority of the judges declined to strike out the requirement as a breach of the equality rights provision of the *Charter*, because they didn't have to in order to rule in her favour. Good win Lynn![75]

Reading this was certainly an affirming moment for me, and I am appreciative of this recognition.

PART EIGHT

Some Final
Thoughts

Chapter 24

Defeating the Wiindigo

While this strategy may sound neat and altruistic in hindsight, in the moment I had to manage some very human emotions of fear, sadness, shock, and anger. My personal and professional support system was critical in helping me process my emotions, so that I could make the best decisions instead of acting on impulse.
—Cindy Blackstock, "The Complainant"

SHARON DONNA MCIVOR WAITED ALMOST TEN YEARS BEFORE, on January 11, 2019, the UNHRC released its ruling regarding the Sharon Donna McIvor and Charles Jacob Grismer petition on sex discrimination in the *Indian Act*, specifically, on the sex discrimination faced by descendants who traced their ancestry through matrilineal lineage versus patrilineal lineage. The UN committee argued that the provision in Bill s-3, known as the

Government's version of "6(1)(a) all the way," is an acknowledgement by the State party that the only effective remedy for the ongoing sex discrimination in section 6 of the *Indian Act* is one which accords full section 6(1)(a) status to all Indian women and their descendants born before 1985, on the same basis as Indian men and their descendants born prior to that year. Through these additional provisions, the State party has demonstrated that it knows how to fix the problem. The State party declares that the Government's version of "6(1)(a) all the way" means that all persons will be entitled to the same status as persons on the paternal line, no matter how many generations removed from the women who lost status upon marriage, and that both will have the same ability to transmit status. It appears that the intention of that amendment is to eliminate the sex-based hierarchy. If the Government's section "6(1)(a) all the way" amendment were brought into force, the authors would become entitled to section 6(1)(a) status at long last.[1]

While Canada continued to present arguments against the need to resolve the 6(1)a–6(1)c hierarchy issues, the UNHRC ruled in favour of McIvor, stating that

the State party is under an obligation to provide the authors with an effective remedy. This requires it to make full reparation to individuals whose Covenant rights have been violated. Accordingly, the State party is obligated, inter alia, (a) to ensure that section 6(1)(a) of the 1985 *Indian Act*, or of that Act as amended, is interpreted to allow registration by all persons including the authors who previously were not entitled to be registered under section 6(1)(a) solely as a result of preferential treatment accorded to Indian men over Indian women born prior to April 17, 1985, and to patrilineal descendants over matrilineal descendants, born prior to April 17, 1985; and (b) to take steps to address residual discrimination within First Nations communities arising from the legal discrimination based on sex in the *Indian Act*.[2]

On February 19, 2019, following this wonderful UN ruling, Senator Lillian Eva Dyck urged the government of Canada to sign an order-in-council and bring into force the remaining provisions of Bill s-3.[3] We still had work to do. Canada was ordered to comply with the United Nations ruling within 180 days. But the question remained, would Canada comply?

I was excited to have the opportunity to participate in a 2019 Indigenous Women's Symposium in the city of Peterborough, where I live. One of the organizers contacted me and asked if I would be willing to speak on a panel with my Indigenous sisters: Sharon Donna McIvor, Jeannette Corbiere Lavell, and Yvonne Bédard. Despite my joy, disenfranchisement is a bitch, especially when your sisters and so-called feminists are complicit....

On the second day of this event I attended a discussion because Gwen Brodsky and Mary Eberts, two lawyers who had been working on the issue of sex discrimination in the *Indian Act* for years, were speakers on the panel. Shelagh Day and Judy Rebick, two strong feminists, were also speaking on this panel. I wanted to listen to what they had to say, so I put on my best hat and bravest heart and off I went. After all, I had over thirty years invested in the struggle. During this panel discussion it became obvious that members were calling for more immediate community involvement. Shelagh was doing her best to stress the need to stand behind Sharon and her January 2019 United Nations decision, where the UN had ruled that Canada had to eliminate all the sex discrimination in the *Indian Act* and meet the demands of "6(1)a All the Way!" that we were calling for. While I certainly did not want to take a lead role, I felt I needed to further support Sharon and act on Shelagh's call.

During her talk Shelagh explained that Prime Minister Justin Trudeau needed to sign the order-in-council to enact the last sections that would bring the "6(1)a All the Way!" clauses of Bill s-3 into law. She stressed that it had to be done before Parliament's summer break because once Parliament came back, its members would move into election mode and thus be less likely to do it then. Shelagh further explained that cabinet members meet every Tuesday and that seventeen Tuesdays remained before the summer break on June 21. It was at this time, while sitting in the audience, that I realized I had to do something to help. Shelagh wanted it; actually, she seemed to be begging for people to act. Shelagh was doing her best to emote the need for action.

The panel featuring Sharon, Jeannette, Yvonne, and me as panellists, with Dawn Lavell Harvard, Jeannette's daughter, as the moderator, took place on the second evening of the symposium. Dawn began by asking Sharon the first question, but Sharon directed her to ask me first, as I had thus far been denied the opportunity to speak during the symposium. I had been disenfranchised. Dawn then directed the question to me, whereupon I began with my traditional opening, speaking in Anishinaabemowin. Then

I said I was grateful to be there and to have the opportunity to speak alongside my Indigenous sisters. Certainly, I continued, to have my contribution ignored would be an incredible experience of disenfranchisement, not only because of all the work I have done challenging the sex discrimination in the *Indian Act* but also because Peterborough is the city I had lived in for seventeen years.

Then I broke into a discussion of how I very much needed to say miigwetch to my partner, Nik Gehl, who was an invaluable support to the cause—even though he had been ignored the day before—and also miigwetch to the many community people and community organizations who had stood with me and behind me, such as Alice Olsen Williams, Lynne Porter, and Jim Abel of the Kawartha Truth and Reconciliation Support Group; Roy Brady of the Council of Canadians; Dorothy Boddy and Jill Jones of the Older Women's Network; Charmaine Magumbe of the Community and Race Relations Committee; and Melodie McCullough of *Journey Magazine*. In doing this I invoked the network and strength of community people who had worked with me outside of institutional power where racism, sexism, ableism, nepotism(!), and their intersectional effects thrive and thus serve to disenfranchise important knowledge holders and change makers. It was, in part, my goal to express to the two organizers of the symposium that they had underestimated me and the community support I have had in the work I do.

As the panel questions and answers moved along, I was asked, "What was your role in continuing to challenge the sex discrimination in the *Indian Act*?" This, I felt, was a bizarre question in that it was pretty obvious what my role was: the plaintiff on the matter of INAC's unknown and thus unstated paternity policy; an anticolonial theorist who created and developed the concept of the "Indigenous Famous Five"[4]—which morphed into the Canadian Feminist Alliance for International Action's "Indigenous Famous Six"—and the very "6(1)a All the Way!" concept that we were all rallying around; and a writer of possibly over 100 community-based news articles, blog posts, and posters published on the topic. Indeed, this was my very response. I further said that I was in the process of pitching to a publisher a new book on my work and effort. This is the book you have in your hands.

Returning to Shelagh's plea for community mobilization, I acted because I wanted to support Sharon. After the weekend symposium I decided it was best for me to remain objective regarding the larger goal we all had. I decided I would campaign outside of the office of the Minister of Women and Gender Equality, Maryam Monsef, every Tuesday until the parliamentary summer break. I had little choice as I wanted to support Sharon in real, concrete ways. So I took my silly sandwich board out of storage and painted "6(1)a All the Way!" on the back of it, and every Tuesday from noon to 1:00 p.m. I asked community members to join me in my protest and they did. My goal in doing this was to gain local and national media coverage as well as to do my best to make sure the issue remained in the consciousness of community members and Monsef herself. My last Tuesday protest was on June 18. Unfortunately, the summer break came and went without the prime minister issuing the order-in-council. Fortunately, the story does not end there.

The National Inquiry into Missing and Murdered Indigenous Women and Girls released its final report on June 3, 2019, and it firmly called for Canada to eliminate the sex discrimination in the *Indian Act*.[5] Then, on August 14, federal ethics commissioner Mario Dion ruled that Prime Minister Trudeau had violated the *Conflict of Interest Act* when he pressured former attorney general Jody Wilson-Raybould to halt the criminal prosecution of SNC-Lavalin.[6] Possibly feeling the heat within this broader political context, it was on August 15 that the prime minister issued the order-in-council enacting all the "6(1)a All the Way!" clauses into law, effectively eliminating all the sex discrimination that we all had worked so hard to end. In issuing the order-in-council Trudeau took Canada out of the Dark Ages—and did more for Indigenous women than any other prime minister had done—by doing something Indigenous women had been asking for for fifty years. After decades with Sharon as our leader, we finally defeated the wiindigo.

Afterwards, Shelagh Day was quoted as saying, "We welcome the coming into force of the final provisions of Bill s-3, which eliminate the 143 years of discriminatory treatment of First Nations women and their descendants. Finally, after a long struggle, First Nations women have achieved formal equality in the law."[7] However, this does not mean Indigenous women gained the substantive equality we need.

Chapter 25

I Danced and I Danced; My Heart Was Full

O NE DAY POSSIBLY THIRTY-FIVE YEARS AGO—WAY TOO MANY years ago—when I was in my twenties, Chief Robert Whiteduck of what was then called the Golden Lake Indian Reserve, now Pikwàkanagàn First Nation, asked me something like, "When will you go through the process and become registered as a Status Indian?" In doing that he reified within me, or made it real for me, that doing the work was my responsibility. There is a small part of me that wonders if he is aware that this was how I understood his question.

On August 15, 2019, thohahente, a Mohawk friend, came to my newly acquired home to gift me with an Eagle Feather. Having just had the house key placed in my hands, my mind and heart were slow in understanding what was happening. It was a ceremonial moment; thohahente told me the Eagle Feather was a gift, removed from his traditional headdress, to honour my work on the achievement of "6(1)a All the Way!" It turns out thohahente's grandmother had married a non-Indian man, and as a result she was a victim of Canada's genocide and enfranchised into white society. It was through Bill C-3, when the *Indian Act* was amended in 2011, that he and his mother became eligible for Indian status registration. Coming from this history of sex discrimination, thohahente was very aware of my work, was able to navigate through its contradictions, and valued my effort in real ways. Receiving the Eagle Feather from him was such an honour. I really value it and the social mirroring received through thohanente's recognition; this and the Eagle Feather were the much-needed medicine my soul ached for.

August 17, 2019, was another important day for me. A few weeks earlier, before I received the Eagle Feather, I had received a message from Wendy Jocko, an Algonquin Anishinaabe-kwe who served in the Canadian Forces, including two tours of duty in Bosnia and Croatia, a member of Pikwàkanagàn First Nation, my First Nation community.[1] She messaged me asking if I would like to be included in a special ceremony dedicated to honouring Indigenous Algonquin veterans at which our Algonquin ancestors would be honoured with what is known as a Canadian Aboriginal Veterans Millennium Medal.

I had heard about these medals—that they were special medals that veterans themselves or their descendants could request. At the time I was thinking I would like to have one to honour my great-grandfather Joseph Gagnon's service in World War I. I learned the medals are awarded to Aboriginal veterans of the Canadian Armed Forces, the Merchant Navy, and the RCMP, plus those who had joined the United States Forces in peace or war time. They are awarded to veterans who served prior to and inclusive of the year 2000. I also learned that their creation and delivery was a joint effort by the National Aboriginal Veterans Association (NAVA) and INAC.[2] Further, as Wendy stated, "The Aboriginal Veterans Millennium Medal was first issued at the unveiling of the National Aboriginal War Monument on the 21st of June 2001. At that time 2,500 medals were issued to eligible candidates."[3] When I learned the medals can be requested by anyone who meets the eligibility requirements, I quickly had a question: How do they determine that I am the right person to receive a medal on behalf of my great-grandfather? Probing with this question I learned that the application process would determine if the person requesting the medal was appropriate.

Eventually I came to understand that the process of awarding the medals is a way to carry the knowledge into the new millennium, specifically, the knowledge of what Indigenous veterans did for Canada. Regardless, once I learned there was a fee for the medals, I lost interest, and rightly so because

Canada has taken way too much away from me and my ancestors, such as our right to land, our right to define ourselves, and our right to mino-pima-diziwin. When Joseph came home from World War I he was denied the right to land that was preserved for settler Canadians. Actually, what is worse, he was rendered homeless when he was escorted out of his community. As Wendy offered during the ceremony, "It has been documented that Aboriginal veterans were treated poorly upon their return to Canada, with the government stripping them of their Indian status and often barring them from entering their reserves to visit family and friends. Unfortunately, some of our Algonquin Veterans were subject to this type of treatment. This had a devastating effect on the Veterans themselves and their families."[4]

Through the work I have done and continue to do I am well versed in the history of the treaty process and Algonquin denial: for instance, Canada's Parliament Buildings residing on our very lands; the long history of sex discrimination in the *Indian Act*; the continued destruction of our Algonquin Anishinaabe sacred places such as Akikpautik, which is a just a short walk from the Parliament Buildings; and how Canada's cultural genocide continues today. This lived reality is always in the forefront of my consciousness. Having said all this, when Wendy contacted me and told me that the Aboriginal Veterans Autochtones (AVA) and Pikwàkanagàn First Nation were organizing a ceremony where I could accept a medal on behalf of Joseph, I was grateful and said, "Yes, it would be my honour." I learned that the AVA and Pikwàkanagàn had purchased medals for several Algonquin veterans, of which I would be one of the recipients. I was a little concerned, though, because I had not been to the community in years. My political stance on many things, such as the genocide inherent in the land claim process and the long history of the sex discrimination in the *Indian Act*, made me a particular target for some people, and so for years I had lain low.

A few days after being contacted by Wendy I learned that two of my second cousins, sons of my kokomis's brother Gordon Gagnon, would be accepting Aboriginal Veterans Millennium Medals as well. Earl would accept on behalf of his father, Gordon, who had served in World War 2, and Bryce would be accepting a medal on his own behalf, as he was a member of the United Nations Peacekeeping Force in Cyprus. I was happy to learn this as it helped me cope with my responsibility of receiving a medal on behalf of my great-grandfather, a man who was also their grandfather. Following tradition, I quickly went out and purchased a new dress for such a special occasion. I opted for white linen speckled with beautiful butterflies. I almost went for a monochromatic blue but decided I wanted to celebrate my mythological reality that values the natural world we share with the other beings. My shoes were red and my tote was a gift from Barbara Manitowabi.

What was really wonderful about this ceremony was that Wendy, the officiate, arranged for the recipients to sit in alphabetical order, and as a result I was able to sit beside my cousins: them being Gagnons and me as the Gehl I now am (I took Nik's name when we were married). During the ceremony, recipients were informed that they could indeed dance wearing the medal on behalf of whom it was for. I was happy that I could dance with this medal and with my cousins too. Dancing is an Anishinaabe method or practice of embodying knowledge, personifying knowledge, and celebrating knowledge; dancing is spiritual. I proudly danced wearing the medal pinned to my new dress, holding the Eagle Feather that thohahente honoured me with and with my cousins at my side. Unfortunately, while dancing I bumped into Bryce more often than I would have liked; I had to explain later that I am blind in terms of knowing what or who is to my right. Dancing with us was the Chief of Pikwàkanagàn, Chief Kirby Whiteduck, who accepted an award on behalf of John Baptiste "Jack" Whiteduck, and past Chief Robert Whiteduck, who accepted a medal on behalf of Joseph Whiteduck. Kirby and Robert are the great nephews of these veterans and they are also my third cousins, in that their mother, Anna, was my kokomis's cousin. Their participation made the ceremony and dancing even more meaningful. Moreover, I had the opportunity to meet the child (Wayne), grandchildren (Chris and Charlene), and great-grandchild (Allycia) of one of my kokomis's other brothers, Kenneth Gagnon.

While more veterans would be honoured in the future, on this particular day the Aboriginal Veteran Millennium Medal was posthumously awarded to the following veterans: Arthur Earl Benoit, Glen William Benoit, Michael James Joseph Benoit, Teddy Francis Benoit, Anthony Sylvester Bernard, Marion Closter, Don Cooco, Edward Cooco (Lindsay), James Cooco (Cooke), John Cooco, Gordon Gagne (also Gagnon), Joseph Gagnon (also Gagne), Jocko Joseph James Lamure, James S. Lavalley, Mathew Lavalley, Esmond Peter Meness, Joseph Meness, Wallace Meness, Stanley Sarazin, Walter Sarazin, John Baptiste Whiteduck, and Joseph Whiteduck. The

Aboriginal Veteran Millennium Medal was also awarded to living veterans Bryce Gagnon, Frank Wilfred Lavalley, and Roger Meness.

In some ways this experience was very much like a "coming home" ceremony that Pamela Palmater talks about: a ceremony that welcomes the descendants of Indigenous Peoples who were turned into white people through racist and sexist colonial laws, policies, and practices.[5] I danced and will continue to dance when I can.

Morals before Knowledge

I N THE ANISHINAABE TRADITION THE COLOUR BLACK IS VALUED. The colour black reminds us to respect the unknown and to understand that all knowledge cannot be known to humans. While I value the deep meaning in this teaching—that being that we need to respect human limitations and that sometimes the paternity of a child cannot be known—the manipulation of truth through power represents wiindigo psychosis. Without a doubt, Canada's legal system is the manifestation of the worst thing a human can do to another human, in particular, to Indigenous babies.

Someone once asked me, "Do you think truth must come before wellness and movement forward can begin?" This is a good question to ponder. Having reflected on my determination to get to the truth of things in *Gehl v Canada*, I have come to realize that sometimes you can never know the truth. What I mean by this is that there are some people who will never admit that what they did was wrong. In these situations the truth seeker is left feeling further disenfranchised in what it is they feel and know, because for whatever reason they did not receive a truthful person at the other end. In this way the search for truth actually causes more harm, sadness, despair, and depression.

In terms of my journey to gain truth from Canada, the Department of Indian and Northern Affairs Canada, and the Department of Justice, this too ended poorly. The legal system, as a process of getting at the truth, had me navigate through the Oral Tradition, the archives, INAC, and Canada's court system. This process lasted thirty-two years. The court process, rooted in and framed by the methodology and methods inherent in legal positivism, proved to be miserably inadequate as a truthing process. Throughout the process I was met with the resources and power inherent in the Crown's deep pockets: a team of well-paid lawyers (women, no less) trained to argue in such a way as to win at any cost, even at the cost of tossing their morals, if they had any in the first place, to the ground; a context where it was acceptable for settler women to argue against the human rights of the more oppressed Indigenous women and children; and a place where it was acceptable to break the rule of law, such as by not producing evidence so that the truth can be known. In this context, power prevented truth from emerging. It is my thought that the methodology of legal positivism and the power inherent extracted the morality needed in seeking truth, and this is what proved to fail me in my process.

It was naïve of me to think an objective truth is out there and can be achieved through fairness and reason, particularly from settler women who are willing to walk away from natural law and the moral teachings humans need to remain and manifest the good human beings Creator wants us to be. Today I know all too well that cultural genocide, power, and deep pockets mediate and spoil the truthing process of Canada's legal system. Actually, today I know that Canada's legal system is a tool of genocide. It is the wiin-digo personified.

So, back to the question, "Do you think truth must come before well-ness and movement forward can begin?" No, I do not. Not at all. Foremost, wellness is a relationship you have with other people. What I mean by this is that the person seeking truth and wellness should find good, intelligent, and moral friendships and relationships that are carefully chosen. What I needed was someone to affirm the experiences of racism, classism, sexism, and ableism that I faced and, for that matter, continually face every single day. I needed someone who understood the dangers of structural oppres-sion, so much so that they would and could listen attentively and affirm what I was telling them about how I was feeling and living—to listen in a good way. I have learned that truth and wellness are about relationships of affirmation and good social mirroring because truth is not an absolute, objective, singular entity void of the corruption of power. Sometimes you can never know the truth, and seeking it will only make you fall deeper into despair. This is my debwewin.

Truth is located in morality. But in its human form truth can become corrupted when heartless people extract morals from who they are as human beings. In my life's journey I have learned that while morals come before knowledge, humans can and will extract them to be right or because it is how they make a living. As such, I have come to know that truth and wellness are best explored and valued in good, moral, and affirming intelligent relationships. This is my debwewin.

Lastly, on October 25, 2019, INAC notified me, via email, that my Indian status registration category had been upgraded from 6(2) to 6(1)a.3. Now my many nieces and nephews, the next generation, and many other Indigenous People can become registered as Status Indians if they so choose.

Timeline of *Gehl v Canada*

Pre-2001

1865   Birth of my great-great-grandmother Angeline Jocko.

Aug 1882   Birth of my great-great-grandmother's nephew Paul Lee Jocko.

Apr 1890   Birth of my great-grandfather Joseph Gagnon Jr.

Jan 1891   Birth of my great-grandmother Annie Jane Meness.

Sep 1910   Marriage of Joseph Gagnon and Annie Jane Meness.

May 1911   Birth of my kokomis Mary Viola Bernadette Gagnon.

May 1916   Joseph Gagnon Jr. joins the Canadian military, serving in WWI.

Jan 1919   Joseph Gagnon Jr. demobilized from Canadian military.

Late 1920s Joseph Gagnon Jr. and Annie Jane Meness escorted out of their
            community. They are deemed white people.

Dec 1934   Paul Lee Jocko's birth registered (delayed).

May 1935   Birth of my father Rodney Peter Gagnon.

Jan 1945   Indian agent H. P. Ruddy sends letter to Annie Jane Meness
            informing her that she is now a white woman.

1960   The Canadian Bill of Rights enacted.

May 1962   Birth of Lynn Gehl.

1973   Jeannette Corbiere Lavell/Yvonne Bédard SCC decision. They lose.

1982	Canada repatriates the Constitution adding the *Charter of Rights and Freedoms*.
1985	The *Indian Act* is amended through Bill C-31 to bring it in line with the *Charter*. It fails to address all situations of sex discrimination and creates new forms of sex discrimination: first, the sex discrimination inherent in the 6(1)a–6(1)c hierarchy; second, the cousins and siblings issue; and third, the matter of unknown and unstated paternity.
1985–94	My family oral research and archival research takes place.
Nov 1988	Rodney Peter Gagnon passes away.
Feb 1990	My first contact with INAC.
Jul 1990	Annie Jane and Mary Viola are deemed 6(1)c and 6(2), respectively. Additional archival research is needed to prove both of Mary Viola's parents were Indian so she is able to pass on Indian status to my father.
Dec 1993	My first contact with ALST.
Nov 1994	Although I do not know the exact date, through archival research I find Paul Lee Jocko's birth registration record signed by my great-great-grandmother Angeline Jocko. Through this document, which links my great-grandfather Joseph Gagnon to his Indigenous ancestry and his Indian rights, Mary Viola is upgraded to a 6(1)f. An uncle, a half-brother to my father, applies for registration for himself, his brother, and me.
Feb 1995	As a result of Mary Viola being upgraded to 6(1)f my father is posthumously entitled to Indian status and his half-brothers are also now entitled. The INAC Registrar denies me registration because of an unknown and thus unstated paternity in my lineage. I do not know who my paternal grandfather is.
Mar 1995	I protest the INAC Registrar's decision.
Feb 1997	The INAC Registrar informs me that my name was correctly omitted. I have the opportunity to a second protest.
May 1997	ALST submits second protest with INAC and files a notice of constitutional question.
1998	ALST files a statutory appeal, which is held in abeyance.
Apr 1998	INAC argues it did not violate the *Charter*.

Oct 1998   ALST files notice of appeal with the Ontario court, pursuant to
            section 14.3(1)(b) and 14.3(5)(a.1) of the *Indian Act*. The argument
            is that Lynn Gehl and Rodney Gagnon are both entitled to 6(1)a
            registration.

Aug 1999   ALST applies for funding from the Court Challenges Program of
            Canada as well as INAC's Test Case Funding Program.

Sep 1999   INAC denies us funding.

Nov 1999   Mary Viola Bernadette Gagnon passes away.

Dec 1999   CCPC denies me funding but suggests we reframe our application and
            resubmit the request.

Feb 2000   CCPC approves $50,000 in funding.

2001

May   SoC is filed: *Gehl v Her Majesty The Queen*. The challenge is based
            on section 35 of the Constitution Act and section 15 of the *Charter*.
            Kimberly Murray of ALST asks for compensation as per section 24(1)
            of the *Charter*. Damages are set at $1.2 million. It is argued that as a
            result of INAC's bad faith I have suffered and continue to suffer. The
            case is selected for management by a master as this will prevent INAC
            and the DoJ from delaying.

Jun 26   Murray of ALST responds to an informal motion. ALST refuses to
            change SoC to include a challenge to section 14.2(4) of the *Indian
            Act*. ALST is of the view that the negative presumption of paternity
            is not authorized by the *Indian Act*. Rather, the *Charter* challenge
            is with respect to a government practice, not a statutory provision.
            Section 14.2(4) of the *Indian Act* applies at the protest stage and has
            nothing to do with the negative presumption that applies during the
            application stage. ALST proposes an over-the-counter motion be filed
            amending the SoC as follows: substituting the Attorney General of
            Canada for Her Majesty the Queen.

October   The DoJ motions to strike SoC arguing there is no basis to challenge
            an administrative decision taken by the INAC Registrar. The court
            hears motion to strike.

November   The Ontario Superior Court (Justice Swinton) ruled in Canada's
            favour. ALST appeals this decision.

2002

September   The Ontario Court of Appeal upholds the lower court decision. We are given leave by the court to refile the SoC as a challenge to the *Indian Act*.

October   ALST files second SoC challenging the registration provisions of the *Indian Act*.

November   My case is again managed by a master. The possibility of compartmentalizing the legal issues is discussed, meaning addressing the section 15 *Charter* claim apart from the section 35 Aboriginal rights claim.

December   SoD is submitted.

2003

April   I am told the next step is a case management appointment to set a time table for discoveries. The DoJ lawyers say they need more time because they have found more boxes of documents re: Bill C-31.

June   INAC discloses an internal draft proof of paternity (PoP) policy to ALST.

August   ALST amends the SoC. I don't know why or how.

September   The DoJ sends ALST a letter saying they received the amended SoC and they ask for particulars.

2004

May   The DoJ amends the SoD. I don't know how or why.

August   I complete my MA.

September   I begin a PhD program.

2005

May   Murray of ALST says discoveries are set for January to March 2006. She suggests we will not go to trial until the end of 2006 or beginning of 2007.

June   At the request of the Law Society of Upper Canada I speak as a panel member regarding sex discrimination in the *Indian Act*.

Jun 28   NWAC and QNW organize a protest walk to Parliament Hill regarding the continued sex discrimination in the *Indian Act*. Senators Lillian

Eva Dyck and Sandra Lovelace Nicolas as well as Jeannette Corbiere Lavell and her daughter and grandchildren, attend.

2006

Discovery/Production period. ALST receives more than 7,000 documents. I do not read them.

March   My case is no longer managed by Master Dash. At this time my case is proceeding by action with damages under 24(1). ALST will speak to the DoJ about switching action to an application. This means we will not have to deal with the documents that INAC/DoJ dumped on ALST; instead, affidavits will be relied upon. Also, we would proceed on the section 15 *Charter* arguments only and not the section 35 Constitution Aboriginal Rights argument because I am told it cannot be done on an application. Converting to an application would also eliminate awarding of damages.

May   Both parties agree to switching case from an action to an application. Justice Campbell proposes we schedule a motion to determine a legal issue: separating *Charter* rights from Constitution rights. He gives us leave to schedule SJM and leave to rely on affidavits and viva voce witnesses. The SJM is set for ten days in June 2007.

Nov 4   Pursuant to the agreed timeline, Pikwàkanagàn First Nation Chief Kirby Whiteduck and I provide evidence by affidavit.

2007

March   Amy Briton-Cox of ALST has a teleconference with the DoJ and Justice Belobaba, the new judge assigned to hear the case. Wanting to keep the hearing streamlined, he suggests we not call viva voce witnesses. This way my affidavit and cross-examination will be before the court and I will not have to testify.

April   The DoJ provides six affidavits.

June   Coming out of so-called British Columbia, Sharon Donna McIvor court judgement is released. The judge orders the elimination of all the sex discrimination inherent in the 6(1)a–6(1)c hierarchy.

ALST cross-examines INAC witnesses: John Paul Fournier, Bonnie Tolstoy, Allan Tallman, Marion Amos, and Linda McLenachan.

We were unable to meet the dates for the sjm hearing because of two factors: (1) the DoJ's delay in getting its affidavit evidence; (2) ALST's difficulty in locating an expert on Indigenous demography. The hearing is rescheduled for January 2008.

July   Canada appeals *McIvor* decision.

Sep 13   I am cross-examined regarding my affidavit two days after submitting the first draft of my doctoral dissertation. In attendance for the plaintiff: Kimberly R. Murray, Mandy Eason, Lori Mishibinijima, and Nikolaus K. Gehl. In attendance for the defendant: Dale L. Yurka, Gail E. Sinclair, and Catherine Phillips.

Sep 14   The DoJ cross-examines Kirby Whiteduck regarding his affidavit.

December   The DoJ's expert report by Stewart Clatworthy is submitted.

2008

March   In addition to demographer James Frideres, ALST continues to seek a second expert on unknown and unstated paternity.

2009

Stéphane Descheneaux, Susan Yantha, and Tammy Yantha file SoC in the Quebec Superior Court. The case addresses sex discrimination in the *Indian Act* in terms of cousins and siblings.

April   Court of Appeal narrows *McIvor* judgement, thus leaving the sex discrimination inherent in 6(1)a–6(1)c hierarchy intact. The court only addresses the discrimination in situations of the double-mother clause, which is a narrow remedy.

August   The DoJ advises ALST that information from the INAC Registrar relied upon by Clatworthy was incorrect. Therefore, he has to revise his expert report.

My SoC requires amending. I don't know why or how.

November   ALST has a conference call with the DoJ regarding particularization to my SoC that section 6 of the *Indian Act* violates the equality provisions of the *Charter*. It discriminates against applicants whose ancestors are born out of wedlock or who do not know their own or their ancestor's paternity. ASLT is also proposing to amend the SoC to request a declaration that my father be entitled to be registered pursuant to section 6(1)a. Maybe this means ALST is no longer arguing that I too am entitled to 6(1)a? I really do not know what this is about.

2010

Feb 16   ALST files the amended amended SoC. The DoJ consented to the proposed changes. Again, I don't know the details.

Mar 22   Amended amended SoD is submitted. Again, I don't know all the details.

March   ALST receives revised Clatworthy expert report.

April   Kimberly Murray leaves ALST. Mandy Eason takes over my file until she leaves shortly after.

May   I complete the PhD program.

Jun 1   During the Marche AMUN protest I create the slogan "6(1)a All the Way!"

          ALST appears in court to provide a status hearing update. I do not remember the name of the lawyer who did this on my behalf.

September SoC is amended, again I am not sure why, how, or by whom. Turning to social media I begin my public process to raise awareness regarding unknown and unstated paternity.

          ALST expert report from Frideres is due; however, it is delayed.

November   McIvor's lawyer files a petition with the United Nations because Canada refuses to address all the sex discrimination in the *Indian Act*.

          Frideres's expert report is submitted. We receive a draft but I am told it requires revisions.

2011

          Via the *McIvor* decision the *Indian Act* is amended through Bill C-3 leaving much of the sex discrimination inherent in the 6(1)a–6(1)c intact. Canada argues it needed to have a second-stage consultation process.

Jan 31   Frideres's final expert report is submitted to ALST.

March   ALST, continuing to look for another expert, approaches Michelle M. Mann. She agrees. Karen Spector of ALST is now working on my file and we are striving for the October 31, 2011, deadline for the SJM.

April   Mann's expert report is submitted to ALST.

May	Crista Big Canoe is hired by ALST and takes over the "Gehl file."
August	The DoJ opposes Mann's expert report. The DoJ suggests that experts Clatworthy and Frideres meet to narrow the issues.
October	More DoJ discussion about the need for the experts to meet.
November	Now I am told that Frideres requires Clatworthy's code, because his method of analysis regarding his projection of unstated paternity cases is unclear. Also, the DoJ is not happy that Mann is not a demographer and thus continues to oppose her expert report.

Big Canoe of ALST informs the DoJ that we are not willing to deal with more delays regarding the experts. Having experts meet is off the table. The DoJ continues to suggest a conference between the expert witnesses. ALST advises the DoJ that we want a timeline in moving forward or we will ask for a case management meeting.

Although considering it, ALST has not yet formally waived viva voce evidence.

2012

INAC posts its unstated paternity policy online. It fails to address situations of unknown paternity.

March	ALST believes there is no need for me to do viva voce as my SoC and affidavit are strong and it is best to have Mann do viva voce as she contextualizes social-cultural issues. Yet the DoJ will not consent to Mann's report or her viva voce testimony.

The DoJ points to justifiable discrimination as costs alone can meet the criterion for a section 1 *Charter* waive, meaning the sex discrimination is justified.

April	We begin canvassing for court dates.
Nov 1	ALST is notified that the *Gehl* case is ordered dismissed with costs due to delays.
Nov 16	The DoJ consents to ALST notice of motion to set aside the order dismissing the action.
Nov 19	The notice of motion is drafted, arguing that (1) a dismissal would deny me access to justice and (2) council for the plaintiff and defendant have been making efforts in good faith to determine a mutually agreeable time frame and date for SJM.

Nov 26   The court hears the motion. I do not attend. On reading the materials
            and joint submissions the court determines the order dismissing the
            case for delay be set aside. The court orders parties to appear before
            the scheduling motion court to set an SJM hearing date.

2013

January   Master Graham requests a deadline by which the case shall be set down.

Apr 24   ALST receives another revised Clatworthy expert report.

May 10   Big Canoe and Darcy Delisle of ALST attend motion scheduling court
            to set the SJM hearing. The date is established: May 26–28, 2014.
            The judge also sets a date for viva voce evidence by the two experts:
            October 15–16, 2013.

Sep 26   Expert conferencing takes place for the purpose of a joint statement.
            Frideres says Clatworthy's numbers are too high for the section 1
            waive of the *Charter* justification argument. Clatworthy says
            Frideres's numbers are too low.

October   I initiate an online petition to raise awareness and disseminate
            information about my court case. I also create the construct of the
            "Indigenous Famous Five" as a way to give the matter more currency
            in the public.

2014

            I publish my doctoral dissertation in book form.

April   Andrée Good, my mother, passes away.

Ontario Superior Court Time Crunch

April   Expert viva voce evidence is officially cancelled due to a joint expert
            statement.

            We lose the May date for SJM. I am told the court dates were not
            registered in the computer system. Amanda Driscoll of ALST confirms
            new dates: October 20–22, 2014.

May   ALST files the notice of motion for the hearing. This sets out the
            general arguments. The more substantive arguments will be in our
            factum. The joint motion record (JMR) is being compiled. ALST
            anticipates the DoJ will provide it by June 15 so we have time to
            review it before our factum is filed on June 30.

Jun 15　　　The JMR due; however, it is late. I do not know why.

Jun 30　　　The JMR is complete. I am told the volume of documents is over
　　　　　　7,000 pages. I do not read them.

　　　　　　Driscoll of ALST informs me our factum is late but we received a two-
　　　　　　week extension. It will be completed and filed July 15. The DoJ will
　　　　　　have until September 30 to file its factum.

Jul 15　　　ALST completes our factum.

Sep 30　　　The DoJ's factum is due, but due to sickness they ask for an extension
　　　　　　to October 14. ALST agrees to an extension but only to October 8.
　　　　　　The DoJ files a motion to adjourn the SJM.

Oct 3　　　　Hearing date regarding the DoJ's attempt to adjourn the SJM. ALST
　　　　　　is concerned that there will be no court time in 2014 if the delay is
　　　　　　too lengthy, but if by some chance there is time in November 2014
　　　　　　then we may soften our position. The judge refuses adjournment and
　　　　　　instructs the DoJ to provide its factum by 2:00 p.m. on October 10.

Oct 10　　　Joint Book of Authorities is complete.

Oct 20–22　 SJM hearing in Toronto with the Honourable Elizabeth M. Stewart
　　　　　　presiding.

2015

New Evidence / Court of Appeal Time Crunch

January　　 In Quebec, INAC employee Linda McLenachan testifies in
　　　　　　Descheneaux. This testimony is significant to my case. Mary Eberts of
　　　　　　LOME is present.

Jun 2　　　 Justice Stewart renders her decision in my case. I lost! She argues
　　　　　　that all applications are treated the same, and therefore no race or sex
　　　　　　discrimination exists. We appeal.

July　　　　Mary Eberts of LOME sheds more information about evidence that
　　　　　　emerged from McLenachan's testimony, specifically the post-*McIvor*
　　　　　　directive policy shift in situations of unknown and unstated paternity.

Jul 3　　　　ALST files appeal arguing three errors of law. Our materials are due
　　　　　　December 2015.

August　　　Judgement in *Descheneaux* comes out. Descheneaux, Yantha, and
　　　　　　Yantha win on the cousins and siblings issue. Judge Masse gives
　　　　　　Canada eighteen months, until February 3, 2017, to remedy the issues.

Aug 11   ALST and LOME order McLenachan's testimony transcript.

September   Canada, under the guidance of Prime Minister Stephen Harper, appeals the *Descheneaux* judgement.

Sep 4   ALST and LOME receive McLenachan's testimony transcript and learn about *two* post-*McIvor* policy directives.

Sep 23   ALST and LOME request the two post-*McIvor* policy directives from INAC/DoJ.

Oct 1   Mary Eberts of LOME becomes lead council on *Gehl v Canada*. There is some discussion about scheduling the Court of Appeal as LOME and ALST require the two post-*McIvor* policy directives, yet INAC/DoJ are not cooperating. Our materials are now due January 8, 2016, with the DoJ materials due March 7, 2016.

2016

Jan 7   LOME and ALST once again request the post-*McIvor* policy directives and receive *one* of these directives at the end of the day. *It is date-stamped January 10, 2012, well before my court date in October 2014.* LOME and ALST request the other directive; however, INAC/DoJ are stalling.

Jan 8   LOME and ALST were to submit materials to the Court of Appeal today. Big Canoe of ALST tells me they asked for a second extension because of the reluctance of INAC/DoJ to provide the second directive. Through a fresh evidence motion research process, a 2011 internal memorandum surfaces. ALST requires additional knowledge about this, as it is a guide regarding matters of unknown and unstated paternity. ALST and LOME are expecting the evidence on January 22.

Jan 22   The DoJ sends a letter to LOME and ALST and a second INAC policy directive. *It is date-stamped June 13, 2011, well before my court date in October 2014.* Although date-stamped to an earlier date this is a second policy directive regarding how INAC determines non-Indian paternity issues. According to the DoJ the first policy directive sent on January 7, 2016, was the incorrect directive.

Jan 23   LOME and ALST ask the DoJ what policy, approved or not, formal or informal, existed between 2007 and 2011 as they are not satisfied the DoJ met its undertaking in respect to this issue. LOME and ALST request a new schedule be established before February 5, 2016. I am not sure if additional evidence arrives.

February	Upon being elected prime minister, Justin Trudeau drops the appeal regarding the *Descheneaux* decision.
Feb 8	Emilie Nicole Lahaie of ALST informs me that the new schedule for LOME and ALST to submit our factum is May 13, 2016, and the DoJ has until July 29, 2016 to submit its response. This is agreed on to provide time to request a case management meeting and produce a factum that considers all the new evidence.
Mar 17	ALST sends me a copy of the letter regarding the case management meeting. We are denied but it is suggested that we file a motion of new evidence.
May	ALST files a motion for new evidence.
May 13	ALST informs me we did not meet the deadline to submit our appeal factum. It is now due on June 13. I am told that an order from Justice Stewart was missing.
June	Regarding Bill S-3 the Liberal government begins speaking about a two-stage approach to resolving the broader sex discrimination inherent in the 6(1)a–6(1)c hierarchy. This is nonsense as it was also promised in 2010 after the *McIvor* decision.
Jun 13	Our factum of appeal is submitted.
Jun 15	Because of our delay the DoJ's new deadline to submit its factum is September 16, 2016.
Jul 12	We hear from the Court of Appeal. Our court date is set for December 20, 2016. LEAF is filing for intervener status.
Aug 9	The DoJ asks for an extension until November 4 to submit its factum, leaving the December 20 court date as is.
	Suddenly, the two senior DoJ lawyers, Dale Yurka and Gail Sinclair, who have been on the case since at least 2004, are changed. Through this move they will not have to answer to the failure to disclose evidence. The DoJ's new counsel is Christine Mohr and Andrea Bourke.
	LOME and ALST discuss INAC's announcement to amend the *Indian Act* through Bill S-3. ALST and LOME request an invitation to testify and make a submission. It is suggested I do the same.
Aug 12	Big Canoe of ALST calls and tells me about her discussions with the DoJ. She tells them they could have a two-week extension to September 30, not November 4 as requested. ALST thinks this is a

better option than having to contend with a motion and a potential change of court date. The DoJ requests to submit the materials regarding our motion for new evidence on October 14. ALST and LOME agree to this.

September LEAF gains intervener status.

Sep 12 ALST completes motion and affidavit of new evidence for Court of Appeal.

Oct 24 LEAF files its factum.

Bill s-3 Moves through the Senate and House of Commons

Oct 25 The first reading of Bill s-3 takes place in the Senate. Advocates such as McIvor, Corbiere Lavell, and Descheneaux are not happy that this bill continues to keep much of the sex discrimination intact.

Nov 17 Second reading of Bill s-3 takes place in the Senate. Advocates, me included, are not happy.

Nov 30 During Senate testimony, Minister of Crown-Indigenous Relations Carolyn Bennett says she is embarrassed about the poor handling of Bill s-3.

December Senator Lillian Eva Dyck, chair of the Standing Senate Committee on Aboriginal Peoples, refuses to pass Bill s-3 on to third reading in the Senate.

Dec 20 My case is heard in the Court of Appeal. Big Canoe of ALST and Eberts of LOME present their arguments. LEAF makes arguments as well. Junior DoJ lawyers Christine Mohr and Andrea Bourke present their arguments, while senior DoJ lawyer Dale L. Yurka is seated in the gallery observing the outcome of a case she worked on for many years.

2017

January The Liberal government requests more time to consult on Bill s-3 and the court grants six extra months through to July 2017.

Apr 20 *Gehl* Court of Appeal judgement is released. Through administrative law, I win. The INAC Registrar has to be reasonable. While I win, I also lose. The ruling provides me with only 6(2) status. This means the sex discrimination inherent in the 6(1)a–6(1)c hierarchy limits me to 6(2) status.

May 16   I offer oral and written testimony to the Standing Senate Committee on Aboriginal Peoples. Many are surprised about my victory because Bennett is arguing that Bill s-3 addresses all known sex discrimination.

May 17   Clause-by-clause reading of Bill s-3 takes place in the Standing Senate Committee on Aboriginal Peoples. Senator Murray Sinclair drops one of the *Gehl* clauses. All senators, except for Sinclair, accept the "6(1)a All the Way!" clauses.

Jun 1   Bill s-3 third reading takes place in the Senate and unanimously passes with the "6(1)a All the Way!" clauses intact. During this time a friendly amendment is made adding the second *Gehl* clause previously dropped.

Jun 2   First reading of Bill s-3 in the House of Commons.

Jun 8   I offer oral and written testimony to the House of Commons Standing Committee on Indigenous and Northern Affairs. Bennett testifies the same day claiming the "6(1)a All the Way!" clauses could potentially add between 80,000 and 2,000,000 Status Indians. She exaggerates.

Jun 13   Second reading of Bill s-3 in the House of Commons.

Jun 16   The House of Commons Standing Committee on Indigenous and Northern Affairs Canada determines it cannot include the "6(1)a All the Way!" clauses without consultations.

Jun 21   Third reading of Bill s-3 in the House of Commons. Bill passes without the "6(1)a All the Way!" clauses enacted, but they remain in the text of the bill. The government representative in the Senate, Peter Harder, stays further debate until the fall.

Nov 9   Senator Dyck concedes to the House of Commons on Bill s-3 as she does not want to risk the removal of the dormant "6(1)a All the Way!" clauses. She urges the advocates to continue.

Dec 12   Bill s-3 receives royal assent and becomes law. Again, this version of the *Indian Act* contains the dormant "6(1)a All the Way!" clauses, so all that is needed is for the prime minister to issue an order-in-council.

2018

Apr 17   "The Indigenous Famous Six," a creation of the Canadian Feminist Alliance for International Action, are introduced in the Senate chamber. Through my effort, Yvonne Bédard is included. Sadly,

Jeannette Corbiere Lavell is delayed by weather and does not make it to the ceremony.

November   Through a Freedom of Information request I learn the DoJ billed INAC more than one million dollars to litigate *Gehl v Canada*.

2019

January   The United Nations rules on McIvor petition. Canada is told to eliminate all of the sex discrimination in the *Indian Act*. In the decision the UN relies on the "6(1)a All the Way!" concept rather than the legal clauses.

March/June I take on a seventeen-Tuesdays campaign protesting weekly outside MP and Minister for Women and Gender Equality Maryam Monsef's office in Peterborough, Ontario. Many Peterborough community members support this effort. They know me because I live there too.

August   Prime Minister Trudeau signs the order-in-council enacting all the "6(1)a All the Way!" clauses just days after the Office of the Conflict of Interest and Ethics Commissioner determined he was guilty of interference in the SNC-Lavalin situation. This SNC debacle also led to the demotion of Minister of Justice Jody Wilson-Raybould, an Indigenous woman, her removal from the Liberal cabinet, and eventually her being ousted from the Liberal Party altogether.

Aug 15   I accept a Canadian Aboriginal Veterans Millennium Medal on behalf of my great-grandfather Joseph Gagnon Jr.

Oct 25   INAC informs me that my status registration category is upgraded from 6(2) entitlement to a new subcategory of 6(1)a: 6(1)(a.3).

Notes

Dedication

1   Canada's history and current policy of genocide is a topic for settler people and politicians to listen, read, think, and learn about. Both the Truth and Reconciliation Commission of Canada (2015) and the National Inquiry into Missing and Murdered Indigenous Women and Girls (2019) concluded that the genocide of Indigenous Nations, Peoples, and women and girls was and remains colonial policy in Canada. The MMIWG provided a legal framework that begins with Raphael Lemkin's broader definition of genocide and draws on scholars and legal experts in the field of genocide. In my work I rely on the discourse of cultural genocide, a more insidious form of genocide because it can happen through laws, policy, and practices right in front of people who will not be able to see and perceive it. Gehl, "Seven Key Learnings."

Preface

1   Gehl, *Claiming Anishinaabe.*

Introduction

1   It is important to qualify here that the word "father" may not be the best way to refer to a man who impregnated a woman through sexual violence.

2   Alcantara, "Old Wine in New Bottles?"

3   For more on this perspective, see Gehl, "Seven Key Learnings."

1. Fighting for Recognition

1   "Wholistic" is my preferred spelling. I am not talking about a hole but rather a whole.

2   Miller, ed., *Sweet Promises*; Milloy, "Early Indian Acts."

3   Williams, *Savage Anxieties*.

2. The Personal Implications of the Discrimination in the Indian Act

1   These categories have since been changed. This is in part what this book is about.

2   For exact dates, readers can review the timeline in the appendix.

3   ALST is now known as Aboriginal Legal Services (ALS); however, it was Aboriginal Legal Services of Toronto (ALST) at the time my case began, so this is the name and abbreviation I use throughout the book.

3. Long Live the "Algonquin Frauds"

1   Barrera, "Algonquins of Ontario Claim Facing Internal Tensions."

2   Gehl, *Claiming Anishinaabe*.

4. "Love to Me Is the Kids"

1   Lambert, *Travels through Canada*, 533.

2   Charles Bagot, [Bagot Report], appendix EEE, n.p.

3   Speck, *Family Hunting Territories*, 1–30; Day, "Indians of the Ottawa Valley," 3.

4   I am not sure that she was Mohawk; rather, I am telling my kokomis's story about her.

5. Disenfranchised Spirit

1   Indian status registration is the mechanism through which Indigenous Peoples gain access to their treaty rights such as health care and education. Non-Status Indians are not entitled to these treaty rights.

2   The Indian Act criminalized Indigenous culture beginning in the 1880s (see Mathias and Yabsley, "Conspiracy of Legislation"). While this process ended in 1951, many lingering effects persist today.

3   For more on cultural meaning systems, see Castillo, *Culture and Mental Illness*.

4   Some people think a focus on Indian status registration is not progressive in that many First Nations are now establishing citizenship codes. Regardless of this thinking, at the level of practice in most situations Indian status registration, Band membership, and citizenship are not synonymous. It must be appreciated that a shift of discourse does not mean an ideological shift. For example, until recently I was denied Indian status registration and therefore Band membership and citizenship. That said, certainly disenfranchised spirit theory can be generalized to situations of the denial of citizenship.

5 See Bear with Tobique Women's Group, "You Can't Change"; Cannon, "Revisiting Histories"; Day, "153 Years"; Day and Green, "Sharon McIvor's Fight"; Eberts, "McIvor: Justice Delayed"; Gehl, "'Queen and I'"; Gehl, "Canada's Indian Policy"; Gilbert, *Entitlement to Indian Status*; Jamieson, *Indian Women*; Lawrence, "Gender, Race"; Lawrence, *"Real" Indians and Others*; McIvor, "Aboriginal Women's Rights"; McIvor, "Aboriginal Women Unmasked"; Miller, *Sweet Promises*; Monture-Angus, *Thunder in My Soul*; Palmater, *Beyond Blood*; Palmater, "Genocide"; Silman, *Enough Is Enough*; Stevenson, "Colonialism"; Furi and Wherrett, "Indian Status."

6 Statistics Canada reports that by the end of 2002, more than 114,000 individuals gained status registration through the 1985 amendment. It has been estimated that through the 2011 amendment as many as 45,000 grandchildren of Indian women once enfranchised for marrying out will gain the right to status registration. O'Donnell and Wallace, "First Nations."

7 In this chapter, the terms "emotional dimension of the human condition" and "heart knowledge" are used interchangeably.

8 Hall, "Question of Cultural Identity."

9 Hall, "New Ethnicities."

10 Yon, interview with Stuart Hall.

11 Hall, "Introduction," 4.

12 Hall, "Cultural Identity," 226. As a person with a disability, I find these terms offensive. Contradictorily, though, I also see their usefulness. I apologize if my use of these terms offends the reader.

13 Jenkins, *Social Identity*.

14 Schultz and Lavenda, *Cultural Anthropology*, 22.

15 Jenkins, *Social Identity*, 21.

16 Jenkins, 174.

17 Diamond Jenness and A. Irving Hallowell worked with the Ojibway, who are one Nation of the larger Anishinaabe Nations situated around the Great Lakes region of what is now called Canada and the United States. See Jenness, *Ojibwa Indians*; Hallowell, *Role of Conjuring*.

18 Jenness, *Ojibwa Indians*, 18–28; see also 90–111.

19 Hallowell, *Role of Conjuring*.

20 Hallowell, 172–82. It should be noted that a traditional knowledge holder and Elder has informed me that humans cannot lose their soul. While this may have been the case traditionally and prior to colonization, I do not think it is true today. We need to remember that Elders are not necessarily critical thinkers.

21 In this chapter it is best to understand the words "soul" and "spirit" as having the same meaning. Benton-Banai, *Mishomis Book*, 57.

22 Lawrence, "Gender, Race," 4.

23 Quoted in Eberts, "McIvor: Justice Delayed," 31.

24 Duran and Duran, *Native American Postcolonial Psychology*, 27.

25 Duran and Duran, 24.

26 Napoleon, "Aboriginal Self Determination," 41.

27 See Day and Trigger, "Algonquin"; Sarazin, "220 Years."

28 Gilbert, *Entitlement to Indian Status*; Monture-Angus, *Thunder in My Soul*; Gehl, "'Queen and I.'"

29 There are many spellings for this name, such as Jocko, Jacco, and Jacque.

30 All quotations of Skip Ross were provided to me through the Oral Tradition, unless otherwise noted.

31 INAC requested that Skip search the records for both Jocko and Jacob because Jacob is the maiden name of Sarah's mother. Also, the surnames Jacob and Jocko are often used interchangeably.

32 Both Skip and I have left the Algonquin land claim. I left because through my doctoral work I now fully understand that the process is a colonial process. Skip's reason is that the process is wrought with too many issues.

33 The blood-quantum criterion was eventually changed to descent only. See Gehl, "'Queen and I'"; Gehl, "Rebuilding of a Nation."

34 Gehl, "'Queen and I.'"

35 "Proud Day," *Renfrew Mercury*, August 22, 2000, 7.

36 Skip Ross, *Oral Tradition*; see also R. Pappin, "Algonquin Elder," 8; N. Kruzich, "Recovering the American Eel," 15.

37 R. MacGregor, L. Greig, J. M. Dettmers, W. A. Allen, T. Haxton, J. M. Casselman, and L. McDermott, "American Eel in Ontario," Environment Canada, "American Eel of the St. Lawrence," Government of Canada, April 6, 2009; A. Millington, "Reviewing the Basin's Importance."

38 With the advent of the second-generation cut-off rule in the 1985 amendment to the Indian Act, over time more and more people may feel spiritually disenfranchised.

39 Skip Ross died in October 2018 at the age of eighty-five.

7. Great Gathering against Bill c-3

1 IPSMO is now called Indigenous Solidarity Ottawa.

2 All quotes in this chapter were provided to me via the Oral Tradition.

9. The *Indian Act*'s Legislative Silence

1 *Canadian Charter of Rights and Freedoms*, s 15(1), Part I of the *Constitution Act, 1982*, being Schedule B to the Canada Act 1982 (UK), 1982, c 11.

11. Canada's Unstated Paternity Policy Amounts to Genocide against Indigenous Children

1 Lemkin, *Axis Rule in Occupied Europe*.

2 Readers should not read this short chapter and interpret it as encompassing all that is needed to be known on this topic of genocide. I suggest people read

A Legal Analysis of Genocide, a supplementary report of the 2019 National Inquiry into Missing and Murdered Indigenous Women and Girls (2019), and also *Honouring the Truth, Reconciling for the Future*, the Truth and Reconciliation Commission final report (2015).

12. Canada Is Carrying Out Cultural Genocide with a Smile

1 See Alice Olsen Williams, "Open Letter: Kawartha Group Disappointed with Monsef's Voting Position on Bill s-3," letter to the editor, *Anishinabek News*, August 28, 2017, http://anishinabeknews.ca/2017/09/05/open-letter-kawartha-group-disappointed-with-monsefs-voting-position-on-bill-s-3/.
2 Gehl, "Insidious Nature."

13. "The Queen and I"

1 Stevenson, "Colonialism," 67.
2 Voyageur, "Contemporary Indian Women," 100.
3 Stevenson, "Colonialism," 55.
4 Earley is the subject of a new film by Courtney Monture, titled *Mary Two-Axe Earley: I Am Indian Again*, to be released in 2021 by the National Film Board.
5 Bear with Tobique Women's Group, "You Can't Change."
6 Bear with Tobique Women's Group, 206.
7 See chapter 14 for more details.
8 Silman, *Enough Is Enough*; Bear with Tobique Women's Group, "You Can't Change."
9 During a five-year period (from June 1985 to June 1990), the Department of Indian Affairs received over 75,000 applications for registration. Canada, Department of Indian Affairs and Northern Development, *Impact of the 1985 Amendments*, 8. Keep in mind here that marriage to non-Status men was not the only reason for women's enfranchisement, although it did account for the majority of cases. Voyageur, "Contemporary Indian Women," 104.
10 Gilbert, *Entitlement to Indian Status*, iii.
11 Annie Gagnon to [H. P. Ruddy], January 2, 1945, in author's possession.
12 Voyageur, "Contemporary Indian Women," 101.
13 Readers will notice that this stated year of my kokomis's departure from the reserve changes. I am not too concerned about this because I am not good with dates and also because the numeric calendar is a colonial imposition. Indigenous Peoples would, I think, talk about how many snows ago or how many moons ago an event was.
14 Jamieson, *Indian Women*, 13.
15 Jamieson, 1.
16 Norris, "Contemporary Demography," 205.
17 Furi and Wherrett, "Indian Status," 9.
18 Gilbert, *Entitlement to Indian Status*, 16.

19   Archives of Ontario, *Aboriginal Sources at the Archives of Ontario*, handout (Toronto: Ministry of Citizenship Culture and Recreation, n.d.).

20   Terri Harris (INAC), "Investigation," letter, February 13, 1995.

21   Furi and Wherrett, "Indian Status," 5.

22   Furi and Wherrett, 10.

23   Furi and Wherrett, 10.

24   Gilbert, *Entitlement to Indian Status*, 18.

25   Gilbert, 15.

26   The apostrophe is intentionally left out as it implies ownership.

27   McIvor, "Self-Government," 179.

14. Unknown and Unstated Paternity and the *Indian Act*

1   The government of Canada is invested in calling these treaty rights "programs and services."

2   Again, enfranchisement best translates to no longer being an Indian.

3   Miller, *Lethal Legacy*.

4   Francis, *Imaginary Indian*.

5   The full name of the 1857 act was *An Act to Encourage the Gradual Civilization of the Indian Tribes in the Province*.

6   Oftentimes this is referred to as "marrying out," which means marrying a man who is not an Indian person as defined by the Indian Act.

7   Gilbert, *Entitlement to Indian Status*.

8   Jamieson, *Indian Women*.

9   McIvor, "Aboriginal Women Unmasked."

10   Silman, *Enough Is Enough*; Stevenson, "Colonialism."

11   April 17, 2012, marked the thirtieth anniversary of the *Charter of Rights and Freedoms*. Possibly needless to say, I did not celebrate.

12   While at the time AANDC argued that no such written policy existed, they did have a practice. The position that unwritten practices are not policy is a pitiful attempt to shift the discussion in a ridiculous way.

13   The father's signature is required on the child's birth registration form, regardless of marital status, for it to be factored into the process of determining status registration. This also applies to situations where a non-Indian mother has a child with a Status Indian father and the father's signature is not on the child's birth certificate.

14   Again, these rules about section 6(1) and section 6(2) also apply to Status Indian men and their descendants born after 1985.

15   Gehl, "'Queen and I.'"

16   See Gilbert, *Entitlement to Indian Status*.

17   As discussed in the introduction, in situations where a mother did add the father's name, if a signature was not forthcoming the name was removed by officials. It was standard practice. I am not sure if this practice continues today. I address this matter more deeply in a chapter in this book.

18   To recap, at this time my kokomis was registered as a 6(1), my father as a 6(2), and I was not entitled.

19   Gehl, *Claiming Anishinaabe*.

20   It is my thinking that the process of striking my claim was a DoJ strategy of delay, rather than my lawyer taking the wrong action as some people may think.

21   As stated in the introduction, many paternity scenarios are subsumed under this unstated paternity policy. In this way, the policy title is a misnomer and blames mothers.

22   Clatworthy, "Factors Contributing."

23   Mann, "Disproportionate and Unjustifiable."

24   Of course these men are not fathers at all. Rather, they are predators and/or sick people.

25   See also Mann, "Indian Registration."

26   Gehl, "Quick Facts."

15. Protecting Indian Rights for Indian Babies

1   Miller, *Lethal Legacy*; Borrows, "Wampum at Niagara"; Gehl, "Indigenous Knowledge"; Gehl, *Truth that Wampum Tells*.

2   Duncan Campbell Scott (1920), quoted in Troniak, "Addressing the Legacy."

3   Miller, *Lethal Legacy*.

4   Gehl, "'Queen and I.'"

5   Gilbert, *Entitlement to Indian Status*.

6   Eberts, "McIvor: Justice Delayed."

7   McIvor, "Aboriginal Women Unmasked," 108.

8   Jamieson, *Indian Women*.

9   McIvor, "Aboriginal Women Unmasked," 113. See also Monture-Angus, *Thunder in My Soul*; Day, "153 Years."

10   McIvor, "Aboriginal Women Unmasked." See also Monture-Angus, *Thunder in My Soul*; Silman, *Enough Is Enough*; Stevenson, "Colonialism."

11   O'Donnell and Wallace, "First Nations."

12   See Borrows, "Wampum at Niagara." See also Gehl, "Indigenous Knowledge"; Gehl, *Truth that Wampum Tells*.

13   While many may argue that it was in 1985 when the enfranchisement process was removed from the Indian Act, I disagree. It is my contention that enfranchisement has a new form: the second-generation cut-off rule.

14   Cited in Keung, "'Status Indians,'" n.p.

15   Outside of my discussion of 6(1)a–6(1)c and how AANDC applies these sections to Indigenous women and men in an unequal manner, I do not discuss the other paragraphs (subsubsections) of 6(1). Such a discussion is beyond the scope of this work and my expertise. Again, I am neither a lawyer nor trained in law.

16   Eberts, "McIvor: Justice Delayed"; Gehl, "'Queen and I'"; Gilbert,

Entitlement to Indian Status; McIvor, "Aboriginal Women Unmasked."

17 Eberts, "McIvor: Justice Delayed," 28.

18 McIvor, "Aboriginal Women Unmasked"; see also Eberts, "McIvor: Justice Delayed."

19 Day, "153 Years." See also Day and Green, "Sharon McIvor's Fight"; Eberts, "McIvor: Justice Delayed"; Haesler, "B.C. Aboriginal Woman."

20 Eberts, "McIvor: Justice Delayed," 32.

21 Sharon Donna McIvor, email correspondence with the author, October 18, 2017. See also the United Nations ruling on McIvor: UN Human Rights Committee, "Views Adopted by the Committee." In the original publication of this article and a subsequent re-publication, I stated that Sharon's son, Charles Jacob Grismer, was registered as 6(1)c when in fact he was registered as 6(1)c.1. The goal was 6(1)a.

22 Eberts, "McIvor: Justice Delayed," 39–40.

23 McIvor and Brodsky, "Equal Registration Status."

24 Day, "153 Years."

25 Cited in Haesler, "B.C. Aboriginal Woman," n.p.

26 Women's Legal Education and Action Fund (LEAF), "LEAF Urges Government," n.p.

27 Day and Green, "Sharon McIvor's Fight"; O'Donnell and Wallace, "First Nations."

28 Eberts, "McIvor: Justice Delayed," 42.

29 Bagot Report, appendix EEE, n.p.

30 Speck, *Family Hunting Territories*, 21.

31 Day, "Indians of the Ottawa Valley," 3.

32 Palmater, *Beyond Blood*, 218.

33 Palmater.

34 Cannon, "Revisiting Histories," 6.

35 Cited in Gilbert, *Entitlement to Indian Status*, 34.

36 Gilbert, 33.

37 Gilbert, 33.

38 Gehl, "'Queen and I.'"

39 I need to qualify that many girls became pregnant through the sexual violence that occurred during their residential school and day school experience. In these situations it is highly unlikely that the father's signature would be recorded on the birth registration form.

40 While thinking through all these situations we also need to keep in mind that while a mother, grandmother, or great-grandmother may know the father, this does not mean a child, a grandchild, or great-grandchild knows. What is more, these categories—unstated, unreported, unnamed, unacknowledged, unestablished, unrecognized, and unknown paternity—also apply to the paternity of one's grandfather and/or great-grandfather.

41 Clatworthy, "Factors Contributing."

42 Mann, "Disproportionate and Unjustifiable."

43   Clatworthy, "Factors Contributing."
44   Clatworthy, 16–18.
45   Clatworthy, 19–22.
46   Fiske and George, *Seeking Alternatives*, 4.
47   Native Women's Association of Canada, "Aboriginal Women," 1.
48   Mann, "Disproportionate and Unjustifiable," 33.
49   Mann, "Indian Registration," 21.
50   Mann, 26.
51   McIvor, "Aboriginal Women Unmasked," 133.

16. Ontario's History of Tampering and Re-Tampering with Birth Registration Documents

1   Again, it is important to qualify here that the word "father" may not be the best way to refer to a man who impregnated a woman through sexual violence.
2   See Gehl, "'Queen and I'"; Gehl, "Sex Discrimination"; Gehl, "Unknown and Unstated Paternity"; Gehl, "Indian Rights for Indian Babies"; Gehl, "Canada's Unstated Paternity Policy."
3   See Henderson, "Review of Canada"; Mann, "Disproportionate and Unjustifiable."
4   Mann, "Disproportionate and Unjustifiable," 32.
5   ServiceOntario, "Get or Replace an Ontario Birth Certificate," https://www.ontario.ca/page/get-or-replace-ontario-birth-certificate.
6   *Vital Statistics Act*, RSO 1980, c 524.
7   Henderson, "Review of Canada," 1.
8   Henderson, 9.
9   Cited in Henderson, 1–2.
10   The amount of this fee has changed over time.
11   See Franklin, "Ontario Opens."
12   Baute, "Adoptees Can Find Mom."
13   All quotes from Karen Lynn in this chapter were provided to me via the Oral Tradition.

17. Law Society of Upper Canada Talk

1   Stewart, "Address."
2   At the time of doing this talk in 2005, I was ignorant about the difference between a land claim settlement and a treaty and did not understand how Canada appropriates what is meant by a treaty when it calls the comprehensive land claim process the "modern treaty process." The "modern treaty process" is a federal government–driven process that continues the genocide that the Doctrine of Discovery unleashed.

18. House of Commons Committee Testimony

1   This dollar amount increases. I discuss this again in chapter 23.
2   This second statement about the *Gehl* clauses in this paragraph is not correct. See the last chapter for a better discussion of the *Gehl* clauses.
3   This amount has since increased to $800 million.

21. Carolyn Bennett's "2 Million" New Indians

1   This figure is a best guess based on the 1985 and 2011 numbers. Not a good strategy on my part.
2   Pamela D. Palmater cited by Senator Lillian Eva Dyck in Canada, Parliament, *Debates of the Senate*, 42nd Parl., 1st Sess., June 1, 2017, p. 3195.
3   Sharon Donna McIvor, email correspondence with the author, October 18, 2017.
4   Clatworthy and Frideres, "Joint Statement of Expert Witnesses."

22. Valuing Discourse

1   *Descheneaux c Canada (Procureur Général)*, 2015 QCCS 3555.
2   "Quebec Superior Court Grants Extension," CBC News, January 26, 2017.

23. My Last Chapter

1   Monture-Angus, *Thunder in My Soul*.
2   McIvor, "Aboriginal Women Unmasked," 113.
3   McIvor.
4   At this point I now rely on the language of "unknown and thus unstated paternity" when I talk about my court case. See the introduction for a reminder about this shift in language use.
5   *Canadian Charter of Rights and Freedoms*, s 15(1), Part I of the *Constitution Act, 1982*, being Schedule B to the *Canada Act 1982* (UK), 1982, c 11.
6   Gehl, *Truth that Wampum Tells*.
7   Blackstock, "Wanted," 36.
8   The Archives of Ontario is no longer located in downtown Toronto. It is now located at York University.
9   Another way to say this is INAC had a PoP policy or two-parent rule that insisted on proof of paternity.
10 Gehl, *Claiming Anishinaabe*.
11 Dean Beeby, "Justice Canada Chops Research Budget by $1.2-Million," *Globe and Mail*, 11 May 2014.
12 I do not understand why we did not take the route of the statutory appeal. What I do know is that the judges liked to blame us for not taking that route. Further, I do not even know what a statutory appeal means.
13 We did not challenge INAC's new two-parent rule. This was a similar approach as taken in *McIvor v Canada* (Eberts, "McIvor: Justice Delayed").

14 *Indian Act*, RSC 1985, c I-5, s 14.2 (Protests).

15 Mann, "Disproportionate and Unjustifiable."

16 Palmater, "Genocide."

17 Alcantara, "Old Wine in New Bottles?"

18 Ontario, Ministry of the Attorney General, "Fact Sheet."

19 Although it was said that the case shifted from an action to an application, or rather a hybrid between the two, at the Court of Appeal for Ontario the justices still referred to the case as an action. I am not sure why this is.

20 Kirby and I are related. My kokomis and his mother, Anna Whiteduck, were first cousins.

21 See Gehl, *Truth that Wampum Tells*.

22 Clatworthy focused on unknown and unstated paternity, meaning he looked at unknown and thus unstated paternity; and also, known yet unstated paternity. What I am again re-clarifying here is that there is a difference between an absolute unknown father and an unstated father.

23 See Frideres, "Response to the Report"; Clatworthy, "Analysis of Select Population Impacts."

24 Mann, "Gehl v Canada."

25 See Mann, "Indian Registration"; Mann, "Disproportionate and Unjustifiable."

26 Gehl, "Sex Discrimination"; Gehl, "Long Time Sex Discrimination."

27 Gehl, "Canadian Government."

28 I closed this petition in August 2020 with 5,784 signatures.

29 *McIvor v Canada (Registrar of Indian and Northern Affairs)*, 2009 BCCA 153.

30 See Eberts, "McIvor: Justice Delayed."

31 Eberts, 37.

32 Lehmann, "Memorandum."

33 Millan, "Parliament Given 18 Months."

34 Gilbert, *Entitlement to Indian Status*. It is important for me to qualify and state here that the law offices of ALST and LOME relied on statute, meaning legislation, versus secondary sources, as I did here, when addressing INAC's history of legislation on the matter of unknown and thus unstated paternity. In my factum of appeal they listed the shifts as follows: "From 1850 through 1876 any Indian blood was good enough, there was no question of illegitimacy; from 1876 through 1951 any child of a man, illegitimate children of women not included (no presumption of Indian paternity apparent); and from 1951 through 1985, illegitimate children included unless proven that father non-Indian." I will admit that I am not sure how to read this: "from 1876 through 1951 any child of a man, illegitimate children of women not included (no presumption of Indian paternity apparent)."

35 Gilbert, 33–34.

36 *Gehl v Canada*, 2014, at para 94.

37 I explored the option of ordering transcripts, but my case was a civil case, and as such no stenographer recorded the courtroom process.

38   *Gehl v Attorney General of Canada*, 2015 ONSC 3481. See also Indigenous Law Centre, "Gehl v Canada." Sometimes I wonder if the legal arguments on the analogous ground of "unknowable paternity" would have been successful. But again, I am neither a lawyer nor trained in law.

39   *Gehl v Attorney General of Canada*, 2015 ONSC 3481.

40   A good example of the difference between "formal equality" and "substantive equality" is that of a poorly lit parking lot where, as a result of the poor lighting, women are more likely to become victims. Clearly women need extra measures to ensure their safety. A formal equality lens would argue the parking lot is equally lit for both men and women, whereas a substantive equality lens understands the need for extra measures to protect women.

41   Remember, the *Charter* was an improvement over the *Canadian Bill of Rights* because it protected women from discrimination under the law, not just the administration of the law.

42   It is important for me to note here that seven years and nine months earlier, on March 23, 2007, McLenachan had also provided evidence in relation to my *Charter* challenge.

43   Indian and Northern Affairs Canada (INAC), "Memorandum: Deeming Non-Indian Paternity 6(1)(c) Omitted," June 13, 2011, p. 1.

44   INAC, 2.

45   I now have a different understanding. I flesh this out in a later chapter.

46   *Duhaime's Law Dictionary*, s.v. "intervener," accessed February 13, 2019, http://www.duhaime.org/LegalDictionary/I/Intervener.aspxh.

47   *Gehl v Canada*, Factum of the Intervener, 2016.

48   This is another way of saying whoever the man was, he is deemed non-Indian.

49   *Andrews v Law Society of British Columbia*, [1989] 1 SCR 143.

50   *Gehl v Canada*. Factum of the Appellant, 2016, at para 105. See *McIvor v Canada*.

51   *Gehl v Canada*, Factum of the Appellant, 2016, at para 108.

52   INAC, "Non-Indian Paternity"; INAC, "Memorandum: Deeming 6(1)(c) Omitted 'Illegitimate Child' Deceased before September 4, 1951 and Deeming 6(1)(a) or 6(1)(c) 'Illegitimate Child' Alive on or after September 4, 1951," January 10, 2012; both cited in *Gehl v Canada*, 2016, at para 116.

53   *Gehl v Canada*, 2016, at para 134.

54   I can only assume they mean that a boy child is treated the same as a girl child.

55   In this section I rely on the *Gehl* 2017 Court of Appeal judgement (2017 ONCA 319) as well as several secondary sources to inform my analysis. See *Gehl v Attorney General of Canada*, 2015 ONSC 3481; Giroday, "Victory for Woman"; Gonsalves, "ONCA Divided"; Kinsinger, "*Gehl v Canada*"; "More Turbulence in Judicial Review"; Nerland, "Dr Gehl Wins Appeal"; "Ontario Court of Appeal Finds"; Sikkema, "Court of Appeal Justices"; Truesdale, "Lynn Gehl Wins Fight." See the bibliography for complete references.

56   *Gehl v Canada*, 2017 ONCA 319, at para 36.

57   *Gehl v Canada*, at paras 44–45.

58   *Gehl v Canada*, at para 64.

59   *Gehl v Canada*, at para 72.

60   *Gehl v Canada*, at para 73.

61   *Gehl v Canada*, at para 75.

62   As discussed in the introduction, this Trudeau Liberal platform was laden with lies and manipulation, but a discussion of this is outside the scope of this work.

63   Canadian Press, "Carolyn Bennett Admits."

64   Canada, Parliament, Senate, Standing Committee on Aboriginal Peoples, *Proceedings*, 42nd Parl., 1st Sess., May 17, 2017.

65   Galloway, "Feds Say They Can't."

66   This department is now called Women and Gender Equality Canada. I would have preferred "equity" over "equality."

67   Robertson, "Government, Senate at Odds."

68   Canada, Parliament, Senate, *Debates*, 42nd Parl., 1st Sess., November 9, 2017, p. 4160.

69   Canada, "Plain Text Description of Bill S-3."

70   I am indecisive on this because if you read the *Gehl v Canada* (2017) judgement you will see that the reasoning of absolute unknowns is fleshed out.

71   I use the word "could" in this sentence because it depends on the need for evidence as set out in the *Gehl* clauses.

72   Canada, Parliament, *Debates of the Senate*, 42nd Parl., 1st Sess., April 17, 2018, p. 5190 (statement on Equality Day by Hon. Marilou McPhedran).

73   Wikipedia, s.v. "The Indigenous Famous Six," last edited December 16, 2020, https://en.wikipedia.org/wiki/The_Indigenous_Famous_Six.

74   INAC, "Non-Indian Paternity"; INAC, "'Illegitimate Child.'"

75   Murray Sinclair, "Congratulations are due to Dr. Lynn Gehl," Facebook, April 20, 2017, https://www.facebook.com/Sincmurr/posts/463640447301510.

24. Defeating the Wiindigo

1   UN Human Rights Committee, "Views Adopted by the Committee," sec. 5.15.

2   UN Human Rights Committee, sec. 9.

3   Dyck, "Motion to Urge the Government."

4   "The Indigenous Famous Five" is something I created as my way to give the issue of sex discrimination in the *Indian Act* more currency. I was playing on the cultural hegemony of the very controversial Famous Five collective. See Gehl, "Persons Day." Yes, of course I understand the contradiction.

5   National Inquiry into Missing and Murdered Indigenous Women and Girls, *Legal Analysis of Genocide.*

6   Canadian Press, "Trudeau Breached."
7   Smith, "Indian Act's 143 Years," n.p.

25. I Danced and I Danced; My Heart Was Full

1   "Wendy Jocko," Algonquins of Pikwàkanagàn First Nation website, accessed
     January 13, 2021, http://algonquinsofpikwakanagan.com/legacy/chief_
     council_bio_wendy.php.
2   "Honours: Aboriginal Veteran Millennium Medal (AVMM)," Aboriginal
     Veterans Autochtones, accessed February 12, 2021, http://avavets.com/
     honours/.
3   Wendy Jocko, personal communication, August 17, 2019.
4   Wendy Jocko, personal notes, August 17, 2019, in possession of the author.
5   Palmater with Gehl, "Lynn Gehl Challenges."

Anishinaabemowin Words and Meanings

Akikpautik	Creator's First Sacred Pipe
Anishinaabe	Original person
Anishinaabe-kwe	Anishinaabe woman
Anishinaabeg	Original People
Anishinaabemowin	Anishinaabe language
chi-miigwetch	big thank you
dbaajimowinan	a personal story
debwewin	a personal truth that involves both mind knowledge and heart knowledge
kokomis	grandmother
miigwetch	thank you
mino-pimadiziwin	the good life
ogitchidaa kwewag	warrior women
wiindigo	a flesh-eating monster lacking in moral integrity

Bibliography

Alcantara, Christopher. "Old Wine in New Bottles? Instrumental Policy Learning and the Evolution of the Certainty Provision in Comprehensive Land Claims Agreements." *Canadian Public Policy* 35, no. 3 (2009): 325–41.

Andrews v Law Society of British Columbia, [1989] 1 SCR 143. http://canlii.ca/t/1ft8q.

Bagot, Charles. *Report on the Affairs of the Indians in Canada, laid before the Legislative Assembly, 20th March, 1845*. [Bagot Report]. Journals of the Legislative Assembly of the Province of Canada, 1844–45.

Barrera, Jorge. "Algonquins of Ontario Claim Facing Internal Tensions, Accusations Some Involved Are Not Indigenous." *APTN National News*, March 11, 2015. https://aptnnews.ca/2015/03/11/algonquins-ontario-claim-facing-internal-tensions-accusations-involved-indigenous.

Baute, Nicole. "Adoptees Can Find Mom, But Not Dad." *Toronto Star*, December 10, 2009. http://www.thestar.com/life/2009/12/10/adoptees_can_find_mom_but_not_dad.html.

Bear, Shirley, with the Tobique Women's Group. "You Can't Change the *Indian Act*?" In *Women and Social Change: Feminist Activism in Canada*, edited by Jeri Dawn Wine and Janice L. Ristock, 198–220. Toronto: James Lorimer, 1991.

Beeby, Dean. "Justice Canada Chops Research Budget by $1.2-Million." *Globe and Mail*, 11 May 2014. https://www.theglobeandmail.com/news/politics/justice-canada-chops-research-budget-by-12-million/article18598170/.

Benton-Banai, Edward. *Mishomis Book: The Voice of the Ojibway*. Hayward, WI: Indian Country Communications, 1988.

Blackstock, Cindy. "Wanted: Moral Courage in Canadian Child Welfare." *First Peoples Child and Family Review* 6, no. 2 (2011): 35–46.

Borrows, John. "Wampum at Niagara: The Royal Proclamation, Canadian Legal History, and Self-Government." In *Aboriginal and Treaty Rights in Canada: Essays on Law, Equality, and Respect for Difference*, edited by Michael Asch, 155–72. Vancouver: UBC Press, 2002.

Cairns, H. A. C., S. M. Jamieson, and K. Lysyk. *A Survey of the Contemporary Indians of Canada: Economic, Political, Educational Needs and Policies*, vol. 1, edited by H. B. Hawthorn. Ottawa: Indian Affairs Branch, October 1966.

Canada. Department of Indian Affairs and Northern Development. *Impact of the 1985 Amendments to the Indian Act (Bill C-31)*. Ottawa: Minister of Supply and Services, 1990.

———. Parliament. *Debates of the Senate*, 42nd Parl., 1st Sess., June 1, 2017, https://sencanada.ca/en/content/sen/chamber/421/debates/126db_2017-06-01-e#41.

———. Parliament. *Debates of the Senate*, 42nd Parl., 1st Sess., November 9, 2017. https://sencanada.ca/en/content/sen/chamber/421/debates/158db_2017-11-09-e#48.

———. Parliament. *Debates of the Senate*. 42nd Parl., 1st Sess., April 17, 2018. https://sencanada.ca/en/content/sen/chamber/421/debates/193db_2018-04-17-e#11.

———. Parliament. Senate. *Proceedings of the Standing Committee on Aboriginal Peoples*. 42nd Parl., 1st Sess., May 17, 2017. https://sencanada.ca/en/Content/Sen/Committee/421/APPA/22ev-53342-e.

———. "Plain Text Description of Bill S-3, An Act to amend the *Indian Act* in response to the Superior Court of Quebec decision in Descheneaux c. Canada (Procureur général)." Accessed January 13, 2021. https://www.sac-ISC.gc.ca/eng/1478177979520/1572460398953.

Canadian Press. "Carolyn Bennett Admits Bill to Change *Indian Act* Was Badly Handled." *Toronto Star*, November 30, 2016. https://www.thestar.com/news/canada/2016/11/30/carolyn-bennett-admits-bill-to-change-indian-act-was-badly-handled.html.

———. "Trudeau Breached Federal Ethics Rules in SNC-Lavalin Affair: Ethics Commissioner." *Maclean's*, August 14, 2019. https://www.macleans.ca/politics/ottawa/trudeau-breached-federal-ethics-rules-in-snc-lavalin-affair-ethics-commissioner/.

Cannon, Martin J. "Revisiting Histories of Gender-Based Exclusion and the New Politics of Indian Identity." Research paper for the National Centre for First Nations Governance, May 2008.

Castillo, Richard J. *Culture and Mental Illness: A Client-Centered Approach*. Pacific Grove, CA: Brooks/Cole, 1997.

Clatworthy, Stewart. "Analysis of Select Population Impacts of the 1985 Amendments to the *Indian Act* (Bill C-31) and Select Hypothetical Amendments to the 1985 *Indian Act*." Winnipeg: Four Directions Project Consultants, April 24, 2013.

———. "Factors Contributing to Unstated Paternity." Indian and Northern Affairs Canada, Strategic Research and Analysis Directorate, January 20, 2003. http://publications.gc.ca/collections/Collection/R2-255-2003E.pdf.

Clatworthy, Stewart, and James S. Frideres. "Joint Statement of Expert Witnesses for the Defendant (Stewart Clatworthy) and the Plaintiff (James S. Frideres) in the Matter of Lynn Gehl v. Attorney General of Canada." n.d.

Darling, Elysa, and Drew Lafond. "Barring Claims against Discriminatory Legislation: *Canada v Canada*." *ABlawg.ca* (blog), University of Calgary Faculty of Law, June 29, 2018. https://ablawg.ca/2018/06/29/barring-claims-against-discriminatory-legislation-canada-v-canada/.

Day, Gordon M. "The Indians of the Ottawa Valley." *Oracle* 30 (1979): 1–4.

Day, Gordon M., and Bruce G. Trigger. "Algonquin." In *Handbook of North American Indians*, vol. 15, *Northeast*, edited by Bruce G. Trigger, 792–97. Washington: Smithsonian Institution, 1978.

Day, Shelagh. "153 Years of Sex Discrimination Is Enough." Editorial. *Toronto Star*, January 6, 2011. http://www.thestar.com/opinion/editorialopinion/article/916682--153-years-of-sexdiscrimination-is-enough.

Day, Shelagh, and Joyce Green. "Sharon McIvor's Fight for Equality." *Herizons* 24, no. 1 (2010): 6–7.

Descheneaux c Canada (Procurer Général), 2015 QCCS 3555. http://canlii.ca/t/glzhm.

Duran, Eduardo, and Bonnie Duran. *Native American Postcolonial Psychology*. Albany: State University of New York Press, 1995.

Eberts, Mary. "McIvor: Justice Delayed—Again." *Indigenous Law Journal* 9, no. 1 (2010): 16–46.

Fiske, Jo-Anne, and Evelyn George. *Seeking Alternatives to Bill C-31: From Cultural Trauma to Cultural Revitalization through Customary Law*. Ottawa: Status of Women Canada, 2006.

Francis, Daniel. *The Imaginary Indian: The Image of the Indian in Canadian Culture*. Vancouver: Arsenal Pulp Press, 2000.

Franklin, Robert. "Ontario Opens Its Old Adoption Records—Surprise! No Dads!" *Origins Canada*, December 19, 2009. http://www.originscanada.org/ontario-opens-its-old-adoption-records-%E2%80%93-surprise-no-dads/.

Frideres, James S. "Response to the Report prepared by Stewart Clatworthy in the Matter of Lynn Gehl v. Attorney General of Canada." Calgary, January 31, 2011.

Furi, Megan, and Jill Wherrett. "Indian Status and Band Membership Issues." Political and Social Affairs Division, Parliamentary Library, February 1996.

Galloway, Gloria. "Feds Say They Can't Accept Senate Changes to Bill Aiming to End *Indian Act* Sexism." *Globe and Mail*, June 5, 2017. https://www.theglobeandmail.com/news/politics/senate-indian-act-sexism/article35185997/.

Gehl, Lynn. "Canada's Indian Policy Is a Process of Deception." *Briarpatch*, March 2, 2015. https://briarpatchmagazine.com/articles/view/canadas-indian-policy-is-a-process-of-deception.

———. "Canadian Government: Remove all of the sex discrimination in the Indian status registrations provisions of the *Indian Act*—Enough is enough."

Petition to Prime Minister Justin Trudeau, n.d. [2013]. Change.org. https://www.change.org/p/canadian-government-remove-all-of-the-sex-discrimination-in-the-indian-status-registration-provisions-of-the-indian-act-enough-is-enough.

———. *Claiming Anishinaabe: Decolonizing the Human Spirit*. Regina: University of Regina Press, 2017.

———. "Indigenous Knowledge, Symbolic Literacy and the 1764 Treaty at Niagara." Federation for the Humanities and Social Sciences blog, February 15, 2011. https://www.ideas-idees.ca/blog/indigenous-knowledge-symbolic-literacy-and-1764-treaty-niagara.

———. "The Insidious Nature of 'Cultural' Genocide." *Black Face Blogging* (blog), June 8, 2015. https://www.lynngehl.com/black-face-blogging/the-insidious-nature-of-cultural-genocide.

———. "The Long Time Sex Discrimination in the *Indian Act*—Indian Status Provisions." YouTube video, 6:38. May 16, 2014. https://www.youtube.com/watch?v=hkkPwoCh-6g.

———. "Persons Day: The Indigenous Famous Five Contingent." *Canadian Dimension*, October 10, 2013. https://canadiandimension.com/articles/view/persons-day-the-indigenous-famous-five-contingent.

———. "'The Queen and I': Discrimination against Women in the *Indian Act* Continues." *Canadian Woman Studies* 20, no. 2 (2000): 64–69.

———. "Quick Facts on Aboriginal Affairs and Northern Development Canada's Policy on Unstated Paternity." N.d. http://www.lynngehl.com/uploads/5/0/0/4/5004954/unstated_paternity_quick_facts.pdf.

———. "The Rebuilding of a Nation: A Grassroots Analysis of the Nation-Building Process in Canada." *Canadian Journal of Native Studies* 23, no. 1 (2004): 57–82. http://www3.brandonu.ca/cjns/23.1/cjnsv23no1_pg57-82.pdf.

———. "Seven Key Learnings from the MMIWG Legal Analysis on Genocide." *Briarpatch*, March 19, 2020. https://briarpatchmagazine.com/articles/view/seven-key-learnings-from-the-MMIWG-legal-analysis-on-genocide.

———. "Sex Discrimination and the *Indian Act* (yes the saga continues...)." YouTube video, 9:27. June 24, 2012. https://www.youtube.com/watch?v=mYl8_QSDAjY.

———. *The Truth that Wampum Tells: My Debwewin on the Algonquin Land Claims Process*. Halifax and Winnipeg: Fernwood, 2014.

Gehl v Attorney General of Canada, 2015 ONSC 3481. http://canlii.ca/t/gjctm.

Gehl v Canada (Attorney General). (2014). Factum of the Plaintiff. Motion for Summary Judgement.

Gehl v Canada (Attorney General). (June 13, 2016). Factum of the Appellant.

Gehl v Canada (Attorney General). (September 23, 2016), Toronto C60706 (ONCA). Factum of the Intervener [Women's Legal Education and Action Fund (LEAF)]. https://www.leaf.ca/wp-content/uploads/2016/12/2016-09-23-Gehl-Factum-LEAF-Final.docx.pdf.

Gehl v Canada (Attorney General), 2017 ONCA 319. http://canlii.ca/t/h38cq.

Gilbert, Larry. *Entitlement to Indian Status and Membership Codes in Canada.* Scarborough, ON: Carswell Thomson Canada, 1996.

Giroday, Gabrielle. "Victory for Woman Who Argued Sex Discrimination Exists in *Indian Act.*" *Canadian Lawyer*, April 24, 2017. https://www.canadianlawyermag.com/news/general/victory-for-woman-who-argued-sex-discrimination-exists-in-indian-act/274264.

Gonsalves, Andrea. "ONCA Divided on Use of Charter Values in Judicial Review." *CanLII Connects*, July 26, 2017. https://canliiconnects.org/en/commentaries/46141.

Haesler, Neil. "B.C. Aboriginal Woman Taking Status Battle to the UN." *Global News*, November 12, 2010. https://globalnews.ca/news/101762/b-c-aboriginal-woman-taking-status-battle-to-the-un/.

Hall, Stuart. "Cultural Identity and Diaspora." In *Identity: Community, Culture, Difference.* Edited by Jonathan Rutherford, 222–37. London: Lawrence & Wishart, 1990.

———. "Introduction: Who Needs 'Identity'?" In *Questions of Cultural Identity.* Edited by Stuart Hall and Paul du Gay, 1–17. London: SAGE, 1996.

———. "New Ethnicities." In *Black Film, British Cinema* : ICA Conference, February 1988 Edited by Kobena Mercer. ICA Documents No. 7. London: Institute for Contemporary Arts, 1988, 27–31. https://issuu.com/icalondon/docs/blackfilmbritishcinema.

———. "The Question of Cultural Identity." In *Modernity and Its Futures.* Edited by Stuart Hall, David Held, and Tony McGrew. Cambridge: Polity Press and Open University, 1992, 273–99.

Hallowell, A. Irving. *The Role of Conjuring in Saulteaux Society.* Publications of the Philadelphia Anthropological Society, vol. 2. New York: Octagon, 1971.

Henderson, Cathy. "Review of Canada: Illegally Removed Elements from Original Birth Registrations with regards to Article 8 of the UN Convention on the Rights of the Child." Submission to United Nations Committee on the Convention on the Rights of the Child, July 29, 2012.

"Honours: Aboriginal Veteran Millennium Medal (AVMM)." Aboriginal Veterans Autochtones. Accessed February 12, 2021. http://avavets.com/honours/.

Indian Act, RSC 1985, c I-5, s 14.2 (Protests). https://laws-lois.justice.gc.ca/eng/acts/i-5/section-14.2.html.

Indigenous Law Centre. "Gehl v Canada." Indigenous Law Centre Blog, University of Saskatchewan, June 12, 2015. https://indigenouslaw.usask.ca/blog/2015/gehl-v-canada.php.

Jamieson, Kathleen. *Indian Women and the Law in Canada: Citizens Minus.* Ottawa: Advisory Council on the Status of Women, 1978.

Jenkins, Richard. *Social Identity.* New York: Routledge, 2000.

Jenness, Diamond. *The Ojibwa Indians of Parry Island, Their Social and Religious Life.* Ottawa: J. O. Patenaude, 1935.

Keung, Nicholas. "'Status Indians' Face Threat of Extinction: In Some Communities, Last Children with Historic Rights Will Be Born as Early as

2012." *Toronto Star*, May 10, 2009. http://www.thestar.com/news/canada/
article/631974.

Kinsinger, Kristopher. "*Gehl v Canada*: ONCA Grapples with Role of *Charter*
Values." *TheCourt.ca*, October 20, 2017. http://www.thecourt.ca/gehl-v-
canada-onca-grapples-with-role-of-charter-values/.

Lambert, John. *Travels through Canada, and the United States of North America, in
the Years 1806, 1807, & 1808*. London: Richard Taylor and Co., 1813.

Lawrence, Bonita. "Gender, Race, and the Regulation of Native Identity in
Canada and the United States: An Overview." *Hypatia* 18, no. 2 (2003): 3–31.

———. *"Real" Indians and Others*. Lincoln: University of Nebraska Press, 2004.

Lehmann, R. Brent. "Memorandum: Summary of the McIvor Decisions."
Prepared for the National Centre for First Nations Governance by Ratcliff &
Company, LLP. June 14, 2009.

Lemkin, Raphael. *Axis Rule in Occupied Europe: Laws of Occupation, Analysis of
Government, Proposals for Redress*. Washington, DC: Carnegie Endowment for
International Peace, Division of International Law, 1944.

Mann, Michelle M. "Disproportionate and Unjustifiable: Teen First Nations
Mothers and Unstated Paternity Policy." *Canadian Issues*, Winter 2009, 31–36.

———. "Gehl v Canada (Attorney General): Report on Unstated/
Unacknowledged Paternity." Ottawa, 2011.

———. "Indian Registration: Unrecognized and Unstated Paternity." Status of
Women Canada, Ottawa, June 2005.

Mathias, Joe, and Gary R. Yabsley. "Conspiracy of Legislation: The Suppression of
Indian Rights in Canada." *BC Studies*, no. 89 (1991): 34–45.

[McCullough, Melodie]. "A Biography of Lynn Gehl." *Journey Magazine*,
November 2, 2018. https://journeymagazineptbo.com/2018/11/02/a-
biography-of-lynn-gehl/.

McIvor, Sharon Donna. "Aboriginal Women's Rights as 'Existing Rights.'"
Canadian Woman Studies 15, no. 2–3 (1995): 34–38.

———. "Aboriginal Women Unmasked: Using Equality Litigation to Advance
Women's Rights." *Canadian Journal of Women and the Law* 16, no. 1 (2004):
106–36.

———. "Self-Government and Aboriginal Women." In *Scratching the Surface:
Canadian Anti-Racist Feminist Thought*, edited by Enakshi Dua and Angela
Robertson, 167–86. Toronto: Women's Press, 1999.

McIvor, Sharon, and Gwen Brodsky. "Equal Registration Status for Aboriginal
Women and Their Descendants: Sharon McIvor's Comments on Bill
C-3, An Act to Promote Equity in Indian Registration by Responding to
the Court of Appeal for British Columbia Decision in McIvor v Canada
(Registrar of Indian and Northern Affairs)." Submission to the House
of Commons Standing Committee on Aboriginal Affairs and Northern
Development, April 13, 2010.

McIvor v Canada (Registrar of Indian and Northern Affairs), 2009 BCCA 153. http://
canlii.ca/t/230zn.

Millan, Luis. "Parliament Given 18 Months to Amend *Indian Act*." *Lawyers Weekly*, September 4, 2015, 5. http://www.dionneschulze.ca/wp-content/uploads/2015/09/2015-09-04_Lawyers-Weekly_Parliament-given-18-months-to-amend-Indian-Act.pdf.

Miller, J.R. *Lethal Legacy: Current Native Controversies in Canada*. Toronto: McClelland & Stewart, 2004.

——. *Sweet Promises: A Reader on Indian-White Relations in Canada*. Toronto: University of Toronto Press, 1991.

Milloy, John S. "The Early *Indian Act*s: Development Strategy and Constitutional Change." In Miller, *Sweet Promises*, 145–54.

Monture-Angus, Patricia. *Thunder in My Soul: A Mohawk Woman Speaks*. Halifax: Fernwood, 1999.

"More Turbulence in Judicial Review." Blog of IMK Avocats-Advocates, May 19, 2017. https://imk.ca/en/blog/turbulence-judicial-review/.

"Motion to Urge the Government to Bring into Force the Remaining Provisions of Bill s-3." *The Progressives*, February 19, 2019. http://theprogressives.ca/hansard/motion-urge-government-bring-force-remaining-provisions-bill-s-3-adopted/.

Napoleon, Val. "Aboriginal Self Determination: Individual Self and Collective Selves." *Atlantis* 29, no. 2 (2005): 31–46.

National Inquiry into Missing and Murdered Indigenous Women and Girls. *A Legal Analysis of Genocide, Supplementary Report of the National Inquiry into Missing and Murdered Indigenous Women and Girls*. June 3, 2019. https://www.MMIWG-ffada.ca/wp-content/uploads/2019/06/Supplementary-Report_Genocide.pdf.

——. *Reclaiming Power and Place: The Final Report on the National Inquiry into Missing and Murdered Indigenous Women and Girls*, 2 vols. June 3, 2019. https://www.MMIWG-ffada.ca/final-report.

Native Women's Association of Canada. "Aboriginal Women and Unstated Paternity." Paper presented at the National Aboriginal Women's Summit, Corner Brook, NL, June 20–22, 2017.

Nerland, Krista. "Dr Gehl Wins Appeal in *Indian Act* Sex Discrimination Case." Olthuis Kleer Townshend LLP, n.d. https://www.oktlaw.com/dr-gehl-wins-appeal-in-indian-act-sex-discrimination-case/.

Norris, Mary Jane. "Contemporary Demography of Aboriginal Peoples in Canada." In *Visions of the Heart: Canadian Aboriginal Issues*, edited by David A. Long and Olive P. Dickason, 179–237. Toronto: Harcourt Brace, 1996.

O'Donnell, Vivian, and Susan Wallace. "First Nations, Métis and Inuit Women." Social and Aboriginal Statistics Division, Statistics Canada, July 2011. http://www.statcan.gc.ca/pub/89-503-x/2010001/article/11442-eng.pdf.

Olsen Williams, Alice. "Open Letter: Kawartha Group Disappointed with Monsef's Voting Position on Bill s-3." Letter to the editor. *Anishinabek News*, August 28, 2017. http://anishinabeknews.ca/2017/09/05/open-letter-kawartha-group-disappointed-with-monsefs-voting-position-on-bill-s-3/.

Ontario. Ministry of the Attorney General. "Fact Sheet: Civil Case Management."

Effective January 1, 2015. https://www.attorneygeneral.jus.gov.on.ca/english/courts/civil/fact_sheet_civil_case_management.html.

"Ontario Court of Appeal Finds Application of Registration Policy under the *Indian Act* Unlawful." Gowling WLG, May 5, 2017. https://gowlingwlg.com/en/insights-resources/articles/2017/registration-policy-under-the-indian-act-unlawful/.

Palmater, Pamela. *Beyond Blood: Rethinking Indigenous Identity.* Saskatoon: Purich, 2011.

———. "Genocide, Indian Policy, and Legislated Elimination of Indians in Canada." *Aboriginal Policy Studies* 3, no. 3 (2014): 27–54. https://doi.org/10.5663/aps.v3i3.22225.

Palmater, Pamela, with Lynn Gehl, "Lynn Gehl Challenges Indian Affairs Unfair Policy." September 27, 2019, in *Warrior Life*, podcast, audio file, 54:03. https://soundcloud.com/pampalmater/lynn-gehl-challenges-indian-affairs-unfair-policy?.

"Proud Day for Dan Ross and Harold (Skip) Ross." *Renfrew Mercury*, August 22, 2000, 7.

"Quebec Superior Court Grants Extension for Update to 'Discriminatory' *Indian Act*." CBC News, January 26, 2017. https://www.cbc.ca/news/indigenous/court-extension-update-indian-act-1.3953515

Robertson, Dylan. "Government, Senate at Odds over Scope of Indigenous Linage Bill." *Winnipeg Free Press*, June 20, 2017. https://www.winnipegfreepress.com/local/government-senate-at-odds-over-scope-of-indigenous-lineage-bill-429767853.html.

Sarazin, Greg. "220 Years of Broken Promises." In *Drum Beat: Anger and Renewal in Indian Country*, edited by Boyce Richardson, 167–200. Toronto: Summerhill Press, 1989.

Schultz, Emily A., and Robert H. Lavenda. *Cultural Anthropology: A Perspective on the Human Condition*, 4th ed. Mountain View, CA: Mayfield, 1998.

Sikkema, John. "Court of Appeal Justices: Invoking 'Charter Values' Risks Subordinating Charter Rights." *CanLII Connects*, August 28, 2017. https://canliiconnects.org/en/commentaries/46534.

Silman, Janet (as told to). *Enough Is Enough: Aboriginal Women Speak Out.* Toronto: Women's Press, 1987.

Smith, Charlie. "*Indian Act*'s 143 Years of Sex-Based Discrimination Finally Ends, Thanks in Part to B.C. Women." *Georgia Straight*, August 19, 2019. https://www.straight.com/news/1286951/indian-acts-143-years-sex-based-discrimination-finally-ends-thanks-part-bc-women.

Speck, F. G. *Family Hunting Territories and Social Life of Various Algonkian Bands of the Ottawa Valley.* Canada, Department of Mines, Geological Survey. Memoir 70. Anthropological Series No. 8. Ottawa: Government Printing Bureau, 1915.

Stevenson, Winona. "Colonialism and First Nations Women in Canada." In *Scratching the Surface: Canadian Anti-Racist Feminist Thought*, edited by Enakshi Dua and Angela Robertson, 49–80. Toronto: Women's Press, 1999.

Stewart, Jane. "Address by the Honourable Jane Stewart Minister of Indian Affairs and Northern Development on the occasion of the unveiling of *Gathering Strength—Canada's Aboriginal Action Plan*." Ottawa, January 7, 1998. https://www.rcaanc-CIRNAC.gc.ca/eng/1100100015725/1571590271585.

Troniak, Shauna. "Addressing the Legacy of Residential Schools." Background paper. Publication No. 2011-76-E, Parliament of Canada, September 1, 2011. http://publications.gc.ca/pub?id=9.572738&sl=0.

Truesdale, Claire. "Lynn Gehl Wins Fight for Indian Status at Ontario Court of Appeal." JFK Law Corporation, May 12, 2017. http://jfklaw.ca/lynn-gehl-wins-fight-indian-status-ontario-court-appeal/.

United Nations. General Assembly. *Convention on the Prevention and Punishment of the Crime of Genocide*. December 9, 1948. UNTS, vol. 78, p. 277. http://www.ohchr.org/EN/ProfessionalInterest/Pages/CrimeOfGenocide.aspx.

———. General Assembly. *Convention on the Rights of the Child*. November 20, 1989. UNTS, vol. 1577, p. 3. http://www.ohchr.org/en/professionalinterest/pages/crc.aspx.

———. General Assembly. *Declaration on the Rights of Indigenous Peoples*. October 2, 2007. A/RES/61/295. http://www.un.org/esa/socdev/unpfii/documents/DRIPS_en.pdf.

———. General Assembly. *Universal Declaration of Human Rights*. December 10, 1948. 217 A (III). http://www.un.org/en/universal-declaration-human-rights/.

United Nations Human Rights Committee (UNHCR). Communication No. 2020/2010. *McIvor and Grismer v Canada*. UN Doc. CCPR/C/124/D/2020/2010 (November 1, 2018). https://tbinternet.ohchr.org/Treaties/CCPR/Shared%20Documents/CAN/CCPR_C_124_D_2020_2010_28073_E.pdf.

Vital Statistics Act, RSO 1980, c 524. http://digitalcommons.osgoode.yorku.ca/cgi/viewcontent.cgi?article=2036&context=rso.

Voyageur, Cora J. "Contemporary Indian Women." In *Visions of the Heart: Canadian Aboriginal Issues*, edited by David A. Long and Olive P. Dickason, 92–112. Toronto: Harcourt Brace, 1996.

Waban-Aki: People from Where the Sun Rises. Directed by Alanis Obomsawin. 2006. National Film Board of Canada. https://www.nfb.ca/film/waban-aki_en/.

Williams, Robert A., Jr. *Savage Anxieties: The Invention of Western Civilization*. New York: St. Martin's Press, 2012.

Women's Legal Education and Action Fund (LEAF). "LEAF Urges Government to Support Bill C-3 and End Sex Discrimination in the *Indian Act*." News release. May 5, 2010. https://www.leaf.ca/news/leaf-urges-government-to-support-bill-c-3-and-end-sex-discrimination-in-the-indian-act/.

Yon, Daniel A. Interview with Stuart Hall. *Journal of Curriculum Theorizing* 15, 4 (Winter 1999): 89–99.

Zichmanis, John. "The Seasons of Love." *Maclean's*, December 1967, 20–22.

Index

Page numbers in *italics* represent figures and tables.

Aboriginal, as term, xl

Aboriginal Affairs and Northern Development Canada (AANDC). *See* Indian/Indigenous and Northern Affairs Canada

Aboriginal Legal Services of Toronto (ALST), 46–7, 76, 148–9, 150–9, 160, 167–70, 171, 173–9, 199–200

Aboriginal Veterans Autochtones (AVA), 212

academia, xxii–xxiii. *See also* Gehl, Lynn: education

addictions, 25, 28, 30

adoptions, 13–4, 64, 86–7, 101–2, 109

agency, 25–6, 30

alcoholism, 30

Algonquin Anishinaabeg: about, 3; Canadian Aboriginal Veterans Millennium Medal, 211–2; criteria of status, 10, 11–2; dbaajimowinan (storytelling), 3; discussing status, 11; experiences of, 11; and family, 14, 86; and Gehl, 111; government buildings on land of, xxxi; identity and racism, 5. *See also* Anishinaabeg

Algonquin enrolment law, 110

Algonquin of Ontario land claim process, xxxiv, 10, 11, 110, 116, 238n32, 244 Ch.18n3

Andrews v Law Society of British Columbia, 145

Anishinaabe Clan System governance, xxii, 86

Anishinaabeg: and colour black, 215; and dance, 213, 214; morals and heart, xxxviii; morals before knowledge, xxiii; sacred stories, 15; as spiritual, 15, 20–1; theories of human condition, 20–2; and treaties, xxxi; words and meanings, 249

Anishinabek News, xxxiv–xxxv

APPA. *See* Standing Senate Committee on Aboriginal Peoples (APPA)

Archives on Ontario, 8, 25–6, 64–5, 244n8

Article 3 of the UNHRC Convention, xvii

Article 26 of the UNHRC Convention, xvii

Article 27 of the UNHRC Convention, xv, xvii

Assembly of First Nations, 60

Assembly of First Nations Women's Council (afnwc), 38–9, 77

assimilation, xiv, xv, 10–1. *See also* enfranchisement

Bagot, Charles, 14

Bagot Commission Report, 14, 86

"Barring Claims against Discriminatory Legislation" (Darling and Lafond), 169

basic needs, xiv, 44

Bédard, Yvonne, xv, 60, 72, 81, 135–6, 195–6

Belobaba, Edward, 155

Bennett, Carolyn, 55, 114–5, 126, 130–1, 187

Benton-Banai, Edward, 21, 29, 31

Berger, Peter L., 16

Big Canoe, Christa, 157, 169, 182, 186

Bill c-3: discrimination continued, 39–40, 84–5; and new Indigenous Peoples, 126–7; protest against, 37–9

Bill c-31: overview, xv–xvi, 41–5; codifying and neglect, 36; as Eastern Doorway opening, 199; as failed, 9, 67, 82; number gaining status (2002), 237n6; two-stage consultations, 55, 162

Bill s-3: overview, xviii; and Bennett, 55, 114–5, 126, 130–1, 187; and Descheneaux, 127; Gehl clauses, 127, 188–91; as gutted by House of Commons, 55, 189–90; and Monsef, 54, 55–6, 209; and new Indigenous Peoples, 126; number of people entitled (2017), 189; as passed with clauses, 189; siblings and cousin issues, 126–7, 162;

two-stage consultations, 55, 119–20, 130–1, 162, 186–7, 191; UNRHC ruling, 205–6

"A Biography of Lynn Gehl" (McCullough), 196

birth certificates, 96–102, *97*. *See also* tampered documents; unstated/ unknown paternity

Blackstock, Cindy, 142, 165, 205

blood quantum, 25, 86, 238n33, 245n34

book overview, xxxi–xxxii, xxxv– xxxvi, xl–xlii; methods and methodology, 140–3; ten qualifiers, xxxvi–xl

British Columbia Court of Appeal, 84

Cairns, H.A.C., 161

Campbell, Archie, 153–4

Canadian Aboriginal Veterans Millennium Medal, 211–2

Canadian Bill of Rights, xv, 60, 135–6, 177

Canadian Charter of Rights and Freedoms: vs. Canadian Bill of Rights, 177; and Canadian Constitution, xxxi; Court of Appeal for Ontario ruling, 183–5; and *Indian Act*, 67; limitations, 196–7; lobbying, 136; in practice, xxix; section 15 (*see* section 15); and sex discrimination, xvi, 67

Canadian Constitution, xxxi

Canadian Council of Natural Mothers, 96, 101–2

Canadian Feminist Alliance for International Action (FAFIA), 118–20, 206

children: as gifts, 15; illegitimate (*see* illegitimate children; Indigenous women: as unmarried); importance of, 94; and *Indian Act*, 87; orphaned/adopted, 14, 86–7, 101; rights of, 103–4; United Nations Convention on

the Rights of the Child, 45. *See also* Status Indians and children; unstated/unknown paternity
children and status: overview, 35–6; and Bill C-3 issues, 39–40; and Bill C-31 issues, xvi, 41–5; detriment of non-Status, xiv; as Gehl's focus, xxxviii; men acknowledging paternity, xv–xvi; men vs. women, 66–7; number affected by unstated paternity, 76; number gaining status (2002), 237n6; number gaining status (2011), 40; number of children affected, 76; percentage of unstated/unknown paternity, 52; prior to 1985, 87; and second-generation cut-off rule (*see* second-generation cut-off rule); Supreme Court of BC decision, 83
child-support, 44
citizenship codes, 236 Ch.5n4
Civilization Act, 47
Clatworthy, Stewart, 90, 127–8, 158, 159, 194
colonization: Algonquin of Ontario land claim process, 11, 238n32; and Gehl, xxiii–xxiv, 70–1, 109, 148; and identity, xxxiii, 5; and ignorance, 165; and justice system, 48; as knowledge before morals, 216; and manipulation, 16–7, 19, 22, 110; and "modern treaty process," xxxvii, 10, 243 Ch.17n2; new policies with same goals, 183; and orphaned children, 87; and souls, 22, 237n20; through Western knowledge criteria, xxii–xxiii; and vulnerable women, 52, 116; within Indigenous Peoples, 143–4
comparator group analysis, 179
"The Complainant" (Blackstock), 165, 205

Conflict of Interest Act, 209
"Conspiracy of Legislation" (Mathias and Yabsley), 20
consultations: as tactic, xxix, 116–7, 190; two-stage, 55, 119–20, 130–1, 162, 186–7, 191
Convention on the Prevention and Punishment of the Crime of Genocide, 51–2, 52–3
Corbiere Lavell, Jeannette: overview, xv, 135–6; on Bill C-3, 38; Bill C-31 protests, 36; honoured, 194–6; and INAN, 189–90; lack of support, 60; as ogitchidaa kwewag, 81; as role model, xxxvi
Court Challenges Program of Canada (CCPC), 151, 158
Court of Appeal for Ontario, 47, 54, 171, 175–86, 188, 191–4, 244n12
cousin issue, 126–8, 162
Creator's law, 199
Crown-Indigenous Relations and Northern Affairs Canada (CIRNAC), xxxviii. *See also* Indian/Indigenous and Northern Affairs Canada
cultural genocide: overview, xxxvii–xxxviii, xli, 235n1; defined, 51; history of term, 51–2; as insidious, 55–6; and Lemkin, 51; unstated/unknown paternity as, 52, 54

dance, 213, 214
Dash, Ronald, 153
Day, Gordon, 14
dbaajimowinan (storytelling), 3
Department of Indian Affairs and Northern Development, 60–1. *See also* status registration
Department of Justice (DoJ): and affidavits, 154–5; arguments in Gehl case, 167, 169–70; Bill S-3 and consultations, 187; budget of, 200; delay tactics, 241n20;

Department of Justice (DoJ) (*con't*):
and Gehl factum of appeal,
174–5; joint motion record
(JMR), 167–8; lawyer fees,
173; and Masse decision,
164; number of staff, 200;
and paternity language, 131;
and post-*McIvor* policy,
171–2, 173–4, 175, 178–9, 181–2;
striking SoC of Gehl, 47, 150,
151; striking SoD of, 174
Descheneaux, Stéphane, xviii, 126–7,
130, 169, 171, 187
Dion, Mario, 209
disenfranchised spirit, 28–31, *29*,
238n38
"Disproportionate and Unjustifiable"
(Mann), 135, 164
DNA evidence, 167
Doctrine of Discovery, 140, 243
Ch.17n2
double-mother clause, xxxix, 80,
84, 126, 161. *See also* second-
generation cut-off rule
Driscoll, Amanda, xxv, 155, 157, 201,
227, 228
Dumont, Marie-Eve, 187
Duran, Bonnie, 22, 29, 31
Duran, Eduardo, 22, 29, 31
Dyck, Lillian Eva, 187, 190, 196, 206

Earley, Mary Two-Axe, xxix, 81
Eastern Doorway, xii, 199
Eberts, Mary: analysis on the *McIvor*
decision, 83, 84; and APPA
committee, 188; and *Descheneaux*
case, 164, 171; and Gehl appeal,
114, 182; on Groberman, 162;
at Indigenous Famous Six
reception, 196; Indigenous
Women's Symposium, 207; and
O'Bomsawin, 187; and post-
McIvor policy, 171; on sexual
violence and paternity policy,

175; Sinclair on, 189. *See also* Law
Office of Mary Eberts
Elders, 237n20
enfranchisement, xxxix, 72, 73, 80,
239n9, 241n13
enlightenment subject, 18
environmental activism, 28
environmental pollution, 111
epistemological oppression, xxii–xxiii
equality, substantive vs. formal, 170,
246n40
Equality Day, 194–5
equality in *Charter*, xxxi
essentialism, 19, 20, 28–30, *29*
ethnicity, 18–9

factums of appeal, 173–80, 245n34
factums of the plaintiff, 168–9
Famous Five, xv
Federal Court of Appeal, 135
First Nation Band membership, 76,
115–6, 200, 236 Ch.5n4
First World War, 4, 5
Fiske, Jo-Anne, 90
formal equality, 170, 246n40
Frideres, James S., 127, 158, 159, 194

Gagnon, Annie Jane Meness (great-
grandmother), 3–5, *4*, 7–8, 61–2,
62
Gagnon, Gordon (relative), 212
Gagnon, Joseph (great-grandfather),
3–5, *4*, 7–8, 62–3, *62*, 64, 211–3
Gagnon, Mary Viola Bernadette. *See*
Gagnon, Viola (kokomis)
Gagnon, Rodney Peter (father), 8–9,
63, 75, 138, 146–8, *147*, 201
Gagnon, Viola (kokomis), 4, *4*, 8, 14–5,
62, 63, 64, 138, 146, *147*
Gehl, Lynn: accomplishments with
court case, 197–8, 199 (*see also*
Gehl court case); colonization
impact, xxiii–xxiv, 70–1, 109,
148; denied status, 9, 67, 75–6,

148–9, 170–1, 173; education, xxxii, xxxiii–xxxiv, 140–1, 149–50, 153, 154; family history, 3–9, 25, 61–7, 138–9, 143–4, *147*, 201, 219–21; as fighting for equality, xxxi–xxxii; honoured, 194–6; identity, xxxiii, 68–9; and *Indian Act* understanding, xxxvii–xxxviii; Indigenous knowledge, xxiii–xxiv, xxxii, xxxv–xxxvi, 110–1, 140–2; and land claims, 238n32; and land claims understanding, xxxvii; master's thesis, xxxiii–xxxiv, 16–31; McCullough on, 196; and medal for Joseph, 211–3; methods and methodology, 140–3; and Monsef, 55–6; natural law, 144–5; organizing book, xxxv–xxxvi, xl–xlii; Pikwàkanagàn First Nation membership, 200; politics and writing, xxxiv–xxxv; qualifying for 6(1)a status, 9; receiving Eagle Feather from thohahente, 210–1; as section 6(1)a.3, 217; as section 6(2), 114–5, 186, 200; Sinclair on, 201–2; and Skip Ross, 25–8; Status registration overview, 145–9, 170; and truth, 215–7; vision issues, xxxii–xxxiii, 148, 149, 157; water testing job, xxxiii, 111

Gehl court case: overview, 67, 113–4, 148–60, 165–71, 173–86, 188–94, 196–200; as abuse, 198–9; at Archives of Ontario, 8, 25–6, 64–5; barriers to, 114; and Bill S-3, 127; case as mainstay, xvii–xviii; and *Charter* limitations, 196–7; costs involved, 114, 169; Court of Appeal for Ontario, 54, 244n12; Court of Appeal for Ontario ruling, 183–6, 188, 191–4; and *Descheneaux* case, 164; DoJ arguments, 169–70; DoJ delay

tactics, 241n20; DoJ factum, 181; endorsements, 77; errors in ruling, 171; expert report process, 159; factum of appeal, 173–80, 245n34; factum of the plaintiff, 168–9; focus of court battles, xxxviii; funding for, 151, 158; Gehl cross-examined, 154–5; Gehl frustration and exhaustion, 153–9, 160; Gehl's grandfather, 181; history of court challenges, xv–xvii; and JMR, 167–8; LEAF's factum, 180; as non-Status, xxxiv, xxxviii, 9; Ontario Superior Court ruling, 170–1, 173; and other Algonquin people, 111; and other Indigenous Peoples understanding, 142; outcomes, 114–5, 119, 200, 217; as personal injury claim, 153; and post-*McIvor* policy, 173–4, 178–9, 181–2; and power, 138; and Registrars, 47–8, 64, 68 (*see also* unstated/unknown paternity); and SJM, 154, 155; and SoC, 46–7, 150, 151, 152, 155; statutory appeal, 244n12; supporting friends, 182; timeline, 219–33; transcripts of, 245n37; as of 2002, 76; as of 2007, 109; website/social media as national strategy, 77, 159–60; and Women's Legal Education and Action Fund, 175
gender discrimination. *See* sex discrimination
gender-neutral language, 129, 131–2
genocide. *See* cultural genocide
George, Evelyn, 90
Gilbert, Larry, 61, 165
globalization, 18
Golden Lake Indian Reserve, 3–4, 5, 7–8, 63. *See also* Pikwàkanagàn First Nation
Gradual Civilization Act, 72, 240n5
Gradual Enfranchisement Act, 72, 80

Grismer, Jacob, xv, xvi–xvii, xxix, 83–4
Groberman, Harvey, 84, 161–2

Hall, Stuart, 18–20, 28–9
Hallowell, A. Irving, 21, 29, 31, 237n17
Harder, Peter, 190
Harper, Stephen, 186
heart knowledge, xxii, xxxviii, 20
House of Commons, 55
House of Commons Standing Committee on Indigenous and Northern Affairs (INAN), 130–1, 189–91

identity: overview, xiv; and affirmation, 19, 29–31, *29*, 63; Algonquin and colonizers, 5; and colonization, xxxiii, 21–2; as enlightenment subject, 18; and ethnicity, 18–9; and Gehl, 68–9; as postmodern subject, 18; and power, 19–20, 22; production of, 19–20, 29–30, *29*; restoration of, 17; and rights, 61; and rights of children, 103; and settlers, 5, 59; as sociological subject, 18; as subjective reality, 16
illegitimate children: as accepted in Indigenous cultures, 14, 15, 86; as comparator group, 179; and disorganization, 161; and INAC 2012, 171; in *Indian Act* history, 44–5, 87, 165, 245n34; McIvor's parents, 162; and PoP policy shift, 171–2; removal of word in Bill C-31, 44–5, 183; and United Nations declarations, 103. *See also* Indigenous women: as unmarried
illness, 20
INAN (House of Commons Standing Committee on Indigenous and Northern Affairs), 130–1, 189–91
Indian, as term, xl

Indian Act: addressing unknown paternity (*see* unstated/unknown paternity); amendments defined, xl–xlii; and Canadian Bill of Rights, xv, 60; and *Canadian Charter of Rights and Freedoms*, 67; as criminalizing Indigeneity, 236 Ch.5n2; Gehl's understanding of, xxxvii–xxxviii; history of, 59–60; history of challenges, xv–xvii; and inclusion of children, 87; proof of paternity, 152; and protection of vulnerable people, xxxvii; as racism/sexism mechanism, 93; and Registrars (*see* Registrars); remedying, 68, 90–3; two-parent rule, 110, 146, 149, 178, 183; and unmaking of Status Indians, 10, 20, 22; as upheld in court (*see* Supreme Court of Canada). *See also* PoP (proof of paternity) policy; unstated/unknown paternity; *specific sections*
Indian/Indigenous and Northern Affairs Canada (INAC): administrative remedies, 91–3; and archival records, 26; Bill S-3 and consultations, 130–1, 186–7; denying funding to Gehl, 151; and evolution of legal clauses, 114; Gehl's protest 1997, 9; and gender-neutral language, 129, 131–2; lawyers of, 150; and Masse decision, 164; names of organization, xxxviii–xxxix; and nation-to-nation discussions, 115–6; policy vs. practice, 240n12; posting unstated paternity policy online, 130, 165–7; rectifying past decisions, 172; and Registrars (*see* Registrars); and Skip Ross, 23–4, 26–7. *See also* Registrars; unstated/unknown paternity

Indigenous family model, 14–5
Indigenous Famous Six, xiv–xv, 195–6, 208
Indigenous knowledge: overview, xxi–xxiii; and Gehl, xxiii–xxiv, xxxii, xxxv–xxxvi, 110–1, 140–2; morals and heart, xxxviii; storytelling as gaining knowledge, 3. *See also* disenfranchised spirit
Indigenous men/fathers: acknowledging paternity, xvi, xxxvi, 53, 70, 77, 88–9; and "father" term, 235n1; finding children, 101; insecurities, 91; women not disclosing paternity, 90–2. *See also* unstated/unknown paternity
Indigenous Peoples, rights of, 103–4
Indigenous scholars, xxii–xxiii
Indigenous Services Canada (ISC), xxxviii. *See also* Indian/Indigenous and Northern Affairs Canada
Indigenous Title. *See* land claims process
Indigenous women/mothers: vs. all women rights, 136; challenging power, xxxi–xxxii; and Creator, 144, 145; as dependent, 5, 60; finding children, 101–2; in Indigenous culture, 86; marrying non-Status men, 60; not disclosing paternity, 90–2 (*see also* unstated/unknown paternity); as ogitchidaa kwewag, 81–5, 92; and sexual violence, 52; as targeted by unstated paternity policy, 52–3; as unmarried, 39, 96–101, 103, 163; voting, xv; younger mothers, 76. *See also* mothering
Indigenous Women's Symposium, 206–7
Inter-American Commission on Human Rights (IACHR), 118–20

International Covenant on Civil and Political Rights, xv, xvii, 73, 81
intersectionality, xxxii

Jamieson, S.M., 161
Jenkins, Richard, 19–20
Jenness, Diamond, 20–1, 29, 31, 237n17
Jocko, Angeline (great-great-grandmother), 8, 14–5, 64–6, 68, 146, *147*
Jocko, John (relative), 146, 147
Jocko, Paul Lee (relative), 15, 146, 147
joint motion record (JMR), 167–8

knowledge. *See* Indigenous knowledge; Western knowledge
knowledge bundle, xxi, xxii
knowledge production, 140
known yet unstated paternity, 137. *See also* unstated/unknown paternity

Lambert, John, 14
land claims process, xxxvii, 243 Ch.17n2. *See also* Algonquin of Ontario land claim process
Lauwers, Peter D., 182, 184–5
Lavenda, Robert H., 19
Law Office of Mary Eberts (LOME), 171, 173–4. *See also* Eberts, Mary
Lawrence, Bonita, 21–2
LEAF (Women's Legal Education and Action Fund), 85, 175, 180, 182
Legal positivism, 140, 216
Lemkin, Raphael, 235n1
LOME. *See* Eberts, Mary; Law Office of Mary Eberts
Luckmann, Thomas, 16
Lynn, Karen, 96, 101–2
Lysyk, K., 161

Maggie (relative), 63
Mann, Michelle M., 89, 90–1, 96, 135, 152, 158, 164
Marche amun, 37–9

marriage: and enfranchisement, 73, 85, 136, 240n6; and whiteness, 7–8, 60, *62*, 63; women as unmarried, 39, 96–101, 103, *163*

Martell, Moses, 15, 109

Masse, Chantal, xviii, 130, 162, 164, 187

Mathias, Joe, 20

McCarney, Rosemary, 195–6

McCullough, Melodie, 196

McHugh, Kathleen, 38–9

McIvor, Sharon Donna: overview, xvi–xvii, 83–5, 161–2; on Corbiere Lavell court decision, 136; on Eurocentric notions, 68; honoured, 194–6; and INAN testimony, 189; Indigenous Women's Symposium, 207–8; at Marche amun, 38; as role model, xxxvi; and second-generation cut-off rule, 73; and Senate Committee on Aboriginal Peoples, 125–6; and Supreme Court of BC, xvi–xvii, 83; and Supreme Court of Canada, xvii, 85; and UNHRC, xxix, 40–1, 205–6

McLenachan, Linda, 164, 171

McPhedran, Marilou, 188–9, 194–6

medals, 211–3

Medicine Wheel, 21, 29

men. *See* Indigenous men/fathers

methods and methodology, 140–3

Michel, Viviane, 37, 189

Miller, Bradley, 182, 184–5

mino-pimadiziwin (good life), 5, 15, 31, 93

missing/murdered women, 186, 235n1

"modern treaty process," xxxvii, 10, 243 Ch.17n2

monogamy, 144

Monsef, Maryam, 54, 55–6, 209

Montminy, Joëlle, 130–1

Monture-Angus, Patricia, 136

morals: and AANDC, 93; and courage, 142–3; and Indigenous ways of knowing, xxi–xxii, xxiii, xxxii, xxxviii; before knowledge, 216–7

mothering, 13–5, 70–1, 94, 143, 144. *See also* Indigenous women/mothers

Murray, Kimberly, 76, 148, 150, 151–2, 155, 156, 199–200

National Indian Brotherhood (NIB), 60

National Inquiry into Missing and Murdered Indigenous Women and Girls (MMIWG), 186, 235n1

National Strategy to Raise Awareness on Unknown and Unstated Paternity (NSRAUUP), 77, 159–60

nationality, 68–9

nation-to-nation discussions, 115–7

Native, as term, xl

Native Women's Association of Canada (NWAC), 35, 38, 77, 90

natural law, 144–5

negative presumption of paternity. *See* unstated/unknown paternity

Nicholas, Sandra Lovelace (nee Lovelace): overview, xv, 73, 81; Bill C-31 protests, 36; honoured, 195; and INAN, 189–90

non-Status detriments: overview, xiv, 61; accessing information, xxxiv; Anishinabek citizenship, 76; awareness for pursuing registration, 60–1, 68; Band membership, 76; burials, 72; education, 46; freedom on land, xxix; health care, 46; inheriting property, 72; leadership positions, 80; and reserves, 5, 61; women no longer Indigenous, 7–8, 60, *62*, 63

O'Bomsawin, Rick, 187

ogitchidaa kwewag, 81–5, 92

Ojibway people, 237n17

Olthuis Kleer Townshend, 175

Ontario Court of Appeal. *See* Court of Appeal for Ontario
Ontario Native Women's Association (ONWA), 38, 77
Ontario Superior Court, 151, 169–70, 173
Ontario Superior Court of Justice, 47
Ontario *Vital Statistics Act*, 96–8
Oral Tradition, xxxv, 14–5, 64

Palmater, Pamela D., 86, 126, 152, 188, 189
paternalism, 60
paternity, xxxvi–xxxvii, 59–60. *See also* PoP (proof of paternity) policy; Registrars; unstated/unknown paternity
patriarchy, xii, 93, 116, 132, 144, 166. *See also* sex discrimination
personhood, xiv–xv
petitions, 160
Pikwàkanagàn First Nation, xxxiii, 3–4, 5, 7–8, 12, 27, 63, 212–3
PoP (proof of paternity) policy: overview, 94–5, 114, 176; and Court of Appeal for Ontario ruling, 183–5, 191–3; draft and online, 165–7, *166*; as flexible, 181; *Gehl* case accomplishments, 197–8, 199; Mann on, 91, 152; Palmater on, 152; retroactive, 179; and ruling errors, 171; shift in 2011/12, 171–2; years to formalize, 182. *See also* unstated/unknown paternity
post-*McIvor* policy, 171–4, 178, 181–2
postmodern subject, 18
poverty, 68
power: all-encompassing wiindigo, xxxii; and *Gehl* court case, 138; and identity, 19–20, 22; of words, 130, 131–2
protests: Bill C-3 2010, 37–9; Bill C-31 2005, 35–6; Bill S-3 2019, 209

Quebec Native Women Inc. (QNW), 35, 189
"The Queen and I" (Gehl), about, xxxiii, 149

racism, xxxii, 5, 52, 93, 208, 216
rape/sexual violence, 44, 46, 52, 92, 166, 175
Registrars: and Court of Appeal for Ontario ruling, 192–3; demands of proof, 64; and *Gehl* court case, 47–8, 64, 68; Gilbert, 165; and INAC, 41; interpretations and eliminating Status Indians, 36, 41, 47–8, 74, 87; options for PoP, 167; power of, 172, 178, 192–3, 199; and records, 64; removing child's name, 87; removing father's name, 97, 98–102; responsibilities of, 98; years to formalize PoP, 182. *See also* unstated/unknown paternity
Remembrance Day, 3–4
reparations, xvii
reservations: acceptance on, xv; and basic needs, xiv, 44; removal from, xvi, 7, 63
residential schools, 23, 242n39
Rich, Adrienne, 68
Ross, Carol, 22, 83–4
Ross, Harold (Skip), 17–8, 23–31, 238n39, 238nn31–2; ancestry of, *24*; and disenfranchised spirit, 29
Royal Canadian Mounted Police, 5
Royal Commission on the Status of Women, 81

sacred stories, 15
Schultz, David, 187
Schultz, Emily A., 19
second-generation cut-off rule: overview, 73, 74–5, 137–8; and Corbiere Lavell, 82; defined, xxxix; and disenfranchised spirit, 238n38; as eliminating Status Indians, 36;

second-generation cut-off rule (*con't*): and enfranchisement, xxxix, 241n13; and Gehl's family, 8–9, 110. *See also* section 6(2)

section 5 of *Indian Act*, 192

section 6(1): overview, xvi, 41–2, 41, *66*, 74–5; and Gehl's family, 66–7, *147*; as higher status, 8, 83; and McIvor case, 164; and number of children affected, 76; number of people entitled (2017), 127, 194; percentage of mothers affected, 76; and sub-subsections, 82–3, 84

section 6(1)a: overview, 82–3, 84–5, 124, 138; and DoJ arguments, 182; PoP policy shift 2011/12, 171–2; UNRHC ruling, 205–6. *See also* 6(1)a All the Way!

section 6(1)a.3, 217

section 6(1)c: overview, 66, 83, 84, *124*, 138; and DoJ arguments, 182; PoP policy shift 2011/12, 171–2

section 6(1)c.1, 84

section 6(1)f, 110, 146, 147, 149, 178, 183

section 6(2): overview, 41–2, 41, 66, 74–5, 124; Gehl as, 114–5; and Gehl's family, 66–7, 146–8, *147*; and "illegitimate" word, 44–5; as lesser status, xvi, 8, 83; and number of children affected, 76; number of people entitled (2017), 127, 194; percentage of mothers affected, 76

section 12, 87, 165. *See also* illegitimate children

section 12(1)(a), iv, 84

section 12(1)b, 59–60

section 12(2), 87

section 14.2(4), 150–1

section 15 (*Canadian Charter of Rights and Freedoms*), xvi, 43, 138, 150, 170, 179

section 15(1) (*Canadian Charter of Rights and Freedoms*), xxxi

section 24 (*Canadian Charter of Rights and Freedoms*), 150

section 35 of the Constitution, 150

section 35(1) of the Constitution, xxxi

Senate, 55, 130–1. *See also* Standing Senate Committee on Aboriginal Peoples

Senate Committee on Aboriginal Peoples, 125–6

settlers: abandoning children, 14; and Algonquin identity, 5; and identity of others, 59; as ignorant, 55–6; women and Indigenous men, 137

sex discrimination: overview, xiv, xv–xix, 35–6, 72–3, 79–80; and Bill C-3 issues, 37–40, 84–5; and Bill C-31 issues, 41–5; and Bill S-3 issues, xviii–xix; and *Charter* limitations, 196–7; consultation as tactic, xxix, 116–7, 190; Court of Appeal for Ontario ruling, 183, 186; and cultural genocide contradiction, xxxviii; daughters and section 6(2), xvi; DoJ arguments in *Gehl* case, 169–70, 181; and Gehl's status denial, 9, 67, 75–6, 148–9, 170–1, 173; and gender-neutral language of government, 127; men vs. women, 62, 66; and nation-to-nation discussions, 115–7; number gaining status (2011), 40; as obscured, 13 (*see also* Registrars: power of); Ontario Superior Court ruling, 170–1; protests, 35–6, 37–9, 209; and Supreme Courts (*see* Supreme Court of British Columbia; Supreme Court of Canada); UNRHC ruling, 205–6; unstated paternity as targeting women, 52–3; women as appendages, 5, 60. *See also* Gehl court case; unstated/unknown paternity, *all section 6 entries*

"Sex Discrimination and the *Indian Act*" (Youtube video), 77

Sharpe, Robert J., xvii–xviii, 182–3

siblings issue, 127, 162

Sinclair, Murray, 188–9, 192–3, 201–2

6(1)a All the Way! *38*; overview, xviii, xix, 124, *124*; Bill s-3 clauses, 188–91; creation of, 38, 162; and further analysis, 116; hope for, 115; and House of Commons, 55; and Monsef, 209; and new Indigenous Peoples, 126; and UNRHC, xxix; UNRHC ruling, 205–6

Smith, Cynthia, 189

The Social Construction of Reality (Berger and Luckmann), 16

sociological subject, 18

souls, 20–1, 22, 237n20. *See also* disenfranchised spirit

Speck, Frank G., 14, 86

Standing Senate Committee on Aboriginal Peoples (APPA), 130–1, 187–9

statement of claim (SoC), 46–7, 150, 151, 155

statement of defence (SoD), 155, 169–70, 174

Statement of Reconciliation, 109, 112

Status Indians: benefits of status, 72; and community support, xiv; eliminating status, 36 (*see also Indian Act*); identity restoration and wellness, 17, 18, 63; and Indian term, xl; and lesser forms, xvi, 8 (*see also* section 6(2)); and non-Status uniting, 27–8; status as fictional story, 16–7, 31. *See also* non-Status detriments

status registration: importance overview, 61; overview, 236 Ch.5n1; awareness needed for

pursuing, 60–1, 68; and Band membership and citizenship, 115–6, 200, 236 Ch.5n4; Gehl's overview, 145–9, 170, 200, 210, 217; and new Indigenous Peoples, 126–7; number of applications, 239n9; and two-parent rule, 110, 146, 149, 178, 183

statutory appeal, 244n12

Stewart, Jane, 109, 112, 170–1, 173, 180

Strathy, George R., 174

substantive equality, 170, 246n40

suicide, 63

summary judgement motion (SJM), 154, 155

Superior Court of Quebec, 162, 164

support systems, xiv, 205, 208

Supreme Court of British Columbia, xvi–xvii, 83–4

Supreme Court of Canada (SCC): Corbiere Lavell and Bédard, xv, 72–3, 81, 135–6; McIvor and Grismer, xvii, 85

A Survey of the Contemporary Indians of Canada (Cairns, Jameison and Lysyk), 161

Swinton, Katherine, 47, 151

tampered documents, 87, 89, 97–102, *97*, 240n17

Test Case Funding Program, 151

timeline of *Gehl v Canada*, 219–33

Tobique Women's Group, 60

Travels through Canada and the United States of North America... (Lambert), 14

treaties: and Algonquin Anishinaabeg, xxxi; and depriving status, 10; and enfranchisement, 72; and entitlement, 44; vs. land claims settlements, 243 Ch.17n2; as relationships, 111; and status, 72, 73. *See also* Algonquin of Ontario land claim process; land claims process

Treaty at Niagara, 80
Trudeau, Justin, 55, 186, 209
truth, 140, 215–7
Truth and Reconciliation Commission
of Canada (TRC), 156, 235n1
The Truth That Wampum Tells (Gehl),
142–3, 183
two-parent rule, 110, 146, 149, 178, 183
two-stage consultations, 55, 119–20,
130–1, 162, 186–7

unacknowledged/unestablished
paternity, 88–9, 131
United Nations. *See specific conventions
and committees*
United Nations Convention on the
Prevention and the Punishment
of the Crime of Genocide, 104
United Nations Convention on the
Rights of the Child, 45, 103
United Nations Declaration on the
Rights of Indigenous Peoples, 104
United Nations Human Rights
Committee (UNHRC): Article 3,
xvii; Article 26, xvii; Article 27,
xv, xvii; and Corbiere Lavell, 36;
and Lovelace Nicholas, xv; and
McIvor, xvii, xix, 40–1, 205–6;
and Nicholas, 73, 81
United Nations Universal Declaration
of Human Rights, 103
unknown paternity, 89, 131
"unknown/unnamed parent," 131
unrecognized paternity, 89
unreported/unnamed paternity, 89
unstated/unknown paternity:
overview, 8–9, 74–5, 245n34;
administrative remedies, 68, 90–
3; and Bill C-31 issues, xvii–xviii;
births affected by, 127; defined,
xxxvi; differing language, 89, 130,
131–2, 137, 193; father signature as
required, 89, 96–7, 240 Ch.14n13;

father's name removed, 89, 97,
98–102, 240n17; and Gehl's
father, 8–9, 66, 75; and Gehl's
grandfather, 181, 185; Gehl's
website/social media about, 77; as
genocide, 52, 54; as intentional/
unintentional, 90–1; and
morality, 93; number/percentage
of children affected, 45, 52, 76,
194; policy vs. practice, 240n12;
prior to 1985, 164–5; reasons for
unsigned birth registration, 53,
77, 88–92, 242n40; and Registrar
authority, 172, 178; resolving
issues of, 68; and ruling errors,
171; and sex and marriage, 170;
as targeting women, 52–3, 78.
See also PoP (proof of paternity)
policy; *sections of Indian Act*

veterans, 211–3
vision trouble, xxxii–xxxiii, 148, 149, 157
voting, xv

wellness, 17–8, 21–2, 27–31, 63, 216–7
Western knowledge, xxii–xxiii, 68,
140–1
Whiteduck, Kirby, 12, 154, 213,
245n20
whiteness, 7–8, 9, *62*, 63
wiindigos, xxxii, 139, 199, 209, 215
Wilson-Raybould, Jody, 119, 190
Of Woman Born (Rich), 70
women. *See* Indigenous women/
mothers
Women's Legal Education and Action
Fund (LEAF), 85, 175, 180, 182

Yabsley, Gary R., 20
Yantha, Susan, xviii, 127, 130, 162
Yantha, Tammy, xviii, 127, 130, 162, 187
York County Court, 135
Yurka, Dale L., 182

Lynn Gehl, Algonquin Anishinaabe-kwe, is a member of Pikwàkanagàn First Nation. She is an author, advocate, and artist. Her previous two books are *Claiming Anishinaabe: Decolonizing the Human Spirit* and *The Truth That Wampum Tells: My Debwewin on the Algonquin Land Claims Process*. Her current work focuses on Canada's Algonquin genocide and caring for the most vulnerable. She has fought to help and protect those who have been affected by such as matters related to unknown / unstated paternity and the *Indian Act*, and Indigenous women and girls with disabilities who are bigger targets of sexual violence. In all she does, Lynn thinks, writes, and practices from within the Indigenist paradigm. She encourages all people to go back to their ancestral Indigenous knowledge. She lives in Peterborough, Ontario. You can read more of her work at *www.lynngehl.com*.